BẻT
84
75

The Promise of Solidarity

Inside the Polish Workers' Struggle, 1980-82

Jean-Yves Potel

Translated by Phil Markham

PRAEGER

PRAEGER SPECIAL STUDIES • PRAEGER SCIENTIFIC

Library of Congress Cataloging in Publication Data

Potel, Jean-Yves.
  The promise of Solidarity.

  Translation of: Scenes de greves en Pologne.
  1. Poland—Politics and government—1945-
2. NSZZ "Solidarnosć" (labor organization) I. Title.
DK4440.P6713   943.8'055   82-5322
ISBN 0-03-061776-6
ISBN 0-03-062537-8 (pbk)

Published in 1982 by Praeger Publishers
CBS Educational and Professional Publishing
A Division of CBS, Inc.
521 Fifth Avenue, New York, New York 10175 U.S.A.

123456789 145 987654321
Printed in the United States of America

092628

Contents

KSS-KOR (Committee for Social Self-Defence-Committee for Defence of the Workers) is often simply called KOR. Originally set up as the KOR to campaign for the release of workers jailed in the June 1976 strikes, it became KSS-KOR in 1977 to reflect a commitment by the campaign to take up civil rights issues.

MKS is the Inter-Enterprise Strike Committee

PUWP is the Polish United Workers Party

Voivodie, voivode. The voivodie is the Polish equivalent of a province. It is run by a provincial governor, or voivode.

Zloty. At the time of the events described in the book, the official exchange rate was 34 zloty to the $1. In December 1981, a devaluation brought the rate to about 76 zloty to the $1.

Acknowledgements

I would like to thank all those friends, both in France and in Poland, who have helped me to write this book. Without them it would never have seen the light of day. The warm welcome that I received from the Solidarity militants I met, and the interpreters who helped me, enabled me to gather the necessary information and interviews, and their support is deeply appreciated. In France, my warmest thanks are due to the many people who helped me translate my Polish material. In particular, Anna Romanowska and Barbara L; Janina Sochaczewska, who also explained to me a lot about Poland and made valuable comments on my manuscript; and Cyril Smuga, whose comments also proved most useful. I am also indebted to Georges Mink for his advice and criticism. And finally I would like to thank Denise Avenas, Francoise Carthieux, Alain Brossat and Jean-Claude Klein for having read my manuscript.

All this work would have been impossible were it not for the growth of enthusiasm and solidarity in Poland, which has stimulated and encouraged our work.

Jean-Yves Potel

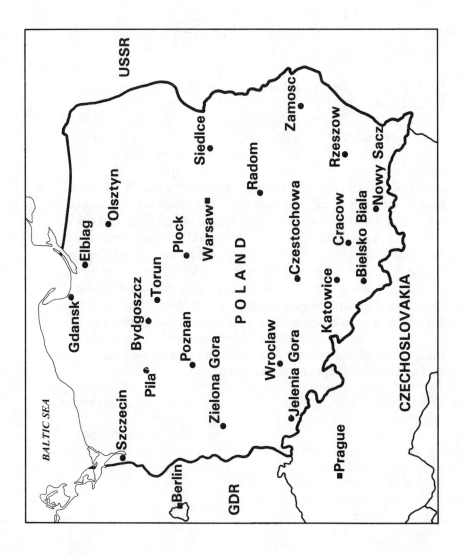

Preface

This book was written a few months after the Baltic seaboard strikes, at a time when the whole of Poland was in a state of crisis. It does not claim to provide a complete history and analysis of the Polish revolution. To write such a history would require one to be able to stand back, and to take into account a whole series of factors which were not available 'in the heat of the moment'. My intention has been more limited. I have tried to give an eye-witness rendering of the early moments of a revolution which, as it blossomed, shook the whole of Polish society to its foundations. For this reason I have thought it best not to edit or alter my account.

I have used these facts as the basis for a series of considerations on the history of the present day. Basically, I believe that the set of contradictions seen in Gdansk carried within them the principal elements which are going to determine future developments. The strike at the *Lenin* shipyard was, and is still, an amazing subject to research. It hastened the gestation of a new social order which had been conceived and dreamt of by only a limited few, and it built it as the property of a whole nation (and particularly of its working class, which had once again become a self-aware historical subject).

This book does not claim to provide a definitive analysis. It outlines the elements which provide a basis for a debate which, in my opinion, interest the international working class movement. Above all, we should not approach Poland with a kind of historical paternalism — however well-intentioned — as if, in the final analysis, the Polish people are only re-running the illusions and mistakes made by more 'advanced' nations. No. We have a lot to learn from this experience, an experience whose outcome is still uncertain.

It is in this same spirit that I have assessed the first defeat of this revolution: the Army take-over of 13 December 1981. With the installation of martial law, General Jaruzelski hoped to check the impetus of an organisation which was carrying the democratic hopes of a whole nation within it. His victory is by no means assured. In the medium term it will depend on the extent to which Polish militants and workers will be capable of analysing the causes of their setback. Once again, I feel that we should avoid over-schematic judgements. I have attempted this in the introduction that follows. The majority of those in whose care lies the future salvation of working-class Poland are, at the time of writing, in prison. Our task, in these early months of 1982, is to do everything possible to get them out.

"We Are Workers; We Will Never Be Slaves"

On 15 December 1981 Western journalists received the second edition of a *Strike Bulletin* published by the Strike Committee of the Huta Warszawa steel works, in which they gave their answer to General Jaruzelski: "We, the steel workers on strike, demand the implementation of the demands of our national strike committee based in the Gdansk shipyards, which are the following: the state of siege to be lifted, and all interned Solidarity members to be freed. We assert that we are workers, and that we will never be slaves, even if you tie our hands and gag us. We have gone on strike, together with the whole of working class Poland, in unity with the whole of our nation." Thus, despite tens of thousands of arrests, the militarisation of the whole country and the cutting of communications, the military junta which was installed on 13 December immediately ran up against resistance from the working class. As yet we do not know the organisational forms, or the future prospect of this resistance, but there is no doubt that it has been massive and determined.

The Junta says that it will not return to the situation existing prior to August 1980. But the danger is that they intend to return further, to the black years of Stalinism in the 1950s. Solidarity, a trade union that was genuinely independent from the state and the Party, was not only the fruit of the strikes on the Baltic seaboard in 1980. It was born from a whole historical experience — the betrayed expectations of 1956, the massacres of 1970, and the strikes of Radom and Ursus in 1976. In these experiences new generations of militants had been formed, and had found a new determination and resolve. Their struggle henceforth would be for an authentically democratic society, combining the humanist traditions of socialism and the idea of the "self-managed Republic". This was something that neither the Kremlin nor the corrupt apparatchiks in Warsaw were prepared to tolerate. For them, ever since August 1980, the Polish revolution had become a nightmare, with its multiple demons of democracy, its pluralism, its desire for self-management, for cultural renewal and political realism. This was the moral upheaval, the hope of a whole nation that had re-established an historical awareness in society as a whole, giving people the strength and the courage to envisage and work patiently for a better future.

Solidarity was (and remains) one of the most formidable revolutionary movements to have appeared in Europe since the Second World War. An inventive movement, based on tolerance, it had many achievements to its credit. Under its umbrella it had succeeded in grouping 95 per cent of the industrial working class, and had, through its activities, polarised whole strata of Polish society: the small peasantry, the intellectuals, the artisans, young school students, etc. Each of these strata had created its own independent organisations in the image of the working-class union. Solidarity saw itself as an organisation combining the characteristics of a social movement and of a trade union. It fought to defend workers and to improve their daily life, and had already achieved important improvements in working conditions, housing and health. It had succeeded in creating an authentic working-class democracy. This was first shown in the course of the strikes, in which workers' committees were set up, comprising elected delegates who were subject to recall and were strictly mandated. Then, as the union was formed, millions of men and women set about defining and putting into practice organisational and decision-making rules and regulations designed to prevent any bureaucratic take-over in the future. In no sense did the union see itself as answerable for the economic crisis and bureaucratic negligence, but in order to deal with them, it created self-management councils in several thousand enterprises throughout Poland. These began by creating a coordination at local level, then at national level, with a view to drawing up, quite independently, the broad outlines for economic policy in Poland. Solidarity also succeeded in winning an unprecedented degree of freedom of speech and artistic freedom, even though the Government restricted its access to the media. Thousands of non-censored newspapers were circulating in Poland, and an independent distribution network succeeded in bringing some of the best Polish artists to a very wide audience. One could fill page after page with the achievements of those months — and one is left with the conclusion that, despite the queues outside shops, despite the endless provocations and the threat from beyond Poland's borders, the Polish people, with the formation of Solidarity, had embarked on a *revolution* in the full sense of the word.

Given all that, how was a military putsch possible? In order to answer this question one must first attempt to reconstruct the elements that led inevitably to this confrontation.

Here, the crisis that began with the Bydgoszcz events on 19 March 1981 seems to have been a turning point. Faced with the repression of its trade union militants, Solidarity mobilised the whole country. An unprecedented general strike was called,[1] and a head-on confrontation was only just avoided, when a hotly-contested compromise agreement was signed on 31 March in Warsaw. From that moment it became clear that, in future, the authorities would either have to give way before the demands of the workers, or would have to confront this powerful mass movement head-on. In the Solidarity camp there was an increasing build-up of accumulated discontent, and people increasingly saw the union as the sole force capable of bringing Poland out of her crisis. The Warsaw compromise was accepted, but it was accepted as a period of truce, a means of gaining time in order to mobilise and focus on the basic questions (trade union laws, economic reform and the full application of the 1980 agreement). The authorities, on the other hand, realised the strength of this working-class organisation, and saw that it would be impossible either to integrate it as such within the state apparatus, or to crush it by an external military intervention. This crisis was the signal for a rearrangement of forces on both sides, and a gradual radicalisation of each other's positions.

Within the state and the Party, the military fraction of the *apparat* began to develop its own policies, as from this moment. The military fraction was represented in government by General Jaruzelski, who had become Prime Minister in February. The reactionary and anti-semitic positions of this bloc were expressed openly in the armed forces daily *Zolnierz*

Wolnosci ("The Soldier of Freedom"). We now know that, ever since April 1981, the infrastructure of the Polish army had been preparing for a scenario of domestic repression. British intelligence sources at that time reported the setting-up of communication systems staffed by Soviet and East German technicians, but without a direct intervention by the Warsaw Pact armies.[2]

At the same time, Kania and Jaruzelski were attempting to rally the Polish United Workers' Party (PUWP), which, at that time, was severely divided and weakened. The ninth Congress in mid-July, under the cover of an apparent 'democratisation', saw a substantial renewal of Party personnel, and the adoption of a 'hard-line' programme of action. A number of the victories represented in the Gdansk agreements were brought into question. But despite this, the PUWP was not strengthened by the Congress. Rather, the Party's organisational base went increasingly into decline, and the military fraction grew in importance. In the successive crises, from one plenary session to another, the military wing provided Kania's principal support. On all the most fundamental questions, the Central Committee took up positions that were hostile to Solidarity's demands. Ever since August 1981, official propaganda had ceaselessly attacked the union; the judicial authorities amassed criminal charges against Solidarity militants (over 200 in October); and the economic authorities sabotaged the distribution of foodstuff. None of the economic reforms were set in motion; the union was refused access to the mass media; and, leaving aside certain concessions made by parliament, the law on self-management went against the union's demands. Thus, at the expense of a thousand minor conflicts and a gradual collapse of the Party as an organisational structure, the military fraction, little by little, began to take power. In mid-October Jaruzelski replaced Kania and now combined the title of first secretary of the PUWP with those of Head of Government and Minister of National Defence.

In the country as a whole, the worsening of the economic crisis forced the union to reconsider its objectives. Up until spring it had refused to take on any responsibility for the management of the economy, but it was now increasingly taking part in discussions on economic reform. It intervened at two levels: the reform of management structures, and broad economic choices. During the summer, following an initiative by committees from major enterprises, Solidarity put forward the demand for authentic workers' self-management as its principal response to the crisis. Within the enterprises, discontent was becoming more acute, and hunger marches and confrontations at a local level began to multiply. Within the union itself, the lessons of Bydgoszcz and the preparations for Solidarity's first national congress, brought with them a quite remarkable development of democracy. The union's rules were defined more closely, and observed in the smallest detail. The regional congresses of June-July 1981, and the national congress in September-October[3] gave the Polish working class a degree of authentic representation which was totally unprecedented. All this served to increase the union's cohesion, its awareness of its own strength, and played decisively in favour of the rank and file of the union, which was fed up with the incompetence at Party and state level.

Inexorably, the movement began increasingly to pose the question of power. In August, Jacek Kuron had noted: "One senses a terrible impatience, which is becoming more and more acute, a feeling that people can no longer tolerate what is going on. For a lot of people this means that the time has come to challenge and overturn the authorities."[4] And in September, Jan Litynski wrote: "At this moment, everybody is perfectly well aware that the authorities are not going to change by themselves, and that it is up to us to do it."[5] However, at this moment the tactics adopted by the Solidarity leadership showed their inadequacy. Z. Bujak, president of the union's Warsaw branch, pointed this out in August: "Our movement is growing weaker. (...) Union members do not understand the tactics adopted by the leadership. (...) I realise this when I went to a meeting in Ursus. It was only when I said that all this self-management activity was leading to taking power, that people understood and said OK. (...) At the moment, people are waiting for a clear programme."[4] In effect, the Solidarity leadership saw the building of self-management as their only means of winning economic power and enabling the country to emerge from the crisis. But the leadership was divided as to the concrete forms which, at a political level, an agreement with the government could take. Furthermore, the self-management movement was developing too slowly. Ten days before the coup d'état, *Tygodnik Solidarnosc* published a balance-sheet of the self-management experience. Jacek Merkel explained that the movement had affected only between 15 and 20 per cent of enterprises. Regional delegates filled out the picture: in Lodz, which is one of the more advanced regions, there are self-management committees in only 150 out of 1,500 enterprises; in Slupsk they were still at the stage of "founding committees", waiting for the government to pass a law; as for Mazowie, H. Wujec explained: "As long as it was a matter of drawing up our statutes, the movement was extremely active. But now that it has become a matter of putting them into practice, the movement has gone a bit slack. (...) We are going to have to prepare the planned referendum in a very precise and concrete manner, because only this will renew and concentrate the self-management movement"; in Gdansk there were between 250 and 300 self-management councils and founding committees; in Bydgoszcz "we have observed among the workers a weakening of the self-management dynamic; hestitations are setting in. It is as if people had lost faith in continuing the movement."[6] In fact, the extension of self-management, (despite the establishment of a National Federation of Workers' Councils in mid-October) was largely determined by the union's central policies, and its relations with the authorities.

A confrontation became unavoidable, and Jaruzelski was thought more readily able to take it on than Solidarity. He anticipated a certain amount of support within the 'silent majority' and the mass of 'don't knows', which had undeniably grown in number during those final weeks. A sizeable section of the population were worn out and fed up with the shortages of goods, as well as being disappointed in Solidarity and confused by government propaganda. Some began to look to the army for a restoration of order. For example, an opinion poll carried out by the union in Warsaw in mid-November, showed that 26 per cent of people supported the abolition of the right to strike being proposed by the central committee of the PUWP.[7] And, compared with previous opinion polls, this was an enormous number. Finally, Jaruzelski's reservations (if reservations there were!) were quickly dispelled under the combined pressure of the hawks within the Party apparatus, and the Soviet Union.

According to official Soviet sources, the general had outlined his plan to representatives of the Warsaw Pact on the occasion of three meetings at the beginning of December. The first in Moscow, with Warsaw Pact defence ministers; the second in Bucharest, with ministers of Foreign Affairs; and the third in Prague, with the heads of the various press agencies. "Thus a three-tier military, diplomatic and ideological operation had been set in motion, as the first step towards martial law. Marshal Khulikov apparently had the twin tasks of overseeing the execution of the operation, and of giving orders to the two Soviet divisions stationed within Poland's borders."[8]

At the political level, the military operation was conceived in two stages, with a view to aggravating dissension within the union. On 4 November, Jaruzelski began negotiations with the Church and with Solidarity, towards an agreement on national unity, but he insisted on putting forward positions that were unacceptable, and he used the mass media, of which he has a monopoly, to spread slanders. He had a precise objective: to make Solidarity publicly responsible for the breakdown of negotiations. On the 22 November, as if to ally suspicions, he ended the deployment of the special military brigades which, since October, had been testing the tension throughout the country. On 24 November Marshal Khulikov arrived in Warsaw, and on 27-28 November, the general announced to the plenary session of the central committee that the right to strike was to be suspended, and that he would be given exceptional powers. From that moment on, events moved very quickly, and the army went directly onto the offensive. The Solidarity leadership was caught up in the trap of negotiations on 'national unity', but they very soon realised the nature of the confrontation which was being prepared. On 3 December, in Radom, the union's praesidium saw the coming clash as unavoidable, and on 11-12 December, the national commission adopted, virtually unanimously, a programme to counter it: an immediate general strike if parliament voted Jaruzelski exceptional powers; a referendum on self-management before 15 February; and free elections. But it was too late. In the night hours of Saturday-Sunday 12-13 December, the army began its wave of arrests, and Jaruzelski proclaimed martial law.

What we have witnessed was a fairly classic process of social polarisation. But while a fraction of the ruling *apparat* was regaining the initiative, within a context in which the Party was falling apart, the Solidarity leadership was hesitating precisely at the moment when it was at the height of its power.

It is this paradox which we need to analyse. The attitude of the military elements within the Party *apparat*, to the extent to which it was encouraged and concretely supported by Kremlin, need not surprise us. It can be seen within the logic of previous upheavals in Eastern Europe. Whether one looks to Berlin in 1953, Budapest in 1956 or Prague in 1968, one sees, on each occasion, albeit with local variations, a continuing determination to break any attempt at a real democratisation of the regime. This reflects without ambiguity the basic source of power of the ruling bureaucracy — that is to say its political monopoly. The means that are employed in order to maintain these privileges — and these can extend as far as mass terror — will be abandoned only if they are judged ineffective. In Poland, as soon as martial law was seen as the only solution, the bureaucracy applied it regardless of the risks.

This is now quite clear, though, unfortunately, the Solidarity leadership seems not to have been fully aware of it. So I would like to turn my attention to the question of the apparent disarray within the union's leadership. I see its main cause in that extraordinary disjunction which has been revealed during the 16 months of struggle — between, on the one hand, the strength, the dynamism and the determination of this social movement, and on the other hand, the weakness and lack of strategic preparedness of its leadership. The two aspects of this paradox must be analysed as they interact with each other; so as to avoid false explanations, such as those which accuse the union of bureaucratisation, Catholicism or nationalism.

The nature of the movement organised by Solidarity is, to a large extent, determined by the specificity of Poland's historical experience. For example, one can clearly distinguish it from the Czechoslovakian experience in 1968-69. In this case one saw a popular mass movement which identified with a part of the Party apparatus, and its current leadership. Like Poland in 1956, one might say. To be sure, both movements had as their reference point the 'democratic' symbols of the XX Congress of the CPSU. But the Prague Spring also had its roots within the history of a Communist Party that was deeply integrated within the national tradition. The Czech Party led the resistance against the Nazi occupation; in 1945-48 it was one of the biggest workers' parties in Central Europe, more important even than the Yugoslav party, at a time when the Polish Communist Party was little more than a group. The power of the Polish Party was imposed from outside by the Red Army, after several years of disorder and civil war. Thus, in order to understand the specificity of the Polish experience we have to distinguish between those people's democracies where bureaucratic power is the product of a convergence between internal tendencies and an intervention from outside, and those where that governing power has been principally imposed from outside. In Poland, people's identification with the state institutions and the dominant Party was, in the 1950s and 1960s, far weaker than in Czechoslovakia. Recently published sociological studies support this view.

First, they show how, throughout this period, the dominant system of values in the population has remained stable. These values combine the social ideals advanced by the regime with patriotism and a continuing religious sentiment. These values tend to reject the central state institutions. People's primary reference groupings are, the family, one's circle of friends, and the nation. Political organisations rank very much in second place. This leads to the following conclusion: "In reality, Poland's objective social structure is clearly equally as complex as that of other industrialised countries. It has a central administration operating at several levels; industrial enterprises which are virtually private in character; political organisations; professional organisations; official national trade unions, etc. However, it appears that none of these institutions is experienced as very important for the majority of Poles, at least from what emerges from the individual interviews. The people interviewed refer to these institutions as 'them', and never as 'us'. In other words, they do not identify with the institutional groups, considering them as foreign to their system of values. Thus our inquiries have revealed the existence of a sort of social gap between people's primary groupings and the nation."

This "social gap" is bound to give rise to frustration and periodic explosions in which the movement changes direction. People move from the individual satisfaction of needs to a collective desire to construct new institutions. And in this case, the ruling Party, the state, and the administration are not seen as instruments to be transformed, but as foreign bodies, which one takes into account only for tactical reasons. Real society awakens and begins to act on dreams that have for long lain dormant. These sociological comments clarify the mechanisms and the scope of a revolution which cannot be reduced simply to popular discontent. The relationship between the PUWP and the working class oscillates between active defiance and indifferent passivity. This does not exclude the possibility of certain illusions, and of reformist movements, but they have a different nature and a different strength compared to those seen in countries like Czechoslovakia, where the Communist Party has deep national roots. In this light it would be interesting to analyse the Gomulka experience in 1956. The documents published in recent months in Poland, regarding the Poznan revolt, for example, show the great gap which existed, in language and ideology between the workers in revolt and the 'revisionist' intellectuals who brought Gomulka to power. And it is probable that these intellectuals' positions were reflected in the writings of the Western Marxist left, which too often limits its analysis to movements within the Party. In fact, the failure of the 'revisionists' was probably not only the failure of a strategy (reform from above), but also that of a political vanguard incapable of expressing the deep aspirations of the working class. And when Gomulka eliminated the most rebellious among them, the Polish proletariat lapsed into indifference.

The experiences of 1968, 1970 and 1976 had a far more radical effect on the political behaviour of the intelligentsia than on that of the working class. The working class rose up with the same violence, even the same slogans, in June 1956, December 1970, July 1976 and August 1980, whereas the intelligentsia each time underwent a change of attitude. They moved from reforming illusions (1956) to revolt (1968), then to indifference (1970), to support (1976) and finally to action (1980). From 1976, the intelligentsia was polarised by the working class movement. These oscillations, which can obviously be traced to the social status of the intelligentsia, were all the greater inasmuch as the new regime in post-war Poland had been obliged to reconstruct an intelligentsia that had been decimated.

These general observations give us three fundamental elements for understanding the characteristics of the crisis opened by the events of August 1980.

The first is the chronic weakness of the PUWP, revealed spectacularly in the recently-ended Kania period (September 1980 - October 1981), and the seizure of power by the military. Despite his tactical cleverness, Kania had been incapable of "reversing the current of events" and of re-establishing even an appearance of social order. The Party was not able to with-stand the shock of the powerful working-class mobilisation; it was rapidly dwarfed by events; it lost its ability to take initiatives, and basically abdicated to the bureaucratic and police apparatus, which itself was divided and weakened by internal factional struggles. Fourteen months after the seaboard strikes, the PUWP had fallen victim to a degree of organisational decay and political paralysis that was unprecedented. It was incapable of building even the smallest of minority currents within the country to support it. The fact that it remained in government as the 'ruling' party was simply the result of a shared desire by both Solidarity and the Kremlin who, each for their own reasons, sought to avoid a confrontation. The nomination of General Jaruzelski to the post of first secretary, and the position henceforth occupied by the military apparatus, represent a final attempt to restore some kind of legitimacy to the central authorities. In effect, they merely confirm the Party's total loss of credibility. From the *apparat*'s point of view, the state of war declared on 13 December, was inevitable.

Second, particular relationship between the Party, the working class and the intelligentsia has produced a working-class vanguard which, in Eastern European terms, is unique of its kind. In the first chapter of this book I trace its evolution, limiting myself to the Gdansk region. A comparison with other towns enables us, on the one hand, to assess the influence of the democratic opposition movement in the formation of this vanguard, and on the other hand, to outline the multiple paths which it has taken. What one finds is a combination of various phenomena. At Gdansk, this vanguard was organised in liaison with KOR and Young Poland, around the newspaper *Robotnik Wybrzeza*; at Szczecin, on the other hand, the group that led the strikes of August 1980 had a quite different history. As one observer has noted: "The Inter-Enterprise Strike Committee comprised 15 praesidium members, of whom five were Party members and twelve had been provincial delegates of the official trade union. The two vice-presidents were Party members (one of them was probably responsible for the very poor reception accorded to Western journalists). The political opposition groupings played no role in the initiation and the subsequent conduct of the strike. Within the leading elements, workers from the Warski shipyard played a dominant role."[9] The political development of this working-class leadership had taken place within a context apparently quite opposite to that of Gdansk, but in both cases the decisive element had been the trauma of December 1970. And they had chosen as leader a welder who had never been a Party member: Marian Jurcik. A very Catholic Polish patriot, he had already been a member of the 1970 strike committee.

The experiences and the political development of the workers within the Solidarity leadership are thus relatively independent from those of the intellectuals. So we are a long way from the vaguely Leninist mythology that underlies some accounts of these strikes. This working-class culture finds its roots within the parallel and private existence of a population which does not recognise itself in the existing social and political institutions. It has its own history, and this largely explains the charismatic power of men such as Walesa and Jurcik, who 'speak Polish'.

Third, and finally, all this contributes to the specific characteristics of political debate within Solidarity. The rejection of dominant ideology (Stalinist Marxism) does not lead to a vacuum, but brings with it a quite astonishing array of political and moral values. A number of ideologies (social democracy, revolutionary syndicalism, national populism, Christian democracy, etc.) which appeared stifled by 35 years of socialism, resurface with unexpected meanings. They express themselves within an extremely powerful working-class movement, and only acquired value inasmuch as they represent the practices and self-questionings of that movement. They are more an indication than a guide. Here lies one of the basic differences between the workers' leadership which led the revolution of 1980-81 and that which emerged in 1956. L. Gozdzik, who, in 1956, led the strike at the Zeran-FSO factory in Warsaw, compared his own failure with the experience of Walesa: "First they taught us that there was a God, and then that there was not. They told me to believe in Stalinism, and then told me of Stalin's crimes. In that quarter-century of my

life, they imbued me with faith, and at the same time with scep-
ticism... As for Walesa, they told him that there was a God,
and then nobody came to take that God away. Perhaps his
quarter-century was somewhat easier than mine." These considerations lead me to disagree with those commentators who
see Solidarity's fatal flaw as having subordinated workers to intellectuals and 'experts' — a flaw said to be caused by the
bureaucratisation of the union.

Other critiques of Solidarity stress the dominance within it
of nationalist and Catholic ideas. Such critiques make too
much of the fact that a number of small nationalist groupings
have been active in the union's wake, or that the mass of its
members worship religious symbols, is not sufficient in itself to
define an ideology of this movement. Rather, one should start
from the movement's social practice and the real political
choices that it has made. For example, one might imagine that
a dominant nationalism might express itself, leaving aside tactical considerations, in a desire to get out of the Soviet bloc,
and in a search for a third 'neutralist' path. Such a tendency
was visible at the time of the Hungarian revolution in 1956.
Solidarity's thinking certainly does not exclude this perspective
in the long term, but it remains within the perspective of a self-
managed socialist Poland. Its general view of alliances is still
based on the idea of a mutual cooperation between countries,
and does not exclude international solidarity with other
working-class struggles.[10] Other, more complex solutions have
also been debated. These range from a 'Finlandisation', suggested by S. Bratkowski of DiP, to a socialist federation of
states of Central Europe (including the Ukraine). The actual
programme adopted in Autumn 1981 states: "Our sense of
reality requires us to take into account the balance of forces
created in Europe after the second world war", and adds:
"Poland can only be a valid partner once she alone has defined,
according to her conscience, her obligations." Thus Polish nationalism comes close to the socialist tradition of the pre-war
Polish Socialist Party, which, at least in principle, sought to
unite the objectives of national liberation and social emancipation. Independent Poland will either be a self-managed Poland
or it will not be.

This perspective conflicts with a number of right-wing
nationalist positions which combine patriotic ideals with a

xenophobic chauvinism. For example, the leaders of groups such as KPN freely admit their anti-semitism and their attachment to the ideas of the pre-war Hitlerite *National Democracy.* This kind of ideology is also to be found within the Young Poland movement, which certainly has a presence in Gdansk. Here again, though, a number of things should be taken into account. The political influence of these groups is not necessarily equal to their prestige in the country as a whole. The arrest and imprisonment of Moczulski and his friends certainly did more for the image of the KPN than did the anti-semitic speeches of its leaders. By keeping them in prison the authorities have turned them into martyrs; symbols of resistance who are bound to generate sympathy. The verbal radicalism of their anti-government statements are widely appreciated. On the other hand, during Solidarity's first national congress, the various tendencies of this right-wing nationalism federated into a Club for the Salvation of Independence (KSN), but their success was limited.[11] The only real support that the KSN — just as the KPN — found was among what somebody at the congress called "the new minority: the true Poles", that is to say, among the most backward fringes of Solidarity's membership. Their political battles within the congress, as well as their manoeuvres against KOR, were a failure. And their degree of representation on the Solidarity's national commission elected by the union was virtually non-existent.

The same observation can be made in regard to Catholicism. The question is not whether Poles do or do not believe in God, whether they draw strength from some moral force, etc... The crucial point was that Catholic doctrine remained secondary within the publications and the activities of the union. The question was debated in the course of drawing up Solidarity's programme. The outline programme drawn up in February-March 1981 cited the "four main sources of its inspiration": "the best of our national traditions; the ethical principles of Christianity; democracy; and the idea of socialism". One of its authors saw this as the union's "moral identity card". This, however, did not prevent lively polemics arising against this somewhat vague allusion. One Catholic intellectual, for example, Marcin Krol, argued: "Formulas like this give you heart, but you don't really know what they mean. What are the 'best national traditions'? A well-meaning interpretation of this formula would be that it means the great sacrifices, the tradition of struggles for freedom and independence, the idea of "yours and ours", etc. But what is the relationship between the 'best national traditions' and 'the political appeal of democracy'? (...) We know that for the past 200 years democracy has rarely been the principal preoccupation of Poles, because the struggle for independence and freedom has created another order of problems. (...) The same goes for the ethical principles of Christianity. Either here we are talking simply of the Ten Commandments, and in that case it would be better just to say so, or the matter is more complex, and should be explained. Within the Christian world there is no single set of ethical values which might be taken as a unique set of Roman Catholic dogma. (...) The notion that such heterogeneous values and sources of inspiration might be able to co-exist without conflict within the realities of social life is based on a dangerous moralising illusion." In the end, the text adopted by congress did not include this passage, and the identity of the union was defined rather by the history of its struggles.

Having dealt with these misconceptions, it now remains to analyse the second paradoxical aspect noted above: the lack of political preparedness of the union's leadership for the military clamp-down. This was recognised explicitly by one of Solidarity's main leaders, Zbigniew Bujak, who has managed to go underground. In an interview with the *New York Times*, he says: "It was becoming clear that the authorities were preparing for a sizeable operation against the union. But we never thought it would be as serious as this (...) I would never have imagined that the whole national commission and Lech Walesa could be thrown into prison." Obviously, these illusions must be related to the power that Solidarity had acquired within society as a whole. No doubt, success had gone to the heads of the leadership. But, more importantly, these illusions were the result of the strategic orientation adopted by Solidarity. Consensus on this orientation was maintained up till the decision taken in October 1981 by the Solidarity leadership to participate in a 'social contract' which was to compromise three inseparable elements: "an anti-crisis agreement" which would be "the first proof of a cooperation between the authorities and society"; "an agreement on economic reform", which would require a "cooperation in the direction of radical change"; and an agreement on the establishment of a self-managed republic which would outline "perspectives and means towards the democratisation of the institutions of public life".

It was on this point, that the principal divergences emerged. The nub of the problem was how to define the precise content of the social contract. Given the level of people's mistrust of the PUWP, signed agreements tend to be seen in the same light as the peace treaties of yesteryear between white Americans and Indians. They are only put into force if the balance of power requires it. Furthermore, the choice of a number of priority objectives — economic reform, self-management, civil liberties, etc. — increasingly led Solidarity's national leadership to seek to concentrate its forces and limit local conflicts. The latter far from being the work of undisciplined militants, were, most of the time, natural reactions to objective situations. Thus, ever since the Bydgoszcz events, the trade union leadership faced a permanent dilemma: either it took up an intransigent position in every single conflict, and in that event ran the risk of bringing about a national confrontation over quite minor issues; or it conserved its strength for dealing with those few basic points. In conditions such as these it is easy to understand the problems and difficulties which the union was experiencing in developing its policies, from the summer onwards. In a sense, the confrontational outcome initiated by Jaruzelski was unavoidable.

Discussions on the national commission and within the Inter-Enterprise Strike Committees dwelt on the question of how to get out of this dilemma, and how, practically, to define the movement's new objectives. People were more and more convinced that, without a firm position on the crucial question of power, it would not be possible to go forward and embark on an effective set of economic reforms. Two positions dominated this debate. The position of Jacek Kuron, supported by Lech Walesa, was conceived within a continuity of the union's original orientation. It was a pragmatic conception. They should move forward step by step. The union should aim at reforming the system, and should remain within the framework of the Gdansk agreements. Poland's geo-political situation could not be modified in the short term. Thus, the government would have to be forced into an agreement.

Concretely, Jacek Kuron envisaged the formation of a "Government of National Agreement". During a debate in Warsaw in mid-September, he explained: "The problem is as follows: can we put forward a programme of gradual reform, and presume at the same time that power will remain in the same hands as at present? Is it not likely that such a reform would prove impossible? One has the impression that this is what life teaches us. (...) Even if the realisation of a programme of reforms from the base were to prove impossible, we would have to gather the whole of society around this programme, because only in this way would everyone come to see the authorities as being responsible for the confrontation, and if it should come to conflict, the government would very soon lose, as happened at the time of the Bydgoszcz events. One could then set up a Government of National Agreement, which would set the date for elections, and would introduce reforms. (...) The USSR would be obliged to accept such an agreement. This government would be formed "in the heat of the moment" within a balance of power that was favourable to the workers, and would have the support of the party, the church and the union.

This notion started from the idea that the Party would not be strong enough to take on a confrontation and turn it to its advantage. Leaving aside the fact that experience has shown the opposite to be true, this notion ran into two major difficulties. On the one hand, the authorities had broken off negotiations since the summer, and did not seem inclined to share their power in any manner whatsoever (even formally); on the other hand, Jaruzelski co-opted this "national agreement" formula by suggesting that it be negotiated without the threat of pending strikes, and by sowing division and dissension within the union. The line of argument put forward by Kuron and Walesa led effectively into a cul-de-sac, and reduced the movement to impotence.

The counter position, while not explicitly breaking with the general framework of pragmatism, felt that the only adequate response to the provocations and incompetence of the regime was to build the self-management movement, and to defend it by active strike action. This tactic was included in the electoral platform of the leadership elected on the occasion of the Lodz regional congress, in July 1981. It contained a clearer vision of the government's manoeuvres. Shortly after the coup d'état, one of the Lodz leaders, Zbigniew Kowalewski, outlined the position[12]: "We were convinced that the regime was evolving in the direction of a military dictatorship, but we thought that it would be a long-term process. We thought that, as Solidarity went on growing and concentrating its forces, the regime would harden into the form of what we called a "military-police" dictatorship. Thus we *did* envisage the possibility of a coup d'état, but in a more distant future. We thought that the dictatorship would use every means in order to guarantee its legality, for example, by voting measures through parliament to support it: and in our view, any such voting in parliament would still be subject to the existing balance of forces. In short, we thought that we still had time left to prepare ourselves."

After the police evacuation of the firemen's college in Warsaw on 2 December, the Lodz militants were of the opinion that "the country was entering a second revolutionary situation. (...) Within the rank and file there was a general feeling, not of frustration, but of the necessity of taking over the management of our own affairs. It is significant that at that stage, the idea of the "active strike" which we had put forward in August, was taken up at the base. An "active strike" means that strike committees take over power within the enterprises, as well as the control of production and distribution: in other words, a seizure of economic power by the working class within the framework created by Solidarity and the self-management movement. The inquiries which we carried out among trade unionists have shown that 65 per cent of workers were in favour of the "active strike" as a means of radical struggle, and that only 12 per cent were in favour of a general strike. In the large enterprises, the number of workers supporting the "active strike" rose to 80 per cent." In mid-November, the idea began to spread to the whole country, and the National Commission meeting of 12 December adopted it as a principle. But it was too late. So, there was an orientation at hand which seemed more effective against the regime's threats, but it was too slowly adopted as an alternative. Furthermore, there was a lack of clarity as to its likely political outcome. Was this orientation expected to lead to a seizure of power, or to an agreement with the government dominated by the Party?

Finally, and this is probably the greatest weakness of this revolutionary process, the various political issues were governed by an overestimation of the extent of the regime's crisis, and an overestimation of the movement's strength. Following the army take-over of 13 December, any resurgence of the Polish revolution will require its leaders to undertake a clear reassessment of this question. The stakes here are high, inasmuch as this movement has raised hopes throughout the Socialist bloc, and any advance of democratic and self-managed socialism within those countries will depend, in large part, on the lessons that are drawn from the Polish experience.

Jean-Yves Potel
15 January 1982

Notes

1. See the strike advice published in *L'Alternative* No. 12 (Maspero, Paris, 1981)
2. "The Secret Count-down", *Sunday Times*, 20 December 1981.
3. See my article "Solidarity's First National Congress", translated in *Revolutionary Socialism* No. 8.
4. *L'Alternative*, No. 13, (Maspero, Paris, 1981)
5. *Robotnik*, 27 September 1981.
6. "The View Before the Battle", a round-table discussion published in *Tygodnik Solidarnosc*, No. 36, 4 December 1981.
7. Opinion poll quoted by L. Dorn during the meeting of the union's National Commission on 3-4 November 1981. Cf. *Tygodnik Solidarnosc* No. 33, 13 November 1981.
8. *Le Monde*, 18 December, 1981.
9. See the dossier on Szczecin prepared by Oliver MacDonald in *Labour Focus on Eastern Europe*, "Poland, Solidarnosc in Action", Spring 1981, p. 18.
10 . See the appeal to workers of the Eastern bloc countries, issued by the first session of the Solidarity's national congress in September 1981.
11. The KSN was set up by about twenty people, including A. Hall (Young Poland), A. Macierewicz (editor of *Glos*), S. Kurowski (economist), etc.
12. A translation of the interview is in *Revolutionary Socialism* 9.

1. The Workers

"So, tell me a little about these Gdansk workers." Maria Komorowska smiled a little before answering. It was Sunday, the first snows of winter were falling, and we had spent the day together. Gdansk was freezing, but the revolution there had been simmering for three months. Maria and I had met during the August strike at the *Lenin* shipyard, where she had spent all her working life. As well as having been elected several times to the Workers' Council in her sector, she was by then information officer of the new union, Solidarity.

Maria was a big-built woman in her fifties, with red hair, a shrewd face, and bright red lipstick. Her face looked tired. Lighting a cigarette, she began to explain: "You know, the workers have changed a lot since the war. Today they're younger, they've studied, they know their history, and they know their jobs. They want to live." She knew them all. That summer you couldn't move in the occupied shipyard without Maria greeting someone, offering advice to another, and asking after the children of yet another. Whenever I found myself up against any kind of difficulty, there she was. "Come along," she would say, and the problem was soon solved. Her spirit, her enthusiasm and her kindness left their mark on that great festival whose air of seriousness and sense of liberation had inspired the shipyard during the month of August. On the evening of the victory she had confided to me: "You can't begin to imagine how proud I am of us, the workers of Gdansk."

I pressed my point. I wanted to find out how it was that hundreds of thousands of men and women had been able to reach such a level of determination in their struggle, such developed organisation and such a calm assurance of final victory.

Maria settled into her armchair. Outside the snow was falling silently. With a plate of sandwiches on the table, she began to talk. In a soft, maternal voice she took me into the realm of that oral history which is so important in Poland where Stalinism has tried to erase historical truth. This oral history, with its myths and legends, may on occasion be an unreliable source, but that evening I knew that this woman would go exploring in her memories and bring me back some of the suppressed truth of the history of the Polish people. A many-faceted remembrance, which the regime has sought to shatter and disperse but which maintains a tenacious hold on life.

"After the war," Maria explained, "all the Germans had to leave the town. They had been living here for generations. They shipped them out by the trainload. Gdansk was then repopulated with Poles from Wilno, who in turn had been chased out by the Russians, who were annexing Lithuania. In exchange we were given Szczecin and the territories to the West."

The war had found Maria in the region of Warsaw, the city where she was born. At the time of the 1944 rising she had fled to the countryside. Afterwards, over the period of a year, she had been involved in welcoming the prisoners freed from the Nazi camps, who were being brought together at the town of Czestochowa. Her own family had disappeared, but one day she received a letter from her mother. She was in Gdansk, and Maria hurried to see her. "I arrived to find a heap of scrap metal and rubble. People were living in there, among machines that were destroyed and burned." But now, despite everything, life had to start again. "We began by putting the place in order, by cleaning out the shipyard. The first sheds were rebuilt, the first machine tools dragged out of the debris, and the old ships were repaired. This was 1945 and it took us a good six months to restore some semblance of normal life. In that period ships were coming from abroad. We were repairing them and repainting them." Wage levels and working conditions were of little importance. People were fired with the enthusiasm of the Liberation; a desire to rebuild their city, an eagerness to taste a liberty that had been crushed by so many years of occupation. The bosses, Nazis for the most part, were replaced by workers. This period too produced its heroes: "I remember one particular worker who was amazing — an ace, a very intelligent man. His name was Stanislaw Soldek. He symbolised our enthusiasm at the beginning of the reconstruction." A hero whom the Government sought to turn into an example: "The first ship to be completed at the *Lenin* shipyard in 1948 bore his name. Later we began to construct cargo boats for the transport of wood, and a factory ship for fishing..."

Today there are eight shipyards in the *Trojmiasto* (the Three Towns — the conurbation consisting of Gdansk, Gdynia and Sopot). Their huge cranes tower in the sky over the bay. They employ something approaching a hundred thousand workers. The most important of them, the *Lenin* shipyard (16,000 workers), produces principally cargo ships, fishing vessels and ultra-modern factory ships. Then comes the *Paris Commune* shipyard (12,000 workers), which specialises in the construction of the bigger ships of more than 20,000 tonnes gross tonnage. Two names which, having for years figured in pamphlets boasting the industrial successes of socialism, will henceforth symbolise the vanguard struggle of Poland's seaboard workers.

These workers, together with the Silesian miners, are among the best paid in the country. "After the war," explained Maria, "you had the yards' recruiting officers and the Party's propagandists scouring the country looking for workers. They made great play of the wage levels and the working conditions: 'There's housing available in Gdansk. It's a good life!' As a result peasants from every region of Poland came to Gdansk. They crammed into workers' hotels like the one where Solidarity now has its office. Most were young. Some of them were content with what they found, but others expected to get everything at once: housing, good wages, etc. But this would have been impossible. These young peasants hadn't a clue about how a ship is built. It took at least three months to acclimatise them, and in that period others were doing the work for them... Because, you know, this intensive recruitment campaign was not allowed for in the planned output levels. It simply meant that the skilled workers were doing double the workload. In those days we were willing to accept a lot. Life by then was becoming easier. Food was not so hard to find, and its quality was better. In the shipyard, there was always an adequate supply of raw materials. It was only at the end of the 1960s that we began to see the absurdities that nowadays you see all around you."

At the end of the war, in the period from August 1944 to March 1945, the whole of Poland embarked on a spontaneous movement in which workers expropriated the factories. The most effective were those under the control of factory councils and trade union committees, which were able to restart production and which, for a number of weeks, maintained the management and successful functioning of the factories. This spontaneous movement represented a collective desire for rebirth, the burning desires of a nation which, after so many sacrifices, had finally found itself. This commitment was sealed by a Government decree signed in February 1945. It was only later, as the monolith of the Workers' Party established its power, that these councils were emptied of their substance and transformed into 'rank and file' bodies subordinated within the trade unions (January 1947). Then, when the trade union movement was centralised, they lost even this role, and from 1948 onwards were transformed into part of the incentive system for increasing productivity. And the final touch came with the 1949 Trade Union Congress which warned the workers of the 'dangers inherent in the idea of workers' management'.

Thus, at one and the same time, the Polish economy had been reconstructed and the working class remodelled. The war had exterminated a large percentage of the skilled work force, and some had also been deported to Germany. The occupying forces had destroyed plant and machinery. The influx of young peasants into the factories, and the rapid development of heavy industry along Soviet lines, were to produce profound changes in the working class. Within five years its numbers had doubled (to reach two million by 1950). Furthermore, the Nazis' virtual destruction of the pre-war workers' movement before the war was carried to its conclusion by the Stalinist administration. Militants of the working-class organisations were either dispersed across the country, or imprisoned. Every available means was used to cut the workers off from their previous political experiences.

It would be wrong, however, to imagine that this historical memory was entirely erased. While a number of veterans moved out of production and into the State and Party apparatus, others undertook training responsibilities. Maria explained to me the situation in the shipyard: "In those days there were still a lot of old workers around. They still had something of the old German discipline. They knew their craft well, having studied it on the job. They said to themselves: 'Without work there will be no bread and no wages.' The idea of going on strike never even occurred to them. They were satisfied. For them the advent of socialism was a source of great happiness. The factory owners had disappeared, and unemployment with them. Also, you had all these young peasants coming from the depths of the countryside, and the old workers taught them their craft. In those days, craft training schools had not yet been set up. The older workers said: 'You must do a good job, you keep your head down, and be a good worker. This will be good for you.' "

Of course, this did not prevent certain conflicts arising against the authoritarianism of the emerging regime. The hegemony of the emerging Workers' Party was not accepted easily. At the time of the trial-run factory council elections organised at the end of 1945, the Workers' Party often found itself in a minority. In fact, in 1946, at Gdansk, Gdynia, Szczecin and Lodz, there were strikes which ended up in street fighting. But all in all, because of the general political conditions and the level of repression, the new regime was able to achieve a temporary stability.

Later on, a lot of things were to change in the factories. The young workers were now for the main part born in the towns, and while the influx from the countryside continued, it was more marginal. Educational standards were rising. "By then," Maria continued, "all the young workers had completed shipbuilding studies in secondary school, and they knew what life was about. In the post-war period, the older workers did their jobs like superb pieces of precise machinery. Then, at the start of the 1960s, they also played an important role when the first wave of school-leavers reached the yards. They had to be taught to be workers. They were still completely green. Each work-team was headed up by a veteran, who was to teach them their craft. The young ones knew shipbuilding in theory, but the old ones knew it in practice. Nowadays things are quite different. During their studies each of these students attends at the shipyard two or three times a week, and when they start as young workers, they already know the basics of their craft, although it takes a while to bring them up to scratch."

Women occupy a very particular place. They number around 5,000 in the *Lenin* shipyard. Their wages and working conditions are theoretically identical with those of the men. "This can be seen in the one sector where they carry out the same work as the men: namely the operation of small cranes." In fact this example is the exception. In general there is substantial sexual discrimination in the division of labour. The majority of women are to be found either in the offices or in the social services. The female blue-collar workers (numbering roughly a thousand) work either in the insulation department, or on cleaning out the ships after welding has taken place. They are in fact employed by a small contractor within the shipyard. As Maria stressed: "Their conditions are terrible. Down in the holds it is very cold, dirty and damp. In winter you slip on the ice, and it's not unusual for people to break a leg. You wouldn't find the men cleaning out the ships. These women lead a terrible life." What is more, like all the workers, they work an average 46 hours per week.

During the August strike I went to visit the shipyard's hospital. The 16 nurses had gone on strike, (unlike the six doctors, who had declared themselves 'happy with the situation'). One of them explained to me the dilemma in which she found herself every day. "The hospital is too small. In this huge yard there is only one nurse for every thousand workers, and you never find more than two doctors on duty at any one time. We are badly equipped, and short of basic medicines. In fact, the hospital services are limited to general medicine and cardiology. The waiting list is always very long, because of staff shortages and lack of equipment. We have to be there 10-12 hours a day, 24 hours round the clock, on a rota basis. Accidents have to be treated outside the yard, because we have no surgeon here." Surely, I suggested, this in itself would have been reason enough for going on strike. She replied: "At the same time, we can't leave the workers without medical care, when you see the state that they are in. Many of them are suffering from chronic illnesses as a result of gas or paint poisoning, or dust in the lungs." In theory, there is a system of rules and regulations supposed to protect workers against breaches of hygiene and safety standards. But these are not observed by the management. On the contrary, explained Alina Pienkowska, all that the managers worry about is the fulfilment of the Plan, and not the working conditions of the workers. And the workers are so anxious about keeping their jobs that they do not complain even when their health is in danger. The manager only comes face to face with the worker when the worker plucks up the courage to claim his rights... and, in that event, he threatens him with the sack, or with not getting the housing that he's spent years waiting for.''

In the shipyard, toxic products are supposed to be controlled and limited to a certain maximum concentration in the atmosphere, the so-called threshold limit value (TLV). But the employers tend to ignore these. This was the situation, for example, in the Elmor factory in Gdansk (which supplies electrical equipment to the shipyard), shortly before the strikes of Spring 1980: "In the cutting sheds, the level of acid fumes was 2.5 times more than the threshold limit value, rising to 3.7 times around the vats. In the chroming shop, the level of acid fumes was 1.7 times more than the TLV, and rose to 8 times the TLV in the immediate region of the vats. This acid does incurable damage to the nervous and circulatory systems. Near the galvanising tanks, the concentration of prussic acid was 5.6 times the threshold limit value, etc." These levels of toxic gases occasionally cause accidents. On 18 June 1980, for example, there was an explosion which severely injured a number of people at the *Lenin* shipyard. It happened in a large ship which, the following day, was due to be handed over to the Russians. Joanna-Duda Gwiazda gathered witness statements at the scene of the accident: "The effects of the accident were horrible to see. Something like a hundred people had been present on the scene. Many of them were burned, or crushed, with broken bones. After the accident they couldn't even find enough first-aid equipment. They had to break into a ship's first-aid cabinet to find some. The first ambulances arrived twenty minutes after the explosion, and they were ferrying the injured for two whole hours. Seventy injured workers were taken to hospital, but there weren't enough beds for them." However this spectacular accident was one of many. *Robotnik*, newspaper of KOR, the workers' self-defence committee, quotes official statistics: "In 1976 almost one in four workers were working in unhealthy conditions. About 2.8 million people were working in hazardous or particularly difficult conditions. The Plan for the elimination of these health hazards was 80 per cent fulfilled in 1976: 60 per cent in the heavy and agricultural machinery industry. For example, in the Ursus factory, 2,200 people were exposed to noise levels exceeding that permitted, and 1,730 to excessive vibrations. Result: 43 cases of work-related damage to hearing, and 13 cases of illness brought about by vibration." Regarding compulsory medical checks,

Robotnik continues: "In 1976 the Plan for periodic medical checks was only 50-70 per cent fulfilled in the furniture, chemical, rubber and shoe industries." As regards protective clothing, which companies are supposed to provide free for their workers, "Requirements for leather gloves were only 35-50 per cent achieved; protective shoes only 60-85 per cent; and security harnesses 75 per cent." On this subject Maria commented: "The most frequent accident in winter is when a worker picks up steel with bare hands. It's so cold that your skin sticks to the metal and is torn away."

The awareness and understanding that the Polish workers revealed in August 1980 and subsequently is the fruit not just of structural transformations and difficult living and working conditions. It has been forged through a long experience of politics, an experience which is particularly rich in Gdansk, a region where the relationship between workers and intellectuals has been less difficult than in the rest of Poland.

Could this have been because of the circumstances in which the reconstruction of the city had taken place? I went to talk about this with Tamara, a teacher at the University of Sopot. She lived in a magnificent villa on the city heights, surrounded by an enormous park and divided into a number of apartments. Tamara had only three rooms (including the kitchen) to accommodate herself, her old mother, her son and her husband. She showed me into a large living room arranged with taste and simplicity. "The School of Fine Arts was born here, in 1945," she told me with pride. Together with her husband, an architect, she had gathered artists from all over Poland. "In 1954 we forced the Government to undertake the reconstruction of the old town of Gdansk. We were still wallowing in Stalinism, and 'socialist realism' had rated as the official theory since 1949. Some people just followed along like sheep, it was indescribable..." But, I asked, didn't others resist? "You can't change the mentality of people, particularly of Poles, with theories like those. At the School of Fine Arts socialist realism was the rule, but actually everyone was doing something else. We are Poles, not Czechs or Germans. It's hard to understand, but that's the way it is! There were official things, and other things which were unofficial. We knew who the police informers were. They would stand for hours at the bar of the only cafe in Warsaw where all the artists met, and where everyone spoke freely. These characters would listen. So we would offer them vodka, they would drink, and then they no longer listened. And that was that.'' This unfair slight on Czechs and Germans rather simplifies a reality which was in fact a lot more painful than this. In fact the thinking of the majority of Polish intellectuals remained 'tame'.[1]

"For us,'' Tamara continued, "the reconstruction was a tremendous opportunity. Bierut ended by becoming a great patron, virtually despite himself, since he understood nothing about art. But he had excellent experts on hand, and did not claim to know everything. He was a simple man, and in these matters he was fantastic. For this he deserves some credit... In Warsaw a group of artists was able to convince him to reconstruct the old city. He was a man who respected our national traditions. The Gdansk artists had to court him for a year, but finally we succeeded in making our case, and in 1954 the great machine was set in motion. You know, Josef Cyrankiewicz, the Prime Minister, was a very cultivated man. Later of course, he was to shoot down workers... but in that period he neither wanted nor was able to kill great artists.''

These succinct explanations underlined Tamara's conviction, her memory that this had been a "very fine era''. She had preserved a memory of it which, for me, evoked rather the Stalinist brochures of the 1950s. "In the process of reconstruction an absolute symbiosis was created between the workers, the intellectuals and the students. A very fine thing. It had a very deep effect on the spirit of the people.'' This was an image already present in Maria's account: "We had rebuilt the old city with enthusiasm: the painters, the architects and the workers worked side by side, with love...'' This shared memory also explains a comparison with recent times: "The intellectuals in those days were not bourgeois,'' explained Tamara. "You could see this in the years which led up to 1956. The bourgeois spirit arrived with Gierek: all the parvenus were capable of discussing was the Spanish tiling in their bathrooms, or their *dachas*. This was what killed the human spirit. Objects killed it. American-style consumptionism in a country as poor as Poland is positively indecent! It creates incredible disparities between waged workers, the ruling class and their hangers-on, and the nouveaux riches. This is something harmful, pitiful and much to be regretted. It is a moral problem."

1956. Poland was getting over the shock of the post-war period, and after a few years was beginning to understand the true nature of the regime left behind by Bierut, who had died a few years after Stalin. An old communist poet, Adam Wazyk, published his "Poem for Adults" in an artistic journal. It laid the blame with the Party leadership. This was the heartfelt cry of a man whose illusions had been shattered: "We see worn-out men, the men of Nowa-Huta who have never been to the theatre, children turned away by criminal doctors, boys forced to lie, girls forced to lie, old women driven out of the house by their husbands, men blackened and defamed, people cast in the streets by vulgar lawbreakers for whom a legal definition is still being sought, men waiting for their papers, people hoping for justice, people who have been waiting for a long time." But this wait did not lead to despair. On the contrary. 1956 was the year of the Soviet Union's XX Party Congress. Kruschev's famous report on Stalin's crimes opened the way for a relative liberalisation which, in Poland, fell on fertile ground. A liberal fraction formed within the Party. Inspired by the working class revolt, it found itself placed at the head of a great anti-bureaucratic movement, the first of its kind in post-war Poland.

Some of the reconstruction efforts of the first Six Year Plan had produced results which translated into formidable statistics: an extremely rapid industrial growth for the period 1950-55, estimated at between 12 and 22 per cent per year. State officials were able to mark up impressive figures on the blackboards of conference halls, even when the objectives of the Plan had not all been achieved. Poland found itself very favourably placed on the competitive world market. The towns had begun to absorb the influx of rural population. But when you emerged from the realm of figures, to walk in the streets, to go into a factory, or to eat in somebody's home, the reality was somewhat more sombre.

The early 1950s saw standards of living stagnating, or even falling. Not only had the wage-system become archaic, but the distribution of goods was badly organised. In certain provinces you would find stocks of products which in others were in short supply. The daily queues began to lengthen, and housing was hard to find. In the factories there were too many work-related accidents, and production lapsed into chaos because of the poor coordination of supplies and the lack of cooperation between factories, which resulted in shortages of materials. It was in this period that the journal *Po Prostu*, the spearhead of the emerging opposition, wrote: "For several years now history has been repeating itself. Twelve times a year, the last ten days of the month become a kind of production nightmare in many of our engineering factories: the FSO car factory, the Ursus tractor factory, and Zispo in Poznan. Men stand by powerless, the demands of production impose themselves inexorably, horribly and inevitably, crushing everything in their path. 70 per cent of April's production at the Zeran factory was produced in the last ten days of the month. At the Zispo plant, more than 70 per cent of planned output was carried out in the last ten days of the month. The average rhythm of output is as follows: the first ten days, 7 per cent; the second ten days, 22 per cent; the third ten days, 71 per cent." In fact, at Poznan this was to prove too much. At the beginning of May 1956, the workers of this old industrial centre (whose traditions date back to the birth of the socialist movement in the last century) reacted. There were strikes and go-slows, petitions to the minister. No reply. The factory committee at Zispo was revived, and decided to send a delegation to Warsaw on 26 June. The workers put forward a whole range of demands. The delegation returned, accompanied by the minister, who beat about the bush. Meetings took place. Then came the strike — the workers came out in demonstrations and occupied the Tribunal building. By 9.30 the strike had spread throughout the city, and thousands of workers were in the streets, shouting for: "Bread, freedom, democracy!"

The authorities were terrified, and gathered their troops. 198 prisoners were freed from the prisons by the crowd, and public records were burned. At midday the armoured cars went into action. They opened fire, and a bloodbath followed. At five o'clock that evening the International Fair at Poznan closed its gates.

The ensuing repression was terrible: 38 dead were reported — of whom a number were policemen who had been lynched by workers; there were 270 injured. Foreigners who had come to sell their merchandise at the International Fair were met by people shouting: "This is our revolution. Tell the world what we are doing. We want the Soviets to go away, we want a new life!"

That day was to shake the whole country. It sparked off a Government crisis which, four months later, was to lead to important changes at the head of the Polish United Workers' Party. Wladyslaw Gomulka, a victim of the Stalinist purges of 1949, rejoined the Central Committee in July, and on 19 October became First Secretary.

The working class had rediscovered its strength. Up until Poznan's 'Black Thursday' collective action had been rare. The influx of workers from the countryside, Stalinism's destruction of all forms of independent organisation (trade unions, councils, the Party), police terror, the divisions within work, the divisive influence of 'socialist emulation' (Stakhanovism), and the structure of the wage system, had turned the Polish proletariat into a heterogeneous ensemble, with no internal cohesion. But it proved impossible to maintain this dispersion and division in the longer term. Gomulka himself was forced to recognise this in his famous speech of 20 October: "The working class has recently given the Party leadership and the Government a painful lesson. By taking strike action and by demonstrating in the streets on that dark Thursday last June, the workers of Poznan have shouted aloud: 'Enough! This cannot go on! The country is on the wrong path!' The working class has never made use of the strike weapon light-heartedly. Especially so today, in people's Poland, where the Government acts in the name of the working class and of all workers, the working class has not taken this step rashly. There is no doubt that things have gone too far, and henceforth such a situation will not be allowed to continue."

This new force, which was seeking an autonomous expression of its own interests, found a form of democratic organisation in the workers' councils. This movement began in October and spread to all enterprises, but at the same time it was identified with the new Party leadership. This leadership had acquired considerable authority and the enthusiastic confidence of the population by just avoiding a Soviet intervention. The tanks were stationed just a few kilometres from Warsaw, and during the night of 19-20 October, Gomulka and Cyrankiewicz negotiated with Kruschev and Mikoyan, who had come by plane from Moscow. These early months of the Gomulka regime are remembered by the working class as days which had given a great breath of freedom.

More than 20 years later, in Gdansk, Tamara was to recall them with nostalgia. "Here a committee was in permanent session at the Polytechnic School. It was magnificent. Workers' delegations were arriving from all quarters, and were able to meet with the intelligentsia. They did not go on strike, for that would have been useless. Each delegation declared its solidarity. Even the Navy sent men. They told us: "We will not fire at our children! Nor on our mothers! We will not shoot on our brothers!" But for all that the Navy's guns were pointing at our backs... Gomulka had everybody with him. People would chant the Polish equivalent of 'for he's a jolly good fellow'. A crazy sort of enthusiasm. His first act was to open the prisons: soldiers of the Resistance who had been persecuted after the war were brought back — that is to say those who were still alive. We embraced the deportees who were brought back from Russia. Then he abolished the the collective farms; he did away with hunger; he brought back works of art, the big national collections; and he stopped persecuting the Church."

However, Gomulka very soon changed his colours. He was trying to maintain a balance between two public factions in the Party. These factions met in towns near to Warsaw: the liberals in Pulawy, and the conservatives in Natolin. The mass movement paid the price of this, thrown from compromise to capitulation, and little by little Gomulka became the plaything of the 'Natolinians'.

One by one he did away with the achievements of that October. The workers' councils were denounced as 'anarchistic utopianism' and the law of 20 December 1958 on 'workers' autonomy' was to set the seal on this process. A number of strikes were broken by the police, and the right to strike was abolished. The journal of *Po Prostu* was banned, and a purge of the Party apparatus began. A prolonged backlash was set in motion.

It is true to say that the Gomulka team initiated a number of economic measures which, despite their timidity, permitted some growth in the country at the start of the 1960s. But while a section of the intellectuals who had emerged from the 'October Left' embarked on a prolonged debate on the nature of this regime, and began to express its discontent, the working class, for the most part, remained passive. Anna Walentynowicz, one of the principal activists in the August 1980 strike, was to explain as follows: "With the arrival of Gomulka there was a real euphoria, a great sense of joy. We felt that the Stalinist regime had come to an end, and the whole of the working class invested a great deal of confidence in him." But it was to prove misplaced.

These different reactions were to give birth to two separate struggles. In 1967-68 the intellectuals and students faced a government offensive, in which the ruling fraction began an intense nationalistic and anti-semitic campaign. The working class, for its part, after a long period of demoralisation and weariness, was to rise up in December 1970. These two tragic experiences were nonetheless decisive in the formation of working-class awareness during the 1970s, and for the emergence of that stratum of vanguard militants — workers and intellectuals — without whom Summer 1980 would have been impossible.

The old communist militant Leopold Trepper summed up the Polish events of 1968 with the following formula: "More than 20 years after the war, in the land of the Warsaw Ghetto, where the Jews had suffered more than anywhere else under the barbarities of Nazism, and under a government which claimed to be socialist, the monster of anti-semitism rose again from its ashes." General Moczar, a former communist partisan, had attempted to take power in 1967 with the support of the army veterans' organisation, which he had transformed into a militant force, and via an enormous campaign of anti-semitism. Taking as his pretext the Six Day War in the Middle East, he claimed to be fighting the 'Zionist fifth column' (n.b. Gomulka's own phrase) which, according to him, was threatening socialism. He put forward a sort of nationalist totalitarianism organised along military lines and backed by racist and populist slogans. Moczar did not achieve his ends (which were to overthrow Gomulka), but his anti-semitic campaign was tacitly supported by the First Secretary and was revived in 1968, at the time of the student rising. The 'Prague Spring' in neighbouring Czechoslovakia stirred the open sympathy of Polish youth, particularly among students. In March the

Government banned a play, *The Ancestors*, written by the Romantic poet Adam Mickiewicz, because it was considered too anti-Soviet. This was the spark that lit the fire. Street demonstrations ended in clashes, and Moczar, as Minister of the Interior, let his 'workers' militia' loose on the University and his anti-semitic hacks set to work in the official Press. A number of the 30,000 Jews who remained in Poland were forced to emigrate, the Universities were purged of 'Zionists', and dissident intellectuals were arrested on charges of 'Germano-Zionist conspiracy', 'imperialist subversion', 'revisionism', or 'Trotskyism'.

The workers, whom Gomulka had encouraged to be suspicious of intellectuals, were indifferent to this repression. In Warsaw and in Silesia the Party even organised meetings against the students. "Here in Gdansk," Tamara explained to me, "a section of the workers understood very well what was going on, even if, in general, the population was hostile to the young people's fight. The shipyards did not strike.

"Many young workers joined in the street fighting between the police and the students. The militia were there to be fought, and it was a pleasure! All the intellectuals took part in the struggle: our hopes for liberty were being crushed. This was the end of the universities, with purges, appointed rectors, an appointed Dean, and all sorts of ridiculous charges being brought."

The example of Gdansk is often cited as a symbol of the mutual indifference between workers and intellectuals. For example, they say that when in 1970 the police fired on striking workers, the workers went to seek the support of the Polytechnic students, who are said to have replied: "Remember 1968!" However, according to other versions, the organisers of the workers' revolt did apologise for their passivity in 1968. Whatever the truth of the matter, the story bears witness to a split which twice had serious consequences, and it illustrates the lessons which many intellectuals and workers subsequently drew. In Gdansk, though, the reality was certainly less clear-cut. The slaughter of December 1970 left a unhealed scar in the memory of the *entire* population: as Tamara put it, it was "a shock from which we never recovered".

On 16 December 1980, a huge crowd was celebrating the inauguration in Gdansk of a monument to the memory of the shipyard workers who had fallen ten years previously. The monument was described in the strikers' August bulletin as follows: "The monument will be thirty metres high, and will be made up of four crosses, with their crosspieces touching, and with anchors attached to the crosses, all arranged in a circle. The figure '4' symbolises the first workers who fell in December 1970 in front of the shipyard's No. 2 Gate. In Poland's national symbolism the cross has for a thousand years represented faith and martyrdom, while the anchor has signified hope. In December 1970 this hope was crucified. The flame which is to burn at the base of the crosses signifies life. Let this monument be a reminder to all those who would seek to take these symbols away from us!"

The international press has already commented excessively on the politicising aspects of that inauguration, stressing, sometimes with justification, the attempt by the Catholic church to co-opt the movement. But the journalists seem to have lost sight of the fact that this was not just an everyday inauguration. For the first time the battered population of the Three Towns was able, with workers from all over Poland, to commemorate that massacre freely and publicly. All the bulletins published by Solidarity carried eye-witness accounts. "It's still very hard for us to talk about it," Anna Walentynowicz confided in me one day in October. When Maria Komorowska spoke to me about it at length one evening in November, the tone of her voice changed with emotion. And for Tamara the story of the revolt was still fresh in her mind. She hunted in a drawer for a copy of *Glos Wybrzeza* dated 28 December 1970, which gave an hour by hour account of those bloody days. She keeps it lovingly, together with poems which were written (or copied) at school by her son at the time, when he was 14 years old. "The children in his class had their heads shaved if they were caught in the demonstrations. At the age of 13 or 14, they were already involved in the events!"

On 13 December 1970, on the eve of the national holidays, the authorities had announced a 30 per cent increase in the food prices. Anger rose swiftly. Maria explained: "We didn't understand why. Since they were increasing prices, they should have increased wages as well. We began to discuss it at work. A number of trusted people — among them Lech Walesa and Anna Walentynowicz — took the lead, and we went to see the director. There were several thousand of us in front of the administration building. They refused to see us. Then we went out towards the Party building. We asked that the decision be withdrawn. No reply. But that evening the reply was clear enough: the First Secretary of the province said it clearly on the television: 'these workers are bandits'."

With the failure of negotiations, the demonstrations turned into riots. One worker who, at that time, had been elected delegate of the repair yard, told the story of an encounter with the local committee: "They led us from one office to another, perhaps in order to find a room which was bugged, or maybe just to wear us out psychologically. Our demands were simple: the withdrawal of the price increases, the release of the previous delegation, which had been arrested, and of the people who had been taken to the old concentration camp of Wejherowo — who numbered at least 3,500! We also demanded food. We cited international conventions, but in vain. When we asked for permission to announce our strike on TV, they grimaced. They were very hostile towards us, and treated us like enemies. This went on for a long time, and in the shipyards people began to get worried. The workers threatened to set fire to the building if we were not allowed out. So then they let us go." For several days there were confrontations between the police and the population and workers of Gdansk, Elblag and Szczecin. "The police," explained Maria, "were wearing Army uniforms. They had surrounded the shipyard with tanks and armoured cars, while the marines occupied the canal. We could see all this from our windows in the shipyard: ships, with their guns trained on us. The women were told to go home. The yard was going to be blockaded, and nobody knew how far it would go. I didn't want to go home — I wanted to stay. But they told me: 'This is men's business, not women's.' So all the women left the yard, under the eyes of the armed police.

"When the workers came out, they were arrested and taken away to an old Nazi concentration camp several kilometres away. Some of them were kept there for up to a week. The shipyard was occupied, but there was no strike committee like the one we have had this year. It was simply that certain workers had more responsibilities than others."

Tamara: "If some sorcerer's apprentice had been trying to stir things up that year, he'd certainly succeeded. Can you imagine — just before Christmas, which is a big festival in Poland, you increase the prices that affect the poorest people! They had actually reduced the prices of Fiats, refrigerators, and out-of-fashion televisions, but the price of smoked herring, white cheese and jam went up by between 40 per cent and 60 per cent. This was completely wrong, quite incredible. When the workers looted the stores, it wasn't to steal the fridges or televisions. They threw them out! The Radunia, the little river that runs in front of the local committee building was full of them! They would not accept rigged price reductions — they would not accept that socialism should favour the rich at the expense of the poor."

A worker: "It took us several hours before we managed to set fire to the local committee building, because the militia drove us back several times. We caught tear gas grenades as they were thrown from the helicopters, and we hurled them through the windows of the building. The building began to burn, slowly. And we saw the smoke rising. Finally we managed to pour some petrol into the entrance hall, through the grille of the main entrance. The blaze flared up — the stairs were covered with carpet. Then we saw a piece of white cloth appear at the first-floor window, and about 15 militiamen came out onto the balcony with their hands in the air. A thin young fellow in blue overalls climbed up the bars and tore down the red flag. He replaced it with the national flag. The crowd sang the national anthem, and we took off our work-helmets. Then the militiamen on the balcony threw down their arms, their helmets, their truncheons and their jackets. They were not sure whether they should take off their trousers or not. They climbed down the bars of the windows, some of them in their trousers and others in their underpants. We put a guard on them and marched them off to the shipyard, and, with the tension relaxed, the crowd dispersed."

Maria: "On the first day the workers found themselves face to face with armed militiamen right in front of the *Lenin* shipyard's No. 2 Gate. The militia fired in cold blood. Four men fell as the crowd was fleeing. A 15-year old youth was struck down at the point on the bridge where the tramlines curve. A police captain who had drawn his pistol narrowly escaped being lynched, and the workers set fire to his car."

Tamara: "Everybody supported the workers. Taxi drivers

were ferrying the wounded, while Gdansk's doctors and chemists gave them shelter. They had the support of the whole seaboard population. The student hostel was locked up so that the students couldn't come out to fight, but some of them shinned down the drainpipes. Anybody who didn't actually live in the region was forced to leave the coast.''

Maria: "At Gdynia it was even worse — sheer slaughter. At the railway station they opened fire with machine guns on people getting off the train.''

The workers of the *Paris Commune* shipyard appealed to international public opinion in an open letter which was published in *The Times* (27 January 1971): "On 16 December 1970, between eight and nine o'clock in the evening, Kociolek appealed to the people to end the strike. The workers concerned returned to work, expecting things to return to normal. To reach the port, the shipyard and other places, they had to cross the railway bridge linking Czerwonych Kosynierow street and Polska street. The first person who came down the steps of that bridge was a pregnant woman. Behind her came four workers, probably from the shipyard. Suddenly, with absolutely no warning, there was the sound of machine-gun fire. The woman cried out: 'Jesus Maria!' and fell from the top of the steps. Another volley followed, and one of the workers crashed onto the railway lines, while the other three slumped down the steps. Panic and terror reigned.'' Two other trains arrived, and the police continued firing on the crowd that was running along the railway lines.

The street fighting of that period has left many a practical lesson in people's memories, as for example the following report by *Robotnik* ten years later: "There were tanks lined up side by side between Gates 2 and 3 of the *Lenin* shipyard. You couldn't see daylight between them... Tanks are not very effective in street fighting. All you need do is to put a lorry across the street. The tank arrives, cuts it in two, fires off a few volleys, but loses its tracks. Then both lorry and tank burn. Then the other tanks crash into them, and also catch fire. Another method: put a fuse in a bottle of petrol, set light to it, and throw it at the tank. It catches fire. A number of workers who had done their military service in tank regiments took their molotovs and jumped up on the tanks. The tanks were enveloped in flames. These workers also stripped off barbed wire and jammed it into the tracks of one tank. These fouled up the cogs, and the tank began to go round in circles. Other workers jammed a pole into the other track, and the tank could no longer move.''

A doctor: ''People's wounds were almost always extremely serious, and in some cases fatal. You could not always see the fatal wounds at first glance. The bullet wounds, the majority of them in the stomach, were small, and did not seem bad enough to cause death. However, we undertook a number of autopsies in secret, and we discovered that their intestines had been torn to shreds. We concluded from this that the people had been killed by dum-dum bullets (...) That evening, after the curfew, a number of refrigerated lorries, which in normal times would be used to transport meat, fish or fruit, were seen out in the streets. These lorries were gathering up bodies. The dead were identified by their papers, and were taken home. The police ordered that they should be buried immediately. Only immediate members of the family were allowed to be present at the burial: two people at Gdansk and Gdynia, five at Sopot.''

The authorities would only admit to 69 deaths. Today, as an official of Solidarity explained to me, a census among the families has revealed between 400 and 500 dead for the Three Towns and Elblag, of whom something like 300 were in Gdynia, and about 100 in Szczecin. This confirms the opinion of a worker from the *Paris Commune* shipyard, on 25 January 1971 (at the time of the meeting with Gierek), when he stated: ''The Press, the radio and the authorities are lying! People here know that 400 people have been killed in the Three Towns, 197 in Gdansk, and 204 at Gdynia.''

''After the massacres,'' Maria explained, ''an indelible hatred for the police was born. We went back to work, but the atmosphere was tense...'' On 23 December Gomulka was dismissed and replaced by Edward Gierek. He released seven billion zloty for wage rises. But the confrontation continued for a number of weeks, in particular to demand the release of the imprisoned workers, a reform of the trade unions, and the resignation of their president. Gierek was forced to come and explain himself before the workers of the Warski yard at Szczecin (24 January) and at Gdansk (25 January). He was evasive in reply to their demands, and a sentence of his still sticks in everybody's memory: ''Comrades, you must help us.''

It was, however, not until the workers in Lodz went on strike on 16 February that the food price rises were revoked.

The Gierek formula seemed strangely similar to Gomulka's solution in 1956. And once again the new First Secretary benefited from the workers' 'investment of confidence' in him. "We thought that he would understand us, that he would give us a better life," Maria explained. Anna Walentynowicz, who was one of the activists in that movement, identified an important difference with the Gomulka period: "Everybody believed in Gierek. He was a miner, he had worked in France and Belgium. He was open to the West. But this confidence was less spontaneous than in 1956. For example, nobody came to offer jewels or to make economies in order to get economic development back on its feet." In Gdansk, in fact, suspicions very soon began to appear. "When Gierek arrived here in January 1971," Maria remarked, "he was very formal. He didn't behave like 'one of the lads'. Just looking at him you could see immediately that he was not going to be what we had hoped. To be sure, after the strike, there had been changes in the unions, and the election of new workers' councils. I was elected in my own sector, but I soon became disillusioned. It was still the same old thing! The unions were supposed to defend the workers, but people who stay in their positions for too long become lazy. They no longer carry out their obligations. They want a quiet life, and they make use of the union to achieve it. They could stay for hours on end nattering, and they would be paid extra for those hours. Very convenient, eh?"

Among the intelligentsia, Tamara explained, "nobody believed in the Gierek idea. This was a clique of technocrats. They did not give Gdansk the justice that had been promised. It was a cover-up job. For that reason I personally have always been suspicious. Of course, Gierek provided a certain stimulus to economic growth in the country, but at what price? Culture, university life, public health, transportation, housing had all fallen into ruins... This was a moral and professional bankruptcy. Little by little people began to see what was happening. For example, these parvenus had easy access to health care. They had their special clinics, their rest homes etc. Medicines were imported from abroad for them. People were quick to see what was happening. How in hell is it possible to build yourself a villa costing millions, when officially you earn 6,000 zloty?

Corruption was there for all to see. Building workers were doing overtime so that the privileged could have their *dachas*.
Everybody knew it. In a socialist society privileges are im-
moral. That should be a fundamental principle. It's a problem
of justice.''

All this led to the creation of a new awareness, particularly
strong in this city whose history has always somehow seemed to
concentrate Poland's destiny. A history of partitions in which
Gdansk, more than any other city, has changed hands many
times since the tenth century: first in the control of the
Teutonic knights, then German, then Polish, and then, between the two wars, a 'free city', under the control of the
League of Nations. A history of uprising: already in the 15th
century Gdansk had risen against the Teutonic knights, who
took the lives of 300 members of a resistance organisation. The
city is a symbol of a lone courage in the face of the indifference
of other countries: the Second World War began with the battle
of Wasterplatte. ''We will not die for Danzig (Gdansk),'' said
the French government of the time, a refrain which was taken
up by the other Western powers.
  The consciousness of the seaboard workers, their unity and
their willingness to fight matured slowly in the fires of this
tormented history. One feels a certain spirit in this town, a
breath of inalienable freedom, which has to do, perhaps, with
the presence of the sea — in other words, of an opening to
foreign parts, to ports and to sea voyages. Gdansk has always
been a refuge, a haven for those refused admittance elsewhere.
Is it just an accident that today one finds there many old
deportees from Stalin's camps? There are many of them in
Poland, but I am assured that there are more here than
elsewhere.
  A fertile ground, then, where men and women have
reflected patiently on this history. They have taken up the
cudgels themselves, and have staked their personal lot. For a
long time a network of trusted militants had already existed in
the factories, men and women who spontaneously represented
their workmates in the face of foremen and management. Rank
and file workers, who were not a proper organisation, but a
kind of counter-power, built on general trust, and in opposition
to the discredited official representatives. ''In every shop or
sector,'' Maria explained, ''there was always somebody who

understood the problems of others, who was able to offer help. When there was a problem, the worker would go to see them.'' These men and women — of whom Maria was one — were, for the most part, not members of the Party. They had no trade union responsibilities, they held no meetings among themselves, but they knew each other well, and were united in the trust which workers invested in them. When they sat on the 'self-management' bodies of the factory (as in the case of Lech Walesa), they would not allow themselves to be talked round, and often paid for their indiscipline with the sack.

In December 1970 they were in the leadership of the strike movement. They organised workers' demonstrations in the factories and went to demand negotiations with the management. This was their first widespread collective action, and in 1976 it was to bring results. In that year, on 25 June, Gierek once again decided on a set of spectacular price rises, to which there was an angry response throughout the country. The workers of Ursus, Radom and other industrial towns stopped work and came out on the streets as those of Gdansk had done before them in 1970. At Ursus, trains were blocked, railway lines were dug up, and the militia attacked the demonstrators with tear-gas grenades. There were between 200 and 300 arrests. At Radom, the workers marched through the streets to the tune of the *Internationale*, shouting: ''No to the price rises!'' There they encountered the Government's reply — 3,000 militiamen, specially equipped for street fighting. There were a number of deaths. At Plock the scenario was the same, like an action replay of the riots of December 1970.

In 1980 the workers of Gdansk sought both to express their discontent, and to avoid a slaughter. In this the experiences of 1970-71 and the influence of the group of militants who had been formed in that period were decisive. A demonstration took place, but it was within the shipyards. Electricians from W4 department marshalled workers in front of the administration block. Terrified, the manager went to find the First Secretary of the Party's regional committee, T. Fiszbach, the prefect and the local president of the union. It was a heated meeting. Fiszbach began his speech by saying: ''Comrades...''. Workers shouted back: ''We are not comrades! We are citizens. It's you who choose to call yourselves comrades, you bureaucrats, you lackeys of the social-imperialist dictatorship.'' The greatest insolence came from the younger workers, and they began demanding wage increases. A young welder stood up: "To feed our families we have to work 300 hours a month. Our fathers fought to get the eight-hour day, and now we have to work 12!" The meeting was inconclusive. The director threatened sackings, "but we wouldn't let him finish his speech. We took his microphone away from him. The representatives of the Workers' Party's local committee suffered the same fate. The representatives of the dock workers, who had set up a spontaneous ad-hoc organisation, went to the microphone and called for strike action if, by seven o'clock the following day, the management had not satisfied the workers' demands. This went on until two in the afternoon. The rest of the day there was no work in the shipyards." At midnight the news came that the authorities had given in.

In all the towns which had been involved in the strikes, the regime replied in the same manner as they had done with previous movements: a large number of arrests, and sackings. They expected that, as before, there would be no response. But this time a *Committee for the Defence of Worker Victims of Repression* (KOR) had been set up by a group of intellectuals. Its aim: "to give juridical, financial and medical support. (...) We are convinced that only by making known the actions of the authorities will we effectively be able to aid their victims. (...) The use of repression against the workers is a violation of the elementary rights of man, rights which are recognised as binding and indispensable not only under Polish law, but also under international law: the right to work, the right to strike, the right to free expression of one's personal convictions, the right of association and of demonstration. This is why the Committee is demanding an amnesty for the people arrested and convicted, and the immediate reinstatement of all the victims of the repression." Among the signatories of this appeal were student movement organisers from 1968, Catholics, leading figures of the pre-war socialist movement, writers and artists. Throughout Polish society an immense movement of solidarity developed, which obtained the workers' release from prison and helped them in their fight with the judicial apparatus. Many of them were subsequently re-instated in their jobs.

Thus the events of 1976 brought the intellectual opposition and the emerging working-class vanguards closer together. This unity in action spread within four years to all sections of

the population, and took many forms, giving rise to independent newspaper and publishing activities. At the start of 1979 a
workers' newspaper, *Robotnik*, which was based on a network
of worker correspondents in Poland's principal industries, was
already being distributed in more than 20,000 copies.

In the coastal region a number of different opposition currents made their appearance. The main one of these was formed
around the *Constituent Committee of Free Trade Unions of
the Baltic* (KWZZ), which had been set up during 1978. It was
established on the initiative of KOR members, and brought
together ex-student militants of 1968 and workers who had
been involved in the leadership of the 1970-71 strikes. Its statement of intent began by summing up the balance sheet of
earlier struggles: "The authorities, with their occasional
retreats (June 1976), or their tactical about-turns (1956 and
1970), have shown themselves incapable of democratising
public life. A broad measure of democratisation is today absolutely indispensable. Society must conquer the right to
democratically control its State. All strata must obtain the right
to self-organisation, and the right to create the social institutions which will make their rights a reality. Only authentic
trade unions and social forms of association will be able to save
the State, because a unification between the interests and
desires of the society and the interests and power of the State
can only be achieved via democratisation." The statement ended
with a definition of the aims of a trade union which was still
embryonic: "Defence of the economic, juridical and humani-
tarian interests of the workers. The free trade unions intend to
help and support all waged workers regardless of their beliefs
or status." It called for "independent forms of representation"
of the working class to be set up, but specified: "We may also
take the path of involving in factory committees independent
militants who will honestly defend the electorate whose interests they represent. We hope that our initiative will become a
stimulus for a number of different independent social activities." Today, after the establishment of Solidarity with its
ten million members, the history of that committee is already
the stuff of legends. Its members played a decisive role in the
organisation and leadership of the August 1980 strikes and it is
sometimes difficult to establish precisely the nature of their activities in the preceding period, particularly as the press has all

too often been vague and uninformative on this question.

Anna Walentynowicz told me some of the history. "At the start, the committee was made up of only three people: Andrzej Gwiazda, Krzystof Wyszkowksi, and a member of the UB whose name I no longer remember." The UB — the old name for the political police — had thus already infiltrated the group. They had offered 200,000 zloty to their informer, a worker by the name of Sokolowski who was frequently ill, and who subsequently died. Andrzej Gwiazda, who remains today one of the pillars of the workers' group of Gdansk, was an engineer in the Elmor laboratories. He was 43 years old at the time. With his wife, Joanna Duda-Gwiazda, a technician in another shipbuilding enterprise (Ceto), he was the prime mover of the committee when it was established in May 1978. They gathered around them a number of 'sympathisers', of whom a number were later to be found in the leadership of the Inter-Enterprise Strike Committee. Some of these worked at Elmor — for example, Alina Pienkowska, a 24-year old nurse, soon to be a leading organiser of the 'health' section of Solidarity, and a young manual worker, a Polish United Workers Party militant, Bogdan Lis. At the age of 26 Lis had, in 1978, been vice-president of the Party's youth organisation. Today he tells how his membership in 1975 (at the time of his military service) had been prompted by the desire to 'do something'. "I would have been just as likely to sign up with an opposition party, if there had been one," he is fond of saying. He was very soon to find himself in sympathy with the activities of Gwiazda.

The police informer was unmasked, and replaced by Edwin Myszk, a young spray painter from the *Lenin* shipyard noted for his audacity. And when Krzystof Wyzkowski left in August to go to Cracow, two organisers of the 1970-71 strikes established contact with the committee: Lech Walesa and Anna Walentynowicz. At the age of 35 Lech Walesa already had behind him a wealth of experience. He was the son of a peasant family from the Lipno region, and had started work at the *Lenin* shipyard in 1967. As a member of the official union, he was one of the leaders of the December 1970 movement, and in January 1971 the strikers elected him as leader of the delegation which was to meet Gierek. He later became a member of the workers' council for his sector, and was sacked on 30 April 1976, after a particularly militant speech during a local union meeting.[2] He didn't find work again until the autumn, when he started in an industrial machinery company at Gdansk, ZREMB. Meanwhile he had been forced to work as a farm labourer in order to support his wife and five children. His first contacts with KOR and the *Robotnik* editorial group date from the end of 1976.

Anna Walentynowicz was 53 when she first met the group of militants organised by Gwiazda. She had spent 30 years in the *Lenin* shipyard, 17 of them as a welder, and then as the driver of an electric crane. Her commitment, she explained to me, was the product of 'the injustices and the lies' practised by the authorities as their mode of government. She had been a workers' delegate at the time of the meeting with Gierek, and "I was in a sense a co-author of that famous 'Help us' statement, since we voted for it. So I felt morally obliged to demand a settling of accounts from the government. We *did* go to their help, we did! But every step I took was lost in bureaucratic indifference. I used to write letters, and never got a reply. So, when I heard on the BBC that there was this committee, I went looking for it. I found it in July 1978, and I think that was a useful step."

In September the first issue of the free unions' bulletin — *Robotnik Wybrzeza* ('The Seaboard Worker') was published. The leadership of the union at that time comprised Gwiazda, Myszk, and a young Elektromontaz worker, Andrzej Bulc. Other names which appeared among the editorial committee of the bulletin were Bogdan Borusewicz, a young 29-year old historian living in Sopot. A graduate of the Catholic University of Lublin, he had been one of the organisers of the student movement in 1968, and had received a two-year prison sentence. He was a friend of Jacek Kuron, and had already signed the founding declaration of KOR. He had also worked closely with Gwiazda since the 1976 strikes. He organised a semi-clandestine workers' university where many of the future leaders of Solidarity met. Subjects included the history of Poland, the 1956 uprising in Hungary and the Prague Spring. "Our relations with KOR were extremely good," observed Anna Walentynowicz. "They supported us with material help, with their publications etc, and their proposals helped us a lot. For my part, I was greatly stimulated by reading books like Stefan Kieselewski's *What is Socialism?* or the pamphlet *The Rights of the Citizen in Relation to the Political Police.* Reading these books helped to lessen the fear that I felt in myself. We also distributed *Robotnik*, which was brought to us from Warsaw. There were only seven people in that committee, but we had a large number of sympathisers who gave us a lot of help." The sympathisers had a lot of young workers among them. For example Jan Karandziej, a welder, who was later sacked from the *North* shipyard on 25 January 1980; or Andrzej Kolodziej, 18 year-old assembler in the *Lenin* shipyard, who was also sacked in January 1980 for having taken part in the demonstration on the anniversary of the 1970 massacre. By the age of 20 he was to be the president of the strike committee of the *Paris Commune* shipyard in Gdynia.

This small group of courageous militants was constantly harassed by the police. "We always had difficulty," explained Anna. "We worked openly and publicly, because it would have been pointless to stay 'underground'. How would people have found us? We distributed *Robotnik Wybrzeza* when people came out of church after mass, and at factory gates. The paper carried our addresses and telephone numbers. Obviously, this made it a lot easier for the police to harass us... The police had us branded, together with KOR, as an 'anti-socialist group', and they wanted to destroy us. They continued to send their spies." At the end of 1979, Edwin Myszk, the young paint sprayer from the *Lenin* shipyard, was also revealed to be in the pay of the police, and, like his predecessor, he was expelled. The committee's leadership was remodelled, and up until the August strike comprised Gwiazda, Bulc and Borusewicz.[3] Meantime, its continuing activities showed the futility of police efforts to crush them during all those years.

The regime was able to reflect on this fact at leisure. For example, at each anniversary of the 1970 massacres. On several occasions, the committee called public meetings in front of the *Lenin* shipyard's No. 2 Gate. In December 1977 only a few hundred people answered the call. The wreath remained in position for only 35 minutes, as did the posters which had been stuck up in their hundreds all over the town. Before the ceremony the militia, the shipyard security guards, and (!) Party militants had been put on a state of alert. In December 1978, by 9.00 am, 3,500 posters had already been stuck up around the town. After a few hours those in the shipyard canteen had disappeared from sight. The police mobilisation was impressive: street patrols, and, on 17 December, preventive arrests among the leadership of *Robotnik Wybrzeża*. But despite all this, on the 18th several thousand people gathered. At 2.15 in the afternoon, shortly before the ceremony, an unusual number of buses parked themselves along the outer wall of the shipyard with their engines running, in order to drown the speeches. The demonstrators gathered round a red and white banner, decorated with the figure "1970" in black. A number of speeches were made, while the police stood by and filmed. There were numerous arrests. Finally, on 18 December 1979, there were almost ten thousand people present. As a demonstration, it was unprecedented. However, the police had taken their precautions — in other words, they had carried out 200 preventive arrests. But there were still militants who spoke out. Lech Walesa made the speech which was later to become famous: "I promise you that next year we will inaugurate a monument here!" And Maryla Plonska read a message: "I speak to you in the name of the militants of the Free Trade Union of the Baltic Coast, who have been arrested," she began. She ended by summoning up the lessons of past battles: "Today, with all the wealth of our past experiences, we are learning to fight for our rights, calmly and with determination. We'll build on our solidarity. We used to have to go out in the streets in order to convince ourselves there were others who felt the same way. Our intransigence and solidarity led to riots. Later some people believed that the regime had changed, and that it too would draw the appropriate conclusions. We did not see to the safety of the members of the strike committee. The strike was chaotic, because we had not been capable of setting up a structure suitable for long-term action. This meant that the birth of independent forms of workers' representation was blocked. (...) So, what did we get from that December? The awareness of our strength, of our rights, and what the regime is capable of doing. Some of us have paid the highest price for that awareness — with their lives. May their memories be honoured!" After this speech prayers were said for the workers who had been killed, and also for the activists of the Czechoslovakian VONS (Committee for the Unjustly Persecuted) who had recently been sentenced in Prague, and for the arrested members of the Polish opposition.[4] They shouted:

"Long live the Free Unions! Down with the Party! Freedom!" And "Free Bogdan!" (Bogdan Borusewicz, whose popularity, as can be seen, was considerable.) All these gatherings, as well as the publication of each of the seven issues of *Robotnik Wybrzeza* were marked by sackings and imprisonments. Walesa, for example, recalls that, during this period, he was summoned to the police station something like 100 times. As a reward for his public presence at the anniversary ceremony in 1978, the management of ZREMB sacked him on 31 January 1979. And when, after several months of unemployment, he succeeded in getting a job at the Elektromontaz factory, the director warned the workforce that an "activist" was about to arrive.

But what was the real constituency of this group of courageous militants, of this committee who caused the whole of Poland to tremble by leading the strike of the seaboard workers? Clearly one is tempted (for this is the stuff of future legends) to imagine that it was quite sizeable, since they clearly reflected the opinions of so many. In fact, the reality is less clear-cut. It is undeniable that this group prefigured the movement that was to arise in the whole of society, and expressed certain deep tendencies at work within it. In this respect it was the vanguard of the vanguard; it distilled years of experience, and represented only the tip of an iceberg, which was the network of trust in the principal factories of the region. Our inquiries among the workers, the statements cited above, reveal that many workers and intellectuals, without any particular involvement in opposition movements, identified with this "long saga of the Polish workers", to use a favourite expression of Walesa. The August strikes were a direct result of their activities. But for all that, the bureaucracy's systems of domination were such that the majority of society at that time remained atomised. The threads of cohesion were tangled in the web of lies, fear and unbelieving. The discontent was smouldering, and only found expression in fits and starts.

This was particularly noticeable at the time of the struggles in which the militants of the free union were involved. For example, in December 1979, the management of Elektromontaz sacked nine workers, of whom one was Lech Walesa. Other workers were transferred. To justify their action, the director referred to a "warning" that Walesa had been given on 18 December, when he was forced to leave his job in order to go hiding before the anniversary celebrations. On 23 December the sacked workers reacted by forming a 'workers' commission'. When Andrzej Gwiazda was interviewed by telephone at the time, he explained why the form of a 'workers' commission' had been chosen. "Because the free trade union was too small, and everybody realised that it was necessary to get organised. By simply creating a factory section, the initiative would never have developed a mass base." The commission published an appeal signed by almost 150 of the 500-strong workforce in the factory. If the sackings remained in force, the commission would announce a strike. As Gwiazda explained: "This appeal was understood by the management, because they took fright and sent the workers home on Friday 1 February, at 11 o'clock in the morning." The commission called two mass meetings in the factory, and summoned all those who had received dismissal notices to contact it, with a view to taking collective action for reinstatement. The management's counter-offensive was bearing fruit, though. Only about 50 people came to the mass meetings. At the doors of the hall, the whole management were waiting, together with Party members, and people were frightened of going in. At the end, the majority of the sackings remained in force. "All in all," Gwiazda commented, "the message was clear. We were not strong enough. We would be unwise to overestimate the opposition's potential. There are seven million industrial workers in Poland, and only 25,000 copies of *Robotnik* are being distributed. The truth is that very few people knew of us."

Another way of assessing the audience of the free trade union and the radicalisation that was taking place within the working class is to analyse the official trade union elections held in Gdansk in Spring 1980. As we have seen, the committee's founding statement explained their intention of penetrating the official structures via democratic elections. This tactic corresponded to a correct assessment of the forms of expression of working class discontent. In fact these elections, far from being discredited, have always provided the occasion for demonstrations of this sort. This time the campaign had even been put back a year. A trade union official had justified this delay by the need to "educate the trade union militants"... a familiar expression, indicating the growing tension between the regime and the workers.

Despite the great difficulties faced by the active workers' groups in expressing themselves or in meeting, the free trade union was able to obtain a number of significant results. At the Marine Technology Centre, the workers of one department sent a letter of protest against the 'clique organised by the vice-president of the company's union council', and they demanded that, in conformity with the law, no department head or manager should figure in the electoral lists. At Techmet, an enterprise employing 600 people, the electoral meeting was transformed into a general protest meeting. At Elektromontaz, after the struggle cited above, the president of the outgoing council — a management stooge — lost his place. But it was the Elmor workers who went furthest. 'A real revolution', as *Robotnik Wybrzeza* put it. Not only did they succeed in electing a number of delegates of their choice, on a platform of genuine demands, but when the management wanted to transfer Alina Pienkowska, she made a direct appeal to the whole of the workforce, and to the enterprise's union council. Its new vice-president — Bogdan Lis in this case — took up her case, and the management was forced to withdraw.

These small victories revealed the strengths and the limitations of the committee's position at the start of 1980. Roughly 2,000 copies of its bulletin were distributed and it was to lay the groundwork for the struggles to come. At the start of the summer, discontent had reached such a pitch that a single spark could set off a blaze.

The spark was provided by the 'Walentynowicz affair'. For almost a year this veteran militant, who was much respected by the workers of the *Lenin* shipyard whom she had always helped and advised, had been a target of repression. She described what happened: "On 23 November 1979 I was accused of having stolen flowers from the cemetery. In fact I had gone there to pick up used candle stubs in order to make new candles." She had wanted to honour those killed in December 1970 in Poland's customary manner. "I wanted to distribute these candles clandestinely to the shipyard workers so that they could put them in front of the gates, where the first victims had fallen. When I returned from the cemetery, the police arrested me in front of my home. The next day they came to search the house. They brought me there dressed in the uniform of a common prisoner. They told my neighbours that I was a thief! They showed them as 'proof' the four kilos of wax.'' After a five-hour interrogation she still refused to admit anything, and was released. ''On 16 December, the eve of the anniversary gathering, a dozen police came back again to search the house. Since I refused to open the door to them, they threatened to batter it down. Then I heard the voice of a friend on the staircase, one of my neighbours whom I had asked to come as a witness to the search. Other neighbours arrived, and I explained to them how these people had treated me — these people who, in 1970, had fired on the shipyard workers. The police even stole two watches from me! They were surprised by the arrival of so many of my neighbours: there were no more searches in my house. My last arrest took place on 22 February last year [1980]. That day they literally tried to kidnap me, by forcing me into a vehicle that drew up alongside me as I was walking along the pavement. Since I fought back, and a crowd was beginning to gather, they gave me a kick. I fell, and this enabled them to drag me into the car. When I was released from this 48-hour detention, a doctor gave me a nine-day sick note. When I started work again at the shipyard, I explained to everyone how the police had behaved, and the director didn't like this. He transferred me. He moved me from my crane-driving job, and sent me into isolation in a warehouse far from the shipyard. I was no longer permitted to go to the canteen, or to speak to anyone. I decided to take legal action, and I won my case. I was to be reinstated in my old job. The director refused. Since I was sick, I got a six-day sick note, beginning 6 August. On the 9th a letter arrived, saying that I had been sacked for... leaving my job.'' On the 14th the strike began at the *Lenin* shipyard, with the reinstatement of Anna Walentynowicz as its first demand. As she was to explain later: ''Workers are no longer afraid. That is the big difference with the early 1950s.''

2. The Strike

The strike that had broken out on the shores of the Baltic Sea one day in August 1980 was an event capable of reviving abandoned hopes. Like an unexpected breeze, it breathed life into them. It set them buzzing. It confounded the sceptics, and worried the strategists. Because this was a most unusual strike. It was innovative, capable of astounding and transforming. It was strong and unified. It shook up a system many had thought immovable. It revived prospects and desires that people had almost forgotten. The march of history was set in motion again.

Such was Poland in the summer of 1980. A Poland where the strike arrived, quietly, and spread, gathering strength, and consuming all around it. Calmly and peacefully.

For the third time, the trigger seemed clear enough. As in the two preceding times food prices were to go up. The authorities had tinkered with the system of meat distribution. Where previously there were two systems — the ordinary shops, which were generally empty, and the 'commercial' shops, which were twice as expensive — they had added a third system of distribution, operating within the factories. Workers could generally find meat there, at normal prices. But lo and behold, on 1 July the Government decided to raise the prices of this factory-distributed meat, in certain provinces, to the levels applying in the commercial stores.

The working class could not accept this. In the factory which had been the spearhead of the 1976 movement — the Ursus tractor factory — three departments stopped work immediately. The following day, 2 July, the factory shop received no supplies. The strike spread to the other departments in the machine shop. On Thursday it was the assembly lines' turn. The whole factory was paralysed — 14,000 workers in all. A similar strike movement began to develop at the other end of the country, in the Polmor factory at Tczew, near Gdansk (3,500 workers), and in the WSK factories at Mielec and Swidnik, two factories producing aircraft and communications goods, each employing more than 10,000 people. At Gdansk, department K1 of the shipyard struck, and the Elmor workers, who were also on strike, sent a delegation to meet Gierek. On that same day, 1 July, work also stopped in the pre-rolling mill of the Huta-Warszawa steelworks, and at the Kaweczynska Street tram depot in Warsaw. On 2 July these were joined by the Pomet workers, and the workers of the Cegielski rolling mills in Poznan, as well as a number of factories in Zyrardow, etc.

The first strike wave was scattered and diffuse. But it marked the beginning of the most formidable working-class mobilisation ever seen in a 'people's democracy'. These strikes concentrated 35 years of discontent, and were to culminate in the show of strength of 31 August. Their spread alarmed factory managers and the central authorities. It threw them onto the defensive, and finally was to bring into question all their policies. Workers were able to win a number of fundamental rights which only a few weeks previously had been unobtainable.

At first the demands were strictly economic, and often very limited. At Ursus, they demanded a wage rise, a threshold agreement, and the establishment of a ten per cent bonus for shift-working as well as an increase in unsocial conditions bonuses from 0.1 to 0.5 zloty per hour. In the Polmo factories, in WSK, in the Gdansk shipyards, in the Pomet factories in Poznan etc, the main demands were limited to an adjustment of wages to prices. Managements in general replied hesitantly, and in most cases gave way. In some places wages were increased, while in others prices were reduced in the factory shops.

But these responses were not sufficient to satisfy the workers, and within two days the whole question was re-opened. Thus, at Ursus, on 4 July, a number of departments went on strike again, because the increase in wages was insufficient. At Swidnik the WSK workers realised, on 7 July, that, contrary to what management had promised, pork chops were being sold at 18 zloty instead of 10.5 zloty. Strikes started again. The following day the Minister for Mechanical Industries arrived. The workers refused to listen to him — they demanded that Gierek himself should come.

The authorities' indecisiveness combined with the fact that

the price rise was then applied to all regions, resulted in an extended mobilisation and widening demands. On 8 July a second, more radical strike wave began. At Zyrardow — a industrial town between Lodz and Warsaw — the rolling mill workers were demanding, in addition to the withdrawal of the price rise, an improvement in working conditions and wages. They demanded a written guarantee that there would be no victimisation against those who had taken part in the strike. On 9 July the movement extended to five textile enterprises, whose mainly female workforce was extremely badly paid. At ZZTT the women workers refused to negotiate with management in the absence of higher authorities. When the authorities arrived, they were presented with a list of 30 demands, including a minimum wage rise of 1,000 zloty, the establishment of a fixed bonus, and a systematic checking of wage levels, which were regularly being reduced. They also demanded — and this was what was qualitatively different — a reduction in the numbers of management, together with a team of Efficiency Control Board (NIK) experts in order to monitor the management of the enterprise and its supply situation.

Not only were the demands new, but so was the geographic extent of the movement. It affected the majority of industrial centres in Poland (Warsaw, Lublin, the seaboard, Poznan, Wroclaw, etc). The strikes were generally short and management generally gave in very quickly, although they occasionally tried to recoup what they had been forced to concede. The basic fact was that the authorities had no intention of going back on the measures that they had decreed. On the evening of 9 July, Gierek said as much on television. He described the situation as 'complicated', and announced that a meeting of the central leadership of the Party and of managers of the economy had confirmed the price rise, although now it was to be limited to two qualities of meat, to lard, to certain poultry, and a number of tinned meats. This limited retreat was aimed simply at playing for time in the hope of blocking the movement.

But the action spread with surprising effect in Lublin, on 14 July. The strike had already affected the nine largest factories (including a lorry factory, a shoe factory, and the abattoirs). It then spread to public transport. Bus and tram workers gave their management an ultimatum. By the 15th railway workers too were demanding wage increases of 1,300 zloty, new factory committee elections, work-free Saturdays, retirement at 55, and family allowance parity with the militia (a 1,000 per cent increase). They refused to let the police or the army into the depots which were on strike. On Wednesday the 16th, all the region's main railway centres were paralysed, with all trains halted. The strike had the town at a standstill. This time, the authorities reacted more sharply, with an attempt to break this mobilisation. They sent a group of railway workers from Siedlce to stand in for the strikers. But these heeded an appeal from the strike committee and went home. The government also began to brandish the threat of Soviet intervention: *Sztandar ludu* published a letter from the political bureau of the Polish United Workers' Party warning of the 'concern which the work stoppages are arousing among our friends and allies'. But in vain. The strike spread to the local newspaper, which stopped production at 7.00 am on the 18th. At 11.00 am the manager decided to grant the wage demand, and most of the enterprises did likewise. A local newspaper was to conclude: "The workers' demands were justified." And in mid-August, at Lublin, the first free trade union elections were held. The organisers of the strike movement did well in these elections.

So, the strikes of July 1980, far from calming people, were to introduce new features, and laid the ground for a more important movement. In mid-July this was commented in *Glos*, a bulletin published by KSS-KOR: "Today one can say that, for the authorities, as also for the workers, the familiar patterns of yesteryear are past and gone. There is nothing new about the authorities trying to bring about a price rise, and then withdrawing it. What *is* new, though, is that, since these strikes started, the regime's representatives have been willing to negotiate with the workers, and have not — at least, not up until the present — used repression. Up until July 1980 there were two models of workers' protest in Poland: the violent strikes, with demands for wage rises, which turn into street demonstrations and clashes with the militia; or strikes which 'don't look like strikes' — in other words, strikes which affect only one or two sections in a plant, generally concerned with the allocation of bonuses, or against production schedules that harmed the workers' interests. Today the workers are not proposing a general withdrawal of the price rises, but are seeking wage rises within their own enterprises — that is to say, they are defending their own particular interests. But, at the same time, these strikes are extending to the whole of the country. When the news arrives that workers of one enterprise have been success-ful, the workers of other concerns go on strike and successfully follow in their footsteps.'' The article also forecast what was soon to become one of the major characteristics of the seaboard strikes: ''This new form of working-class protest is now likely to take the form of aspirations for reforms of the economy, for the establishment of independent trade unions, and a change in the political system.''

The second fundamental characteristic of early Summer 1980 was the appearance of the initial attempts at self-organisation, the election of the first strike committees. Already by mid-July *Robotnik* was spreading far and wide the example of the engineering shops at the Ursus factory: ''The strikers in the 'PS' assembly section elected a delegation of ten members. So did those of the 'PB' sub-frame section, where the delegation numbered 20 workers. In the 'PR' repairs and fuelling section, the workers held a mass meeting, drew up a set of demands, and elected a seven-person strike committee. The management, in an attempt to master the situation, organised meetings of chargehands, supervisors etc, but was not able to get the strikers back to work. Faced with this setback the sec-tion managements embarked on negotiations, either with the delegations, or with the entire workforce, as the situation re-quired. Initially management explained that workers in other enterprises were even less well-treated, and promised increases as from 30 September for those workers who achieved full schedules. In the majority of sections the second and third shifts also joined the strike. By the following day the strike was total. In the presence of a local Party leader, the strike commit-tee presented the strikers' demands. (...) They gave management two hours to reply. After two hours the director, accompanied by his section chiefs, appeared on the scene. They began, as usual, with threats. The workers' reply was to add a further de-mand: that the director should sign a written undertaking not to use repression against the strikers. This the management promised, and then called for a return to work. They said that they were prepared to examine the demands in detail, later, if there was an immediate return to work. This was a crucial moment. But the strikers stuck to their guns, and management had to change tactics. They agreed to negotiate, under the sole condition that the strike committee should change its name, and that the word 'strike' should disappear. The workers accepted this, and this was the reason that the committee thenceforth took the official name of 'workers' commission'. Negotiations began. While awaiting the outcome, the workers began to make preparations for cutting off the hot water supplies, which would paralyse the whole factory, if the negotiations came to nothing. From time to time one of the delegates came out and brought them up to date on the development of the negotiations.'' Having won its principal demands, the 'workers' commission' decided to remain in existence.

However, the example of the Ursus factory remained an exception, rather than the rule. According to an inquiry undertaken by KOR at the time, other examples were rare. Jacek Kuron explained: "In certain of the strikes there was an election of delegates directly from mass meetings, and this was a great success. For example, at WSK-Swidnik the elected delegates won a demand for the [official] trade union council to be at their side at negotiations with management. This was a way of protecting themselves, of not putting their heads on a block. The memory of the repression which was unleashed against the leaders of the 1970 and 1976 movements still remains a powerful brake on self-organisation. There were even some enterprises where the strike committee, elected by secret ballot in the shops, did not reveal themselves openly. This was the case in the huge Stella stocking factory at Zyrardow, where the workforce is principally women, often single and with children dependent on them. We organised a collection for them, because these workers were paid on the 15th of the month, and we suspected that, because of the strike, their wages would not be paid on time, in order to force them to give in. All in all, we have achieved a higher level of organisation than in 1976, but still strike committees are not the rule everywhere. Ursus still remains something of a beacon.''

Finally, we should stress the role of the democractic opposition in this strike movement — basically the KSS-KOR, and its journal *Robotnik*. Right from the start they were involved in initiating and supporting the strikes. On 2 July KOR published a communique that left no room for ambiguity. Its support was total. In cases where its militants were not already present in a given factory, they would immediately go to the spot to check information received. A permanent telephone network was established in a number of Warsaw apartments. The foreign press was kept informed on a daily basis, with precise news and information. In addition to this practical support, KOR also offered advice for developing the struggle. On 2 July their bulletin, distributed throughout the factories, gave precise instructions: "We address ourselves to the workers of all Poland. We should beware of forms of protest which could be used by the authorities to provoke riots. The form of working-class struggle which is most effective for the workers' interests and for the whole of society, and, in particular, is the least dangerous for the whole nation, is self-organisation within enterprises, the election of independent workers' representatives in order to present demands in the name of the whole workforce, to conduct negotiations with the authorities, and to lead workers' action in a responsible and resolute manner. Workers must be aware that only united action can give positive results. Above all the authorities must not be allowed to initiate any kind of persecution of strikers and of real or supposed workers' leaders. We call on the whole of society to unite with the workers and support their demands."

All the elements of success which characterised the August strikes were already present in embryo in the July experiences. KOR's instructions and advice were broadly taken up. Everyone was aware that the movement had only just begun. Perhaps Gierek was the only one to have illusions, as he set off for the Crimea, to take his last holidays as Secretary General. Jacek Kuron, on the other hand, was more far-sighted, in an article that he wrote at the start of August. "In autumn, when inflation will have eaten up the wage rises and when the promises about better meat supplies are broken, these strikes, even if they fade out now, will start anew. Workers' anger will be even greater, and, impossible though it may seem, their suspicion in relation to the authorities will grow too. The regime will find itself in an even weaker position. And then it is virtually a certainty that one of the two parties will lose their patience." This perspective was also put forward in other KOR publications (*Glos, Robotnik*). It became essential to draw up a set of perspectives and tactics for the movements to come. These had been under discussion for several years within the opposition movement. On 11 July KOR had published a long policy statement, putting forward a number of themes which were later to be found, in essence, in the 21 points of the Gdansk Inter-Enterprise Strike Committee. As of that moment, two questions were in everyone's mind: the establishment of an independent union as a guarantee of the required reforms, and the attitude to be taken in relation to the central authorities. In this regard *Glos* wrote in mid-July: "In any action taken by the workers, victory will be all the more assured if they have their own independent organisation and their own free press. KSS-KOR will not be in a position for much longer to fulfil these functions. It was not set up with this aim in mind, and it will never be able to take the place of independent working-class organisations. Thus the responsibility for the present situation lies fair and square with the authorities, but its consequences weigh on the whole of society, most particularly on the most disadvantaged layers. If there is no change in the present system of government, we would continue to move in a vicious circle. This is why, today, the workers bear a great responsibility. In their hands lies the fate of our country. Many things depend on what they manage to win today; among others, the fact that one day Poland will regain its independence. We should have no illusions on this. There is absolutely no chance of achieving it as long as the State is weak and disorganised, as long as society has had all its rights expropriated, and thus has no choice but to raise the flag of revolt, because society does not have the right to participate in government. Today our task is to win back this right of government." Jacek Kuron was more prudent in speaking of tactical considerations. He had in mind more widespread guarantees. He wrote: "I am convinced that the Polish people themselves, even in the face of the authorities, are capable of resolving the crisis and embarking on the road to democratisation. The opposition movement must be the prime mover on this path. We enjoy a certain influence in working class quarters, and we should spread that influence, because they need help, information, and suggestions. It is our duty to contribute, to help the workers organise themselves into independent institutional groups, workers' commissions or unions, or to take over the State unions, as the railway workers of Lublin are likely to do shortly." In regard to the regime,

Kuron spoke in moderate terms: "We have to bear in mind that the Soviet Union and its armies have not simply ceased to exist. But we can reasonably suppose that the Soviet rulers will not embark on an armed intervention in Poland as long as the Polish people desist from overthrowing a government which is docile towards the USSR. Thus, for the moment, we should desist. Our programme for the moment is for a society democratically organised into professional or cooperative associations, economically and locally self-managed. For a while we are going to have to coexist with our Party and our totalitarian state apparatus."

Despite their farsightedness, the opposition militants were taken aback by the extent, the strength, and the outcome of the seaboard strikes. Arising directly out of years of discontent and of accumulated experience, these succeeded in turning history on its head.

Andrzej stood there with seven posters rolled under his arm. It was 5.00 am at the *Lenin* shipyard, Thursday 14 August. He was waiting for Bogdan. Kazik arrived — whom he had also arranged to meet the previous evening. Kazik worked in the W3 section. They went over to the section. A few minutes later, workers changing in that section's locker room saw a poster stuck up under the clock which read: "We demand a 1,000 zloty wage rise, a cost-of-living bonus, and news on the sacking of Anna Walentynowicz!" Groups of workers gathered and asked for more detailed information.

Andrzej left Kazik with his workmates to keep an eye on the poster, and went to the section where Bogdan was due to arrive. He still wasn't there. So he set to work himself. He stuck up a notice on the locker-room door. Cheered on by the workers standing round, he carried on, from locker room to locker room. Nobody knew that a strike had already been decided on the previous night[5] by the handful of militants comprising the Constituent Committee of Free Trade Unions of the Baltic. But already, for several hours, everybody had been talking about striking. Andrzej told everybody what to do: "We all have to meet at nine o'clock in the shipyard's central square." The posters were there for everyone to see, and groups of workers gathered around them. The foremen did not dare break them up, and when one of them tried to interfere, tension rose immediately. Andrzej went to see a squad that he knew well, and explained what he was doing. They approved. He got them to assemble a little further off, in front of the electrode store. Other workers — numbering about 30 — arrived and gathered by the toolroom lockers next door. Andrzej was worried they might disperse, so he went over to them and began talking about the strike in a loud voice: "The whole yard is stopping work. It's to do with wages and the sacking of Anna Walentynowicz." When they had heard him out, the workers decided to go and make up a banner, and then go on to the meeting. But Barc, the department manager, appeared on the scene, amazed at what he saw.

"It's a strike!" Andrzej explained.

"Why a strike? What's going on?"

"Can't you read?" Andrzej retorted, showing him the banner. He gave him some copies of *Robotnik* and the free trade union's leaflet explaining the situation of Anna Walentynowicz.

More and more workers continued to arrive. The banner was already completed when Mazurkiewicz, the secretary of the Party cell, burst on the scene, furious. He tried to confiscate the banner. Not a chance! He was one against many. They stopped him. Red with anger, he shouted: "What does this mean?" They replied: "This is no concern of yours, sir!" Somebody put a pack of leaflets into his hands, and the surrounding workers laughed and made fun of him: the Party secretary looked as if he was going round distributing subversive leaflets! Cowed by the workers' insolence, he walked off, a pitiful sight. Andrzej took the banner and everybody moved off towards the shipyard's central square.

Similar groups were arriving from all sides — cheerful, jostling, and confident. Jurek, for example, arrived with a group of workers. He had left home very early, to do the same as Andrzej. He too, for the first time in his life, had stuck up posters in the locker rooms, distributed leaflets, and had said to all the workers he met: "Here you are, read it! Today the shipyard is on strike." He was fairly confident, having already consulted a number of people the previous evening. If anyone hesitated, he told them that the hull-building sections had already stopped work — though he didn't in fact know whether they had. With a group of 30 workers he too had gone round the shipyard in a demonstration. Workers came out from all quarters to see what was going on, and joined up with them.

In the central square there were by now several thousand men and women, cheerfully waiting there. Neither Andrzej and Kazik, nor Jurek and Bogdan, who eventually arrived with the workers from their department, imagined that this spot would give birth to the most important strike in the history of 'people's' Poland. A tremendous moral power had been set in motion, and nobody was now capable of stopping it. Particularly not Bryczkowski, the section manager's stand-in, who came up and confronted Andrzej's workmates. He came to annoy them, to provoke them. Everyone was gathering in the middle of the square, and while somebody set off a siren, Bryczkowski came down shouting: "Get back to work! Get back to work!" Everybody ignored him. Somebody pointed out the banner: "Read it! Read it! This'll show you what it's about!" One of the internal plant locomotives came to a halt, and its driver began to applaud the proceedings. Bryczkowski continued to bustle around, but was ignored by one and all.

The procession set off again, with the banner at its head. It was a fine morning. They strolled along, whistling, singing, and calling out those who were still in their sections. At the far end of the shipyard, Wojcik, the yard's director, or at least, the man who thought he was still director of the yard, waited. His first words were:

"What's all this about?"

"It's a strike," they all chorused.

"Why?"

"Because you've sacked Anna Walentynowicz."

"Anna Walentynowicz?" replied the director, with feigned surprise.

Somebody refreshed his memory: "She's been sacked without warning. It's disgraceful, somebody like her... A woman who's been decorated with three Orders of Merit — bronze, silver and gold. She's got 30 years of work behind her, and only five months to go before she retires." The director made as if to protest. "We don't want to talk with you now!" shouted Bogdan in his direction. And the crowd set off again, leaving the director to his own thoughts.

The workers began to organise. Some people remained on the canal bridge, to make sure this route was not cut off. Then they all went to Gate No. 2, where, in 1970, four workers had fallen to police gunfire, and a minute's silence was observed to honour their memory. Before long, thousands of workers of all ages were gathered in the square, around the mechanical excavator. Somebody climbed up and made the first speech: "We must elect a strike committee. We need trusted people from each squad..." At that moment the director appeared, with his entourage. They set him up on the excavator, and for a few moments he was able to speak: "What more do you want? You get 9,000 zloty per month — isn't that enough?" He was unable to say much more. From the crowd came a great roar of protest, whistling and people speaking all at the same time. Was the director really so unaware of the huge disparities in rates of pay?!

It was at this point that Lech Walesa came out of the ranks. He had got into the shipyard by shinning over one of the gates. "Do you recognise me? I worked here for ten years. You sacked me in 1976 for being involved in a strike. But I still consider myself a dockworker. I have everyone's trust!" The crowd roared its approval. A number of workers hoisted him on their shoulders, and he said: "We are going on strike and occupying the plant!" The director could not get another word in — he was drowned out by the 'Hurrah! Hurrah!' which rose from the crowd. They demanded that the loudspeakers of the yard's internal broadcast system be connected up, so that everybody could hear what was said.

Somebody shouted: "We must go and find Anna Walentynowicz." Another chimed in: "With the manager's car..." The manager protested, but the strikers were determined, and the driver had to do what they said.

They still had to negotiate the rest of their demands, so they needed to elect delegates and draw up a list of priority demands. They decided to go back into their sections. There were more than a hundred sections in that enormous shipyard. Each section elected one or two delegates, mandated on a set of precise demands, and at the start of the afternoon they got up one after another, perched on the excavator, to present their section's case to the crowd. People cheered and sang, in a kind of relaxed party atmosphere. Then the 200 delegates assembled in the conference hall next to the canteen. This general assembly laid out 11 basic demands, which were far more radical than those of the July strikes. They were both political and economic demands, with the former taking priority. They took as their starting point the advanced demand of the Lublin workers for the dissolution of the (official) trade union factory council. Other demands already pointed to the Gdansk strikers' role as leading the whole of the Polish working class. They demanded the release of political prisoners; the reinstatement of all those sacked; family allowance parity with the militia; and the erection of a monument in front of the shipyard gates to the memory of the martyrs of 1970.

The delegates also set up a 'negotiating committee' of about 20 workers, headed by Lech Walesa. Anna Walentynowicz was also on it. She had just arrived, and visibly moved by this first victory, she spoke to the strikers: "We are firmly resolved to carry forward our movement until our demands are satisfied," she concluded. A workers' militia was set up to make sure that everything went smoothly in each section, and to prevent provocations. Stewards were stationed at the entrances to the shipyard. The 1970 massacres were still fresh in everyone's minds: the shipyard was to be occupied, but they were not venturing out into the streets.

At the start of the afternoon, negotiations began in the conference hall, under the dull gaze of a statue of Lenin erected by the authorities. Facing the workers' delegates sat the yard's manager, accompanied by Tadeusz Fiszbach, First Secretary of the Party in Gdansk. The discussions were stormy, and continued till daybreak. Management gave way very fast on the question of reinstating those sacked, and on the construction of a monument in memory of the victims of 1970. They also undertook that there would be no reprisals against the strike committee, and that family allowances would be brought in line with those of the militia. On the other demands they suggested a fresh meeting two or three weeks later.

This was unacceptable: "If we are going to negotiate, we do it here and now!" said one delegate. The manager would have none of it. He would only agree to a 1,200 zloty wage rise (the workers were demanding 2,000), and said that he was not authorised to negotiate on the other points. Talks were broken off. Management agreed to return at five in the morning. They never came back. The workers were already settling in for their first night in the shipyard.

In Gdansk itself the news of a strike at the *Lenin* shipyard — already the symbol of so many important struggles — spread like wildfire. By four in the morning tram drivers were stopping work in sympathy. Only the electric train serving the Three Towns continued to run. As usual, it unloaded thousands of workers in front of their factory gates. That Friday morning, everybody knew that they would be discussing strike action. For example, the morning shift at the *Paris Commune* yard in Gdynia: from the moment they arrived there was an air of expectancy, and nobody really started working. They talked among themselves. At around 7.30 am, groups of workers gathered in the two largest departments, the K2 and K3 hull-construction sections. A group of them came out and marched towards the management office. Almost immediately the other departments emptied, with workers downing tools and following the demonstration.

Andrzej Kolodziej, a young 20-year old worker, was at the head of the march. He didn't work at the Gdynia yard, but had just spent the night at the *Lenin* shipyard, from which he had been sacked in January 1980. Everyone knew him from his earlier activities. They listened to him and they trusted him. The demonstration marched towards the management building. "This is too soon," Kolodziej explained. "We are not ready. They may organise a provocation to divide us." He led the crowd towards the central square, next to the main gate. This spot was to become the venue for all meetings in the weeks to come. The workers needed to get organised, to decide on their objectives. They elected a 20-person strike committee, of which Andrzej Kolodziej was naturally elected President, and before negotiating they decided to get in touch with the Gdansk workers. *Act together* — that was their main principle.

At first the manager refused to allow them to use the telephone, but was pressured into agreeing. The strikers asked for a delegation to be received. The factory's union council official tried to divert the discussion, and invited the delegates to come into a little room in order to discuss 'calmly'. This was rejected. "Between four walls," warned Kolodziej, "they are always stronger than us. That's a small room, and we would never all get in." So they remained in the open air, and, ignoring the presence of the director, the workers discussed their demands. At the *Paris Commune* shipyard the strike was by now total.

That morning the movement that had been started by the *Lenin* shipyard spread to almost all the other yards in the bay, to the ports, and to other enterprises involved in the ship-building industry (Techmet, Opakomet, Elmor, Klino etc), covering about 60,000 people. The first western journalist to arrive on the scene, the Agence France Presse correspondent, described the atmosphere in front of the *Lenin* shipyard's No. 2 Gate: "A heavy silence weighs over this yard, which normally teems with people and echoes with the sound of sheet steel being worked. The huge arms of the cranes stand still. The main gates of the shipyard are closed. Strike pickets are keeping a vigilant guard on the gates, and systematically empty any bottles of vodka they find in people's lunch-bags. In front of Gate 2 (...) several hundred people have come to express their support for the workers. Mothers and wives have brought food to their sons and husbands. Smiling people chat and offer each other encouragement. The huge barred gate opens in front of us, and we find ourselves in among the strikers. Their faces are expressionless at first, but then light up as we are introduced. The strikers replies are laconic. They can be summed up in one single phrase: 'We will stick together!' (...)

"The city of Gdansk is still and silent. The town has been paralysed since Friday morning by a strike of public transport workers. In the streets, housewives hurry about to do their shopping. Queues build up at the butchers' shops, where that rare commodity smoked ham can be seen on display. Enormous queues line up outside the packed bakeries. Is there a shortage of bread? No, replies a cashier, people are laying in supplies. Why? Each of my questions is met with a smile (...)

"In the sleeping city, there is no sign of a police presence. The workers and the inhabitants of Gdansk are angry, but their anger conceals a worry that nobody dares express openly. Everyone realises that the situation is tense, all the more so since the shipyard workers' complaints have now spread like wildfire to other workplaces."

At midday came the first reaction from the authorities. Just as in 1970, they tried to isolate the town by cutting off telephone communication with the rest of the country. At 5.00 pm negotiations began again. As the strike committee's bulletin was later to explain: "Following a management initiative, departmental representatives are also taking part. Some of these are hesitant and undecided, while others are management stooges. This weakens the position of the strikers." In total there were 110 delegates, led by a negotiating committee of 20. The discussions were relayed in the surrounding area by the yard's internal broadcast system. The sticking point of the previous night's negotiations was unresolved. No further progress on wages. The talks broke down again. At Gdynia, negotiations were even more difficult. The director was refusing to allow the discussions to be relayed through the internal broadcast system. The workers replied with an ultimatum, giving him a quarter of an hour to connect up the microphones, otherwise they would do it themselves. "The law is on our side. From the moment the strike was decided, only the strike committee wields power in this enterprise." The manager had no choice but to give in. For the same reason, as from Friday evening, a permanent contact was established between the Gdynia yard and the yard at Gdansk. Late that night, as the workers were settling into makeshift shelters to sleep, they listened enthusiastically to the news of how their movement was spreading. Many of them spent the whole night on the gates. A new information network had now been established between all the enterprises on strike. In fact it wasn't until Sunday morning that the official local radio made any reference to work stoppages in the Three Towns.

On Friday evening, while KOR in Warsaw was publishing a communique in support of the Gdansk workers, Prime Minister E. Babiuch was explaining on television how the authorities intended to react. After a brief allusion to the events of the previous few days, he denounced the "enemies of people's Poland who are seeking to profit from the atmosphere of tension and emotion, for their own political ends". He appealed for people to return to work "calmly, and with honesty and discipline" towards the reconstruction of the ailing economy. He reaffirmed his confidence "in the working masses' understanding of Poland's national interest". Finally, in the course of announcing detailed economic measures to be adopted in September, he promised that there would be no new rise in the price of meat before autumn 1981. A dull speech, which was received indifferently by the strikers.

At the *Lenin* shipyard, negotiations resumed at seven

o'clock on Saturday morning, but proved fruitless. Once again, talks were broken off. They began again at 11 o'clock. This time management offered a 1,500 zloty wage rise plus a cost of living bonus. Outside, the workers, who were following every word of the negotiations, began to shout: "Two thousand! Two thousand!" The negotiator asked for a delegate vote. The majority of delegates accepted the compromise offered by the management, but first it had to be put into writing. After a brief withdrawal, the management returned with a document. It was signed. At 3.00 pm, in line with the majority vote, Lech Walesa announced that the occupation of the shipyard had ended.

At this point the movement entered a critical phase. The decision to end the occupation was not accepted. People wanted to continue. Confusion reigned, and this at first enabled the PAP news agency to announce a return to work. Later certain journalists were to speak of the strike committee having been overruled. In fact the actual course of events seems to have been a lot simpler than this. According to the chronology of events drawn up by the strikers some days later: "Having left the conference room, Lech Walesa spoke with workers, who led him to understand that a considerable number of the workforce were for the continuation of the strike in solidarity with other enterprises, whose managements had been unwilling even to make promises. In the light of this situation, Lech Walesa revoked the decision to end the strike, but he was not able to announce this decision, because where he was the internal radio was no longer functioning." Following this, at the request of the yard's manager, the majority of workers left the yard. Only a few thousand remained. This version corresponds to the account received two days after the events by the special correspondent of *Le Monde*: "When Walesa came out of the conference room he was wildly acclaimed by several thousand workers, who would brook no compromise. They threw him in the air, singing the traditional Polish version of 'For he's a jolly good fellow'. Delegations from other factories arrived at the yard. They were alarmed: 'If you return to work,' explained a representative from a bus depot, 'nobody else will win anything.' He was applauded. Walesa stood up to speak, and in a quiet voice this 40-year old man turned the situation on its head: 'We must respect democracy,' he said, 'and therefore accept the compromise, even if it is not brilliant; but we do not have the right to abandon others. We must continue the strike, out of solidarity, until everyone has won.' And since Lech Walesa is a political man, he added that this strike was different from the first strike, that new shop delegates should be elected, and that those who wanted to go home could.'' Whatever the correct version of the events, it is undeniable that the leadership of the strike showed a certain hesitation, which would have been quite natural, considering what was at stake. Maria Komorowska has this recollection of the events: "The workers had opened the gates and were already about to leave, but then delegates from other factories entered the yard and said: 'We came out on strike with you; you have won, but we are likely to be crushed. There will be an enormous repression, and many people will be sacked. So what are we going to do?' It was at this moment that the name 'Solidarity' was born. Leszek said: 'We will continue, in solidarity with all workers in Poland.' The gates were closed again, and the strike began anew.''

This was a historic moment. Effectively the strike was no longer a simple collective protest, a defence against rising prices. That phase, which had begun at the start of July had now come to an end. In its place came a political offensive by the whole of the Polish working class, an offensive that was better organised and more resolute than ever before.

On Saturday evening the delegates from the *Lenin* shipyard and from 21 other enterprises set up an 'Inter-Enterprise Strike Committee', the MKS. Its numbers were to increase over and over again as the movement was to spread along the Three Towns coastline; by Monday morning it covered 156 establishments, by Tuesday 253, and by Saturday 388. It was led by an organising committee of 13 members, which subsequently rose to 19 — of whom the majority were production workers.

This change in the nature of the mobilisation left its mark when it came to drawing up the demands which were to fix the committee's objectives. Discussions began at midnight on Saturday, and did not end until Sunday evening. They ranged over every conceivable topic, even taking in the organisation of democratic elections in the country. The initial list, drawn up on the night of Saturday/Sunday effectively included a demand for 'all socio-political currents' to be represented in the elections.

The KOR militants understood what was at stake in the movement, and tried to avoid the impossible. Bogdan Borusewicz explained this clearly: "To demand pluralist elections amounts to maximalism. If the Party were to give in, Moscow would intervene. We must not put forward demands which would either drive the regime to the use of violence, or would lead to its decomposition. Remember that it was the abolition of censorship which justified the intervention in Prague. We must leave them at least some exit routes."

Another delegate interrupted: "We've already left them exit routes by allowing them to govern in the first place."

"We should aim more at economic demands," Borusewicz continued, "and political demands which are negotiable. For example, the release of named political prisoners."

At the same time, there was long discussion about the importance to be given to each negotiating point, and the permissible extent of compromise. Not all the points were to be set as preconditions for a return to work. As the strike developed, there was to be a hardening on this initial position, which had been adopted at a time when nobody really realised the extent of sympathy that the movement would excite at the national level. The only precondition set for reopening negotiations was that telephone communications with the rest of the country should be re-established.

The list of 21 points* which were finally adopted on Sunday evening was a programme which many commentators at the time thought would prove unacceptable to the authorities. But the workers were to show that their confidence was matched by their strength. They knew that the Government had no choice but to give in, in the light of the strength of their mobilisation and their unity.

The 21 points were entitled: 'The Tasks of the Enterprises and Institutions on Strike, Represented by the Inter-Enterprise Strike Committee in Session at the Gdansk Shipyard.' The political elements of these 21 points were clearly all-important to the strikers. During my stay at the shipyard, all the strikers

* See page 220 for the 21 demands of the Gdansk strike. The government conceded the demands, at the same time insisting that they be qualified by a statement that re-affirmed the leading role of the Polish United Workers Party within the state.

whom I questioned told me basically the same thing: "If it was just a question of the money, we would have returned to work a long time ago." Their main demand was the first in the list: acceptance of free trade unions, independent from the Communist Party and the employers.' This, together with the right to strike (points two and seven), was the guarantee of all guarantees. In 1956 and 1970 the workers' councils and the 'democratised' official unions were very soon transformed into traps. Once the workers' mobilisation had ebbed, the Party's manoeuvres came to the fore, and the workers lost everything. They had fought in vain. This time, though, they would trust nobody. They wanted *their* trade union, with *all* rights guaranteed. This policy was soon to prove its worth.

The other points give a clear picture of the aspirations of Poland's workers: freedom of expression (point three); the reinstatement of those sacked in 1970 and 1976, and the release of political prisoners (point four); involvement in the major economic choices facing the country (point six); a challenging of the privileges of the *nomenklatura*[6] (points twelve and thirteen). The economic demands concentrated on the main inequalities that had been produced under Gierek's policies and subsequently: wages (points eight and nine); food and rationing (points ten, eleven and twelve); retirement and pensions (points fourteen and fifteen); health and childcare (points sixteen, seventeen and eighteen); housing and transport (points nineteen and twenty); and work-free Saturdays (point twenty-one).

The '22nd' demand, which was not voted on by the strikers, but which was as widely supported as point No. 1, was a song written by an anonymous writer, a worker at the shipyard. It summed up the hope and the spirit, the assurance of a peaceful strike as it began to extend its power. It was a reply to Gierek's numerous calls to 'Help us', and to successive self-criticisms by various Secretary Generals of the Party: "Stop endlessly excusing yourselves, stop apologising. Look at our grey, tired faces, as creased and crumpled as our lives... Stop trying to tell us that we are foolish, that we lack experience, that this is anarchy. Instead of trying to plug the breaches, why don't you start by changing yourselves." Within a few days this cry was to be heard the length and breadth of Poland.

3. "It's No Good Hoping for Miracles"

The man was a shipwright. He walked upright under the grey summer sky, his long white hair combed back, and his pace measured. He worked on the slipway of the *North* yard at Westerplatte. This was where the tourists used to come looking for traces of the first battle of the Second World War, that battle that the whole of Europe sought to ignore. At 60 years of age he should have been entitled to retire, in order to benefit from this new world on whose construction he had been working for so long. But he had nowhere to live. When he squeezed into the tram that creaked across Gdansk-Wrzeczsz, he left behind him a workers' hostel. He mingled with the silent morning crowd. The homegoing evening crowd swallowed him up, and for ten years now he had been waiting for the house he had been promised. It never came. So he could afford to leave neither the workers' hostel, nor the slipway where he worked, building hull after hull after hull. Management treated him politely. "Within two years you will have a house," promised a young man dressed in an English tweed tie. Should he believe this?

What about the union branch? All they did was offer promise after promise. Recently he had made up his mind. "If they don't give me proper housing, I shall ask for permission to stay at the hostel after I retire." But was this a possibility, for a pensioner to stay on in a workers' hostel? He didn't know. If not he would continue everyday to take the creaking tram to the slipway where he built the hulls of ships.

His room-mate at the hostel was a married man. His wife and daughter were living elsewhere, outside Gdansk. He too was waiting for a place to live. For nine years he had been filling in the triplicate forms required for his request, nine years during which, every evening, he had come home tired to this tip of a room. How could anybody find rest in a place like this? How could he be fit for work every morning? Not that his work was very tiring: he was in charge of maintenance of the big

crane in the *North* shipyard. "I have a very responsible job,"
he was fond of saying, derisively, as if to justify the days and
weeks that passed.

Nothing would ever change him. And the same for another
worker — an assembler. One day, crouching there, with his
short black hair, his mischievous eyes, he had refused to work
overtime — just like that. Anyway, it was not supposed to
be compulsory! He laid down his tools and decided to go
home. He walked along the shipyard canal, he crossed the
bridge, and got on the electric train, and watched the countryside go by, next to the huge blocks of concrete, the cranes,
and, in the distance, in the mist, the old reconstructed town of
which the people of Gdansk were so proud. The result: his head
of department crossed him off the bonus list. They had a fierce
row. The head of department went back to his office. But
nobody had defended him. And yet in each shop there was supposed to be a trade union group, a workers' organisation.
Anyway, he had talked about it with his friend, a workmate. A
small-built man who made all the workers laugh with his country dialect.

That day the little man was offended. Not by the injustice
that his friend had suffered — that was nothing out of the ordinary. So, what was he so upset about? The distribution of the
tokens required to buy a car. Who received those tokens?
Everybody knew. It was the arse-lickers, the officials comfor-
tably ensconced in their offices. People like that changed cars
with as much ease as they changed shirts. They showed them off
round the factory. They put their new toys on parade. His
foreman for example, had one, bright and shiny. Workers used
to go goggle-eyed watching these 'people's' cars, these small
FIAT Polskis which were supposed to be built for the workers.

When the women got up to prepare breakfast for their
children, the children were still sleeping. The women had to get
up very early, to plan how to fill their larder, which was always
empty. Silently they walked through the mists that surrounded
the big apartment blocks that had been built after the war.
They walked to the shops, which were not due to open for
another two or three hours. Nobody ever knew exactly what
would be in the shops. They watched daybreak come, while
their men slept and their children cried. They worried about
how to get enough meat for the week. Soon they would be on

the go again, hurrying, running to work, jumping onto buses and hoping to get to work on time. Travel across town. Put up with the foreman's jokes. Get ready for the evening.

It was a cold and rainy evening in August 1980. The train stopped at Gdansk-Wrzeczsz, its doors opened and the men and women emerged in groups. They spoke little. They mingled into the night, which was already enveloping the town in its black mantle. Lights were few and far between — there was a shortage of electricity. It began to rain harder. A few minutes later, at Gdansk-Stocnia, the train was greeted by groups of workers squatting on the walls of the *Lenin* shipyard, under the cover of oilskins. The rain drowned out their voices, but you could see a long slogan painted up on the black-bricked wall: 'The solidarity strike goes on. We are fighting for freedom and justice, for the whole of Poland.'

I left the station, chilled to the bone. No sign of a bus or taxi. So, in the company of two students whom I had met there, I set off towards the city heights. There I found my friends' friends, on the twelfth floor of a bare apartment block.

Little by little, everyday life was being changed by the strike. People were not working. To reach the factories, and meet the strikers, one had to go on foot. Each family had one or two members who were sleeping at the factories. Their families brought them food. Everything was calm. In the streets people chatted and exchanged news. Of course it was more difficult to get around, but nobody was complaining. The atmosphere was very relaxed. People remembered December 1970, and the machine-guns that mowed down the angry crowds. Alcohol was now banned by the strike-committee. People were no longer collapsing, drunk, on benches; the railway station was no longer host to poor souls looking for help, looking for anonymity. The news that went around was slow to arrive, but precise. There was always somebody on hand to explain what had been said at the shipyards. People were waiting. It appeared that the Government was going to recognise the Inter-Enterprise Strike Committee, and that negotiations were under way at Szczecin. At the present moment it was limited to hearing separate delegations who, in any event, would only have been mandated to negotiate on wages and working conditions. So the workers stayed in occupation and continued waiting. People talked of the strike as if it was the most natural thing in the world. The 'people occupying down there' were not seen as strangers, but as brothers and sisters. My hosts explained the situation to me as if they themselves were personally involved, while we drank a glass of tea on the twelfth floor of the new apartment block. Needless to say, other people were frightened. Particularly those who were working in the state administration. They were not willing to go on strike, because they feared for the future. But, I was assured, they didn't count.

Was it possible to find sufficient food? Things were as usual. During the first two days there had been a shortage of bread, because families had been stocking up. But afterwards everything returned to normal. The shops were open, but they were empty. When something arived, a long queue would form. On this estate it was possible to find meat twice a week, if you were willing to go and start queuing at noon, for two or three hours. As regards bread there was no problem. In general people were eating cheese, eggs, vegetables and fish. Of course, it was not always so simple. The young woman whom I was visiting was breast-feeding her baby, and needed a lot of vegetables and meat.

"And has this situation been going on for a long time?" I asked.

"Yes... a long time."

"Several months?"

My question brought a laugh.

"For years... Anyway, you tend to forget about it. You begin to think that things have always been like this."

The *Lenin* shipyard, Thursday 21 August, in the strike committee's conference hall. The delegates approached the microphone, introduced themselves, explained their struggle, and said why they were there. Outside, despite the pouring rain, people were listening and applauding.

The representative of the maritime port's repair yard: "We are contributing 3,770 zloty to the Inter-Enterprise Strike Committee fund, which is authorised to spend this money as it sees fit. Negotiations with our management have been broken off. The director was twice invited to meet with the whole of the workforce in a local bus depot, but refused to come. In fact, he organised his own meetings, with groups of workers chosen by himself! Our director has been like a little boy playing with the factory printing presses. He produced the following leaflet, which I shall now read to you: 'The strike committee is tacitly backing political demands, insofar as it has made no statement repudiating them. I must inform you that this makes it impossible to negotiate on wage rises and the other payments with which the government commission is currently dealing. The strike committee broke off negotiations at nine o'clock this morning. In the light of this situation, I invite all those who identify solely with the economic demands to meet me at one o'clock this afternoon in the company's assembly hall. We will discuss possibilities of raising wages.' So we too addressed a leaflet to the management: 'We would inform you that we are on strike in total solidarity with the Inter-Enterprise Strike Committee in session at the Gdansk shipyards. All their demands and all eventual changes in their demands are equally ours. Our activities are in no way influenced by any political organisation.' There you are!'' (*Applause*)

The representative from Gdansk-Kokoszki: "I arrived here around half an hour ago. We have had a few small problems in our enterprise... I say 'small' because they weren't really very big. (*Laughter*) What sort of difficulties? As you know, several ministers representing different departments have come to see us. Each of them wants to enter into discussions with companies involved in his own sector. We are in the construction sector, and 'our' minister asked us this morning to send three delegates, along with management, to set up discussions. After consulting the whole workforce, and the Inter-Enterprise Strike Committee, we unanimously rejected this proposal. We will not begin discussions. (*Applause*) We have voted and ratified this. Unless of course the minister himself would like to come and see us... We still need time to think. We are not rushing into things. In order to prove that we are indeed with you, and that we will be with you to the end, we have organised a collection in our firm. Here are 4,660 zloty towards the construction of the monument to the victims of December 1970... Thank you. We will stand by you!'' (*Applause*)

The representative from the Marine Institute: "At their meeting of 21 August 1980, the workers of the Marine Institute expressed solidarity with the positions taken by their strike committee and they authorised the committee to represent them in negotiations with the government commission. Appended is the list of resolutions and demands passed at the Institute. We address this to the Inter-Enterprise Strike Committee, to the government commission, to the management, and to the general council of the union of sailors and shipyard workers." (*Applause*)

— "Ladies and gentlemen, as I already explained to you yesterday, in our enterprise, namely WPRWIK at Gdansk, there has been an attempt to frighten us. The management has given us an ultimatum. They have told us that if the strike was not called off by two o'clock this afternoon, the company would go into dissolution. This morning at about ten o'clock, all members of management went off in private cars to an unknown destination. And what happened then? A number of managers returned, and went to the departments which were not actually out on strike, to encourage them back to work. And when they returned, ladies and gentlemen, there was indeed a collapse: a collapse by management! (*Applause*) Where the negotiations were being conducted by the Second Secretary of the Party, no sooner had he arrived than all the workers, including the staff, joined in the general strike at our enterprise" (*Applause*)

On the Thursday there was news that the police were preparing to come and destroy the shipyard's printing presses. A round-the-clock guard was organised. Henceforth members of the strike committee were to spend the night sleeping in each . of the yard's sections. Friday 22 August: in the Inter-Enterprise Strike Committee hall the procession of workers' representatives continued. News had arrived that the government commission was just beginning discussions with the Szczecin workers. Would it soon be Gdansk's turn? Preliminary contacts were already under way.

— "I represent the rural transport cooperative of Pruszcz-Gdansk. We organised a 15-minute collection among our fellow workers this morning (roughly 70 of us). We collected 4,580 zloty. (*Applause*) At the same time, I would inform you that when our committee — numbering three people — decided to come here, the director general told us: 'Gentlemen, beware. You run a risk that you won't be coming back.' We have to admit that our director was not far wrong... We had travelled no more than two kilometres when we were arrested by the militia. Their car was parked in a side-street, and drove out after us when we passed. It pulled over ahead of us. The militia men took our driver away with them, and then confiscated our car. They wanted to take us to the commissariat, but we flagged down a taxi, and the driver dropped us off here free of charge. Thank you." (*Applause*)

— "I represent the UNIMOR enterprise. Our workers have sent a letter to the provincial committee, demanding that the authorities order the police to leave our factory gates! And I ask (*Applause*) that the delegates here notify all enterprises so that they do the same."

Lech Walesa: "I declare officially that if the authorities do not stop calling in KOR militants and the militants of other social and political organisations for questioning, then negotiations will *cease*. (*Bravo! Bravo! Applause*) These people are not our leaders — because we lead ourselves — but they are offering us assistance, just as they offered assistance before... They had foresight, and helped many of us understand... our history and what our demands should be. (*Applause*) There are other cases too. Like the people who were running our press and publicity ... Around 20 of them are in prison... I appeal to the authorities: I want to see them here, because we cannot really go on negotiating if you apply methods like these. This is not the way to do things! These are not solutions!"

— "Good day, ladies and gentleman... I am from the Powisle cooperative of Kwidzyn. We are joining with you — sorry if we're a bit late, we are all united, and we number around 2,000 — and we support all your demands! (*Applause*) You must excuse me, I am not a public speaker, excuse me..."

— "Here is an announcement for all those leaving the shipyard this evening: we have the registration number of the white Fiat which the militia are using: GV-30-12... GV-30-12... A white Fiat 125."

— "Hello... This is 'Polmozbyt' car factory speaking... That Fiat stopped us twice yesterday. It's a white one, an oldish model. It's not a Fiat MR with the big headlamps. It's easy to spot it. The driver drives without his cap — but when he approaches you he puts it on. To 'civilise' himself a bit, presumably. And in front they've got a camera..."

Andrzej Gwiazda: "On the platform here we have a gentleman who has been sacked for having gone on strike. Marian Lewicki. He comes from Zary... Listen to what he has been forced to sign: 'I terminate my contract as from 21st August 1980, with no notice, because of having committed a serious offence against the duties of a worker, namely having committed a breach of the peace at my place of work. Under Article 52, paragraph 1 of the Labour Code...' And here is his work certificate: 'Marian Lewicki has been employed at the Przodownik invalids' cooperative as a Grade IV metal stamper, earning 11.50 zloty per hour. He has been on piece work. Average monthly wage: 2,869 zloty' He will now tell his story."

Marian Lewicki: "Workers, delegates, all of you here on the committee represent the rights of the workers... I have come from the other side of Poland to see you. I am very moved. When I saw this great crowd, I began to cry... Do not be surprised. I've calmed down now, and I will tell you what has happened... (*Applause*) I was a worker, the same as each of you. I was a worker, but today I am no longer a worker... Yesterday they sacked me for having gone on strike. Because I fought for a better future, so that my children might have something to eat. (*Applause*) I was working in a stamping shop... a very dangerous job. One moment of carelessness, one moment's lapse of attention, or perhaps a machine-fault, and there you are, disabled. For us there is no longer any... help, or aid, because without hands we would no longer be fit for work. (*Applause*) And for a job like this the enterprise was paying us 3,000, 3,500... up to 4,000 zloty. Is this the way to reward the labours of a worker who has given his all... his sweat, his blood, his exertion, to get an honest wage? Are we really asking too much? Workers, tell me! (*Applause*)

"I will explain to you how we ended up going on strike. The story might turn out a bit long. I hope you won't find it boring. I have crossed the whole of Poland to get here. I got up at 4.30 this morning, and I came here to be with you, and to explain my case. Who else could I tell? Who would understand me? Who would listen to me? (*Applause*)

"Our strike happened in the department where people earn the lowest wages. Three weeks previously, we had had a meeting with management. We said that our wages were too low... There had been tension and misunderstanding with the chargehands, just because our rate for the job was not high enough. The management promised that they would increase the rate. We waited. They told us that on piecework we would be able to earn 200 zloty more if... we were not drunk. The coming days were to show that all we would earn would be 70... 80... maybe 130 zloty more. So why should we work? After discussing among ourselves, we decided to go on strike. A drastic step. But nobody had wanted to listen to us. The chargehands were making fun of us. The foremen used to tap their heads when they talked about us, making out we were crazy. But we said: 'We workers should go on strike. We should go on strike, and maybe we will get a rise...' And we went on strike. Yesterday morning we came out, with a banner — the banner that I have here — a banner which is dear to me like no other thing in my beloved Poland..." (*Applause*)

"Where are you from? What's your town?"

"From Zielona Gora."

"But what town?"

"Zary. I am from Zary, in the province of Zielona Gora. Gentlemen, workers. Look... Our banner. How could they have sacked workers with a banner like this? Look at it, please..."

The President: "This is very moving... Too, too moving. Yes, thank you. Carry on, please..."

Marian Lewicki: "OK... I shall now explain how the strike ended. It did not last long. Barely two hours... All of a sudden management appeared, shouting: 'You are all going to be sacked! Come on! Everybody back to work! Otherwise you will all be out the gate, and the militia will arrive!' People were afraid, and went back to work... So, that's what I wanted to tell you. Thank you for listening to me."

Another day, in another part of the old town. The sun was finally shining, picking out the silhouettes of the Renaissance roofs. The sky was as blue as the sea. I was talking with three schoolgirls. Beata, aged 14, Agnieszka and Ania, aged 15. They were on holiday, and all three of them liked football. But not as players: "We are spectators, fans." Agnieszka, the girl with brown, short hair, talked a lot, and was always laughing. For her, to be a footballer was a job, like any other. She thought it was wrong to say that the members of football teams were amateurs. There was discontent among the workers of factories where sportsmen were employed. They claimed that they never saw them at work; they grumbled about these layabouts receiving a wage for doing nothing. But Agnieszka stood firmly by her idols.

Ania loved music, and read a lot. And football? For her it was a 'superb' game, and it was unfair to hold a grudge against the footballers. If anybody was responsible for corruption, it was the Federation officials. "All Party members, mind you..." She said that with a knowing smile. Beata took up the point: "In the factory where my Dad works, the fellow who washes the bottles has to pass them from his left hand to his right hand. Now, if he wanted to do it the other way, it would be impossible. A Party directive says that he can't change directions." We all laughed at this unlikely story.

Ania supported the shipyard workers: "They are the voice of people who, for 30 years, have not been able to speak. They are the voice of the people." The three of them explained: "After the war, when the communists came, they said: 'Things are going to improve... There will be no more unemployment... Life will be wonderful.' Well, that was perfect on paper, in theory. But reality showed something else. Socialism is a utopia. It's impossible."

"There is no difference between capitalism and socialism," Agnieszka stated. "Both of them are sick, and we've got to find something else." For Beata, "the principles of socialism are wonderful; they are very fine, but unrealisable". Why? She wasn't very sure.

"The higher the principle, the more magnificent the principle, the harder it is to achieve. They built a castle out of all this, and from time to time they tell us that one brick is bad, and that it must be changed. Otherwise it will all collapse. But in our country, it's not just one brick. The earth itself is rotten."

Agnieszka was planning to be a journalist, Ania a pianist, and Beata a psychologist. What newspaper did Agnieszka want to write for? She didn't know. And supposing that, in order to get a job, she had to join the Party? What would she do? Never! "Ever since she was little," Ania explained, "she has known that the Party is bad, that it stinks of corruption."

Beata's brother was five years old. He and his friends had invented a new game: they went 'queuing': for three hours they would wait in front of a door, to get meat. In the evening, he would tell his mother: "Ah, I'm really tired. I've been queuing all day!" Everyone at home laughed.

Yesterday evening Beata's mother came back worn out: she had not been able to find either bread or butter. Only cheese.

Ania showed me her history book. She read a sentence: " 'On 17 September 1939 the Soviet armies entered the Eastern provinces of Poland, in order to protect the Ukrainians and Bielorussians...' That is completely false! It was a massacre. Everyone knows that this book is false."

We drank tea, more tea. I talked to them about the shipyard. They hoped that everything was going to turn out well. But, as Agnieszka explained, "we have sunk too low to be able to change everything in just a few days."

So, the strike went on, and collective powers developed. They brought with them every kind of hope, and generated strength and determination. They showed their power, against those who had been repressing them for 35 years. They also generated new illusions. But for how long?

I spoke with a woman worker from Elblag. Her face was wrinkled from work, her hands misshapen: "In 1956 Gomulka came. My mother cried with joy, because she believed that he would put Poland on its feet again. Then Gierek came. My comrades in the factory asked me where this man came from. I told them that he had done great things in Silesia. He had invited us, us workers, to help him. I cut two tons of cloth a day to keep my side of the bargain, so as to help Gierek. Nobody ever came to ask us how much money we were getting for working so hard. But with what is going on today, the women in the factory have been asking me if they should resign their Party cards. I told them: 'Aren't you ashamed to abandon the Party at this moment, when it has so many problems. I know where all this is leading... We must look the workers in the eye.'

'Look,' they protested, 'there are people in the Government who are enjoying themselves, on Poland's money, who are consuming our money for their own ends.'

'Yes, that's true, and that's the reason why the strikes have broken out.' The Polish people are suffering a lot. I told my workmates that if, in our enterprise, the strike only gave us a 2,000 zloty rise, we would start striking again for 4,000. They won't take us for fools this time. Our ministers do their sums with pen in hand. They are sending too many things abroad. I can't find sugar here, or meat, or butter. We have to control our trade. And that's what I told the women in the factory: 'Get this into your heads. It's no good hoping for miracles.' ''

4. Inventing Democracy

"We are going to win." They were certain of victory, sure of
their unity and their rights. They were bound to win. 'They'
were the several tens of thousands surrounding the *Lenin*
shipyard, with their families. They were listening to the
negotiations relayed via loudspeakers from within the factory.
They had brought money, or food, sacks filled with potatoes or
tomatoes. They went to the flower-decked gates, hugged each
other and gave encouragement. The children were there too,
and around this vast shipyard an enormous crowd was waiting
for the Government to respond to the demands of the region's
300,000 strikers. A silent, serious crowd. Eager for news. From
time to time somebody would throw a packet of leaflets in the
air. People rushed to get one. A scuffle here and there, but
order returned very quickly. In fact everyone would get a
chance to read the leaflets, even if they were crumpled and badly
printed. Once read, the leaflets were passed on.

   The shipyards were not open to all comers. Only journalists and factory delegations were allowed over the threshold.
The strike committee maintained a watchful eye. After being
checked several times, each visitor received a pass. This gave
them access within the compounds. The Inter-Enterprise Strike
Committee was meeting in the health and safety committee's
building. They always extended a warm welcome. Four hundred
delegates were in permanent session there, in a large conference
hall. Everything was clean: not a dog-end on the floor, and the
water in the jugs always fresh. A statue of Lenin stood behind
the platform, and on the table, in among bunches of flowers,
stood a little man carved out of wood, with his two fists raised
— obviously the work of one of the workers.

   Here the democratic leadership of the strike sat in permanent session — a permanent conference, meeting day and night.
Each delegation had the name of their enterprise written on a
piece of card. There were daily shuttles between this conference

hall and the various factories. The general level of organisation was extraordinary, outdoing even the most perfect textbook democratic strike.

You could ask anyone, and they would explain how each striker had a part to play in this democratic movement. For example, a young woman worker representing the 750 workers of a canning factory (where 90 per cent of the workers were women). "I have been here for six days, and strike action at our enterprise was only really decided on yesterday. First of all the director suggested that we should go to meet the provincial governor and he himself picked out three delegates, with no consultation whatsoever. Obviously those negotiations came to nothing. I came here, and when I went back to the factory we elected our committee. 12 women workers, one per department, elected by show of hands after due discussion. Now there are two of us here, and we report back twice a day on what has been happening. As for the director, he has disappeared." I asked her if her factory was occupied. She showed me an Inter-Enterprise Strike Committee document: "We are continuing to work. What we produce is useful to the strikers. We have a permit from the Inter-Enterprise Strike Committee." There were in fact several enterprises in this position. And the trains which served the Three Towns were also still running, every ten minutes. This was essential. Often the trains were decorated with Polish flags as a sign of solidarity. I put the same question to several of the delegates meeting in the hall. They had all been elected in the same manner as the woman worker from the canning factory, and all represented strike committees. "We elected 12 people, to cover 800 workers, one per shop," explained a young man from a repair yard. "I am president. Every day we hold section meetings, and I give the news about the factory occupation." The same reply came from an electrical construction plant, employing 1,500 people, and an agricultural machinery factory employing 3,000: 14 delegates per strike committee, elected by show of hands. One of the representatives from the *Paris Commune* shipyard in Gdynia explained to me the advantages of this procedure: "The names are put forward at general mass meetings. It's impossible to make a mistake, because workers know whom they can trust. Because people know each other in the departments, obviously. In this way we appointed 14 delegates, by show of hands. All of them workers — I am the only technician. Four of us remain permanently here in session with the Inter-Enterprise Strike Committee, and we travel back to the plant twice a day in order to carry news and information, and to discuss our mandate. For ten days now the majority of workers have been in occupation, and are staying in the factory." What was the role of the strike committee at Gdynia? "Everybody has a particular job. Some are involved with information. Others with food supplies, others with stewarding, or keeping in touch with families. In Gdynia the whole population is with us."

These delegates revealed a level of scrupulous collective organisation in the factories of the region. They arrived at about 7.00 am, and left after discussion had ended, often very late at night. A new way of life had been born. A woman worker from a food distribution enterprise (200 workers) explained to me how their workplace had changed into a source of supply for the strikers: "In our enterprise, with an 80 per cent female workforce, we have five on the strike committee. After the mass meeting, we took our demands to the director's office. He went off in a huff. We locked the gates. Since then we only open the gates for organising distribution of food, in liaison with the agricultural workers. We redistribute foodstuffs to the other factories."

The first rule of the strike was that those elected should be genuinely representative. The election of committees was not a new thing, but this time it was organised more precisely and systematically. In December 1970 and in January 1971, the strike committees had been elected less methodically. For the most part they consisted of natural leaders, confirmed collectively in the course of mass meetings. At Szczecin, at the time of Gierek's visit in January 1971, negotiations were not able to begin until the workers had had time to elect a delegation. In 1976, at Ursus, Radom and Plock, the workers barely had time to organise themselves; they came out immediately into the streets and confronted the militia. Then the repression set in. Finally, as we have seen, in July 1980, democratic organisation was still a rarity. The example of Ursus, as publicised by *Robotnik*, was not much followed. Some strike committees, fearing repression, remained clandestine. Thus the seaboard workers had taken a decisive step in choosing forms of representation which would limit the delegation of power, and which would establish a relationship of mutual confidence between the mass of workers and their mandated delegates. At the start the chosen form for elections followed the untiring explanations offered by the columns of *Robotnik*. In the *Charter of Workers' Rights*, signed and widely distributed in 1979, it said: "We must begin by freeing ourselves from our passivity. (...) We must find and take up new and effective methods of struggle." Among these they recommended, in times of strike action, "the election of representative delegates who will oversee the negotiation of demands." Shortly before the stoppage of the *Lenin* shipyard, a leaflet entitled *What to Demand? How to Go on Strike?* was distributed. It explained: "The group that decides to take action must draw up a list of demands, and visit all job locations with their list. When the workforce has reached agreement on taking action against management, each section, shop or department then proceeds to the election of its delegate. The elected delegation goes to management and presents the demands in written form, asking, in the name of the workforce, that management answer their case. In the best of circumstances, management agrees to negotiate and decides to meet the demands along lines emerging as a result of the negotiations. In that case it is not necessary to go on strike. If it is, the delegation then becomes a strike committee, and the workforce stops work. However, it is not advisable to strike in those jobs which would involve enormous losses — for example on blast furnaces, or when the action would have an unpleasant effect on the public — for example, in power stations. Workers should come to the factory as usual, but not so as to work. During this time they are represented by the strike committee. The latter must see to the maintenance of order in the workplace, as well as preventing acts of hooliganism, and the consumption of alcohol. In the end, the authorities will be obliged to negotiate with the strikers." This rule was to be applied in all the coastline factories.

It was backed up with modern communications technology too. Workers were so used to hearing men and women speaking 'in the name of the workers', and they had so often been misled, that they wanted an on-the-spot means of assessment. Each delegate was provided with a tape recorder; they recorded everything said in the conference hall and during negotiations.

When they returned to their factory, they gave a summary of events, but they also produced their cassettes. These were relayed inside the workplace, and to the people gathered outside, via the internal works broadcast systems.

Ah, those broadcast systems! They had caught more than one bureaucrat unawares. The factories were effectively supplied with an internal radio, which in normal circumstances would broadcast music or messages from management and the union. Under a guise of democracy, the system was conceived as a means of controlling the working class. But now — as we saw in Gdynia — many strikes began with a battle for control of this internal broadcast system. Workers immediately recognised the democratic use to which it could be put. In every corner of the shipyard, which spread over more than a kilometre in length, one could hear, by direct relay, what was happening in the conference hall. Every shop had its loudspeaker, and in front of each loudspeaker was a tape recorder. Similarly, in the streets flanking the shipyard, and in front of the gates, the people of Gdansk were following the latest developments. When nothing particularly significant was happening, they would rebroadcast the previous day's highlights. They would also call strikers' families down to meet them at the gates, where clean clothes could be passed across, and where children could be hugged.

This form of direct democracy ingeniously combined a system of delegation with a system of continuous control by the rank and file. Each striker thus became responsible in their own right. Everything was crystal clear, everything was clearly understood. Insofar as the delegates were recallable, everybody had a leadership role. Thus Henryka Krzywonos explained to me how she had been elected: "I am a tram conductor. The first day we elected a delegate to go and see what was happening in the shipyard. He came back talking rubbish, telling untruths. Nobody believed him. So another team was elected. I went, along with two or three other drivers, and when we returned people told us: 'You are good delegates. You can represent us down there.' " So, with great pride, at the age of barely 25, she found herself elected to the praesidium.

The stewarding organisation was provided by the *Lenin* shipyard's strike committee — as distinct from the Inter-Enterprise Strike Committee — and was divided into three groups. They could be recognised by coloured armbands, with the letters KSSG on them (Strike Committee of the Gdansk Shipyard). The red armbands were worn by the 'flying militia', who saw to the safety of the praesidium members, and who were able to intervene quickly in the event of provocations. Other workers were in charge of protecting ships under construction, as well as plant and machinery in the shops; they wore blue armbands. The areas surrounding the shipyard were guarded by workers from the adjoining shops. These sentries spent the night in tents or makeshift canvas shelters, set up along the perimeter wall. One of their jobs was to make sure that no 'unidentified force' tried to rub out or paint over the slogans that decorated the shipyard. These guards relieved each other promptly, and with good humour. Often, as I returned in the evening, I heard guitars and voices singing songs of the strike. Finally, the organising committee, with their red and blue armbands marked 'Thoughtfulness and Solidarity — SG', were responsible for controlling the shipyard gates and the conference rooms. In this way there was a strict control of all movements. A worker from the shipyard would, under normal circumstances, not be able to go out. But by the end of the strike there were special dispensations which required special passes. Furthermore, no-one was allowed to enter the Inter-Enterprise Strike Committee building (unless they were delegates, or attached to the stewarding organisation). Thus delegates (and journalists accredited by the Inter-Enterprise Strike Committee were checked three times before they reached the conference room: first, at the yard's No. 1 Gate; again at the building's front entrance; and again at the entrance to the conference hall. These checks were very strict, and reflected the strikers' determination. Wheeler-dealing and subterfuge would have been impossible.

The reception of journalists, which at first was improvised, was soon organised by Maria Komorowska. In the final days there were to be more than a hundred journalists. A proper accrediting system was set up, with union cards being checked, and passes being issued. Each journalist had to give their name and the name of their newspaper, which occasionally created difficulties insofar as most of the journalists had only tourist visas. There were a dozen interpreters, wearing yellow armbands indicating which languages they spoke. These were for the most part students, but also included a number of workers. Finally, photographers were allowed into the shipyard, but only within a limited area.

Other aspects of the stewarding organisation were less well known. I asked on several occasions whether any preparations had been made for police attacks. I got no precise answer, but was led to understand that with the material and tools used in this shipyard... However, when on 21 August, the alarm was raised about a possible militia attack on the printshop, the stewarding organisation received the following instructions: in the event of dubious individuals climbing the walls, they were to be driven back if they were civilians, but if they were in uniform they were not to be resisted. Also it was clear that the committee had at their disposal a very effective information service. They were able to monitor troop movements in the region, and they maintained a constant check on the radio network linking the militia vehicles. And, as a committee member informed me, the Inter-Enterprise Strike Committee was regularly up to date on road, air and sea traffic in the Baltic region. All these stewarding activities were organised by a special commission of the yard's strike committee, the KSG.

Thus, between six and ten thousand people were safely ensconced in the *Lenin* shipyard. They slept in workshops and offices, and were provided with the basic necessities: camp beds, air mattresses, stoves, tea etc. At the *Paris Commune* yard in Gdynia, the strikers built huts out of the planks, or corrugated iron, and named them according to their fancy: 'Hotel Orbis', 'Dacha', etc. Food supplies were the responsibility of the *Lenin* yard's strike committee. It too depended on support from the population, along with some ingenuity. The food, which was bought with the money collected by the Inter-Enterprise Strike Committee, came from the town. The ex-treasurer of the factory committee, a member of the official union, who was also responsible for the yard canteen, effectively refused to sell any of his supplies. Now, the strike committee was spending something between 60,000 and 70,000 zloty a day on food. Fortunately, those in charge of buying food found enthusiastic support among the public. The market traders regularly added ten free kilos of fruit to any order; and the owner of a patisserie regularly brought cakes for nothing. One time, a farmer from Paszczyn arrived at No. 1 Gate wheeling two cookers — one gas, one electric — on his cart. A present for the strikers. The region's poultry farmers one day sent 5,000 eggs; somebody brought a barrow full of potatoes, someone else a pig. Peasants from the surrounding villages even wanted to give 20 cows... And there were some extraordinary efforts... for example the Macki cooperative dairy. Having approved the workers' demands, the director organised a regular supply of milk and cheese to the Gdansk yard. He was also the first to join the new union in September. Volunteers from among the strikers even went to help in milk production, and in distributing it to the factories.

A number of ploys were, however, necessary to transport the food. Since, at the beginning of the strike, the militia had blocked the roads leading to the shipyard, between 30 and 40 workers used to transport boxes of cheese, vegetables and bread by climbing over the fence next to No. 3 Gate. Later on, kilos of foodstuff were to arrive in the shipyard hidden in the van belonging to the PKF (Polish Film News). Finally, had the yards been completely cut off from the town, two private fishing boats were on hand to bring food in via the canals.

Every day between 700 and 1,000 free lunches were served at the yard's canteen for delegates and observers. The food was basic: a soup, a small piece of meat (pork or poultry) with vegetables, bread, fruit and a non-alcoholic drink. The meals were prepared by volunteers trained by the regular canteen employees.

Naturally enough, the organisation of the Inter-Enterprise Strike Committee's transport needs fell to the transport sector delegate on the praesidium, Henryka Krzywonos. She saw to the allocation of petrol and the organisation of taxis. As she told me: "We had a lot of money, but no petrol. So, with a few mates, I went, at the start of the strike, to find the fuel tanker used by the public transport authority. We brought it here, to the yard. Only lorries and cars authorised by the Inter-Enterprise Strike Committee were allowed to have petrol. And they needed a document with my signature." One day even the militia came to ask for petrol. Henryka refused them. She also organised the taxis. There were 300 striking taxi drivers, who now worked solely for the Inter-Enterprise Strike Committee. They were permanently parked in front of the main gate of the *North* yard, while five cars were parked next to the *Lenin* yard.

"If we suddenly found that we needed 20 taxis," Henryka explained, "I signed a chit, and they arrived immediately."

Henryka was one of the few women members of the praesidium, where she represented a sector where three quarters of the workforce were men. I asked her how women were involved in the struggle; "Like men. No particular problem..." Not satisfied with her answer, I pressed further. She found my question stupid, and ended by telling me that in her workplace mothers had to continue seeing to their children. They left the depot to take them to school, and to bring them home again. Often their husbands were also on strike, which meant that they had to find someone to look after the children. Failing all else, grandmothers stepped in to help. "But there's always a neighbour or an old person at home," Henryka explained. "In fact childcare was organised spontaneously. There are many women who don't go to work, and who offered their services to do the housework, and look after the children of strikers. They come to the depot, and the children are allocated. This is a tremendous movement — there are even waiting lists. A tremendous solidarity... And if you leave money on the table at home, you can rest assured that nobody will steal it." Interestingly, some time after the strike, the police were to remark that the weeks of the strike had seen not a single theft. "I had not been on speaking terms with my neighbour for a long time," Henryka admitted, "but there she was, one day, come to do my housework and wash all my dirty laundry!"

However, these forms of support still kept women in their traditional roles. The woman delegate from a cement works where 90 per cent of the 140 workers were women, explained how the women in her enterprise 'made do': "The majority of women are not able to remain in permanent occupation. Only a small group stays for the whole night. This is a different group every night, organised on a rota. But everyone comes in during normal work hours, from 7.00 am to 3.00 pm. We organise discussion groups. The factory is a hive of activity; we are getting to know each other. Last Saturday — a 'free Saturday' — all the women came with their children. We organised games. It was fantastic." In general, whenever I touched on this area of discussion, I encountered two parallel attitudes. On the one hand, every striker, whether male or female, thought it natural that women should have the same responsibilities as men. The same attention was paid to women's opinions as to men's. So at this level there was no particular display of sexism. But on the other hand, Catholic morality came to the fore in the allocation of jobs. The woman striker was a woman in subjection, sacrificing herself. She was like the Virgin Mary. She was seen differently from the pinup girls pinned up around the walls in a lot of departments. Anna Walentynowicz often presented both points of view simultaneously: yes, women were equal with men in this strike; yes, they should be prepared for great sacrifices, for this was their destiny.

We have no figures on the number of women among the Inter-Enterprise Strike Committee delegates. Going on my own observation I would estimate them at something less than a third, whereas 40 per cent of the Polish industrial workforce are women. As to the praesidium, it had only three women out of a total of 19 members (less than 20 per cent). This meant that the sexual discrimination which prevailed in the organisation of work was undeniably reproduced in the organisation of the strike. And this, despite the initiatives described above, was a point of weakness.

These forms of organisation were reproduced, in varying degree, in all enterprises in the region. The number of delegates in session at the *Lenin* yard reached 1,000 by the end of the month of August, representing more than 600 enterprises. During negotiations they were led and represented by a 19 member praesidium. Most of the praesidium was working class: it comprised 14 workers, the majority of them skilled (fitters, metalworkers, electricians, crane drivers, welders and labourers), four technicians and engineers, and a writer. They came from 15 enterprises (the metalworking industries, the four principal shipyards, electrical construction, transportation, a refinery, and the ports of Gdansk and Gdynia). The three most important workplaces (the *Lenin* yard, the *Paris Commune* yard, and Elmor) had two representatives each, who were, at the same time, the movement's main leaders: Walesa, Walentynowicz, Lis, Gwiazda, Kolodziej etc. Before the strike all these had been involved in the activities of the Constituent Committee of Free Unions of the Baltic. They formed a tight team, bonded by several years of shared experience, which, despite differing opinions on individual questions, was capable of giving a firm and resolute leadership to the struggle. This, however, did not prevent certain modifications in the composition of the praesidium. Two members, Joanna Duda-Gwiazda and Lech Jendruszewski were removed in the last week of the strike — for reasons I could not ascertain — and were replaced by Tadeusz Stajenny and Alina Pienkowska. The division of labour was more theoretical than actual: "It is difficult to say who exactly does what," Florian Wisniewski, an Elektromontaz worker and member of the praesidium, told me. "The truth is that everybody does everything." However, during negotiations each person had a particular brief to defend in discussions with the minister: Gwiazda for the free trade union, Walentynowicz for the political prisoners, Badkowski for censorship, Pienkowksa on health, etc. Also, it is incorrect to assume, as the media so often did, that the negotiations were solely a dialogue between Jagielski and Walesa. Each individual member contributed to the whole, and praesidium decisions were reached according to a precise procedure which had been adopted by the delegate assembly of the Inter-Enterprise Strike Committee on 22 August. On this subject two motions had been presented by Bogdan Lis. The first said: "The decision to stop negotiations, to proceed to a vote, and the results of that vote will be made known to all the delegates by the president of the Inter-Enterprise Strike Committee, Lech Walesa. Voting will be by a show of hands and will be accompanied by a written ballot. We will vote by writing 'Yes' or 'No' on ballot papers and by raising hands as we deposit the ballot papers. All decisions, with the exception of the final decision vote, will be taken by a two thirds majority." As regards procedure within the praesidium: "On the Inter-Enterprise Strike Committee praesidium voting on each of the 20 demands, and on the ending of the strike, will require a two thirds majority. Lech Walesa, as president, will each time have a right of veto. Having heard his arguments there will then be a new vote, which again will require a two thirds majority. During negotiations, the decision to take the matter to a vote has to be taken unanimously. Praesidium votes will only be valid if obtained with a two thirds majority. If the two thirds majority is not achieved, there will be a vote of delegates in the hall, after the two sides' arguments have been heard. The vote in the hall will be taken on the basis of a two thirds majority. Failing this, a fresh vote will take place." In addition to the president, two vice-presidents were named — Bogdan Lis from Elmor, and Andrzej Kolodziej from the *Paris Commune* shipyard. They had no particular duties, other than to stand in for Walesa as occasion required.

A word on the role of the president. The media always strive to reduce the struggle between social forces to a matter of differences between individuals. They have consistently and excessively personalised the leadership of the strike. Lech Walesa, the 'man of the year' for many mass circulation magazines, was painted as a kind of messiah, as a 'man of the people', adored by his 'troops'. The Press inquired into his childhood; they questioned his friends from military service days; and they delved into his past for the secret of what was happening in Poland. In short, they turned this worker electrician into a religious hero, who turned to God (or, failing that, to the Pope) to find the inspiration necessary for his mission. They preferred to show Western workers a religious mass, rather than a mass assembly of democratically elected delegates that might have given them ideas... This so-called 'news' was a measure of the worries which these workers' struggles were beginning to arouse among governments of East and West alike.

The reality was far more simple. Lech Walesa, as president of the Inter-Enterprise Strike Committee, was a spokesman for strikers who were perfectly conscious of their struggle, and answerable to it. His role was due entirely to this level of democracy. His talent as a speaker, and the path he had followed since the 1970 strikes, had made him the natural mouthpiece of these men and women. He was, and remained, a worker like themselves, despite the presence of some minister or other dignitary. He spoke their language. You had to have seen this small, dapper man, laughing with the crowds gathered at the shipyard gates, not haranguing them, but talking to them, like an ordinary human, about this and that. He always seemed to say the right thing at the right time. He knew how to put a rude or smarmy minister in his place. When they carried him across the shipyard, when they chanted the traditional 'May he live a hundred years! A hundred years!', they were confirming that he had done what they wanted him to do. If he proved wrong, if he put forward a mistaken proposal, people did not hesitate to contradict him, to put an opposite point of view. In this situation democracy ruled — the democracy of the vote — an if somebody was in a minority, he simply went along with the majority.

Walesa was during that period the voice of the strikers. But that was all he was. His weight in the decision-making process was not based on any particular prestige. Furthermore, he often represented a moderate viewpoint in discussions, influenced by the Catholic expert Tadeusz Mazowiecki. Other members of the praesidium, such as Andrzej Gwiazda, had at least as much influence, if not more, at critical moments. They were more political, and had more of a feel for understanding the balance of power than Walesa did. The tremendous responsibility shown by the strikers, and their magnificent organisation, were not the work of some superhuman. And anyway, they had plenty of other means of expressing themselves.

On Saturday 23 August publication began of the daily strike news bulletin *Solidarnosc* ('Solidarity'): this was an A4-format leaflet, folded in two, in tiny print. It gave the latest news, published Inter-Enterprise Strike Committee communiques, as well as commentary, reportage and poems. Numbers 12 and 13 were taken up with a detailed chronology of the events. Fourteen issues were produced in the space of ten days by two young militants: Konrad Bielinski of KOR and Mariusz Wilk. In the final edition they wrote that: "the bulletin has been produced by a small editorial committee, separate from the Inter-Enterprise Strike Committee." Nonetheless, all the workers identified with it. The appearance of each issue was accompanied by vast queues up the stairs of the Inter-Enterprise Strike Committee building. Factory delegates queued to wait for their packets. There were never enough copies to go round. On the final day people were saying that a copy of No. 1 was now worth nine copies of no. 13!

Two printing presses were involved in its production. Duplicators were brought to the *Lenin* shipyard and run by militants of the unofficial *Nowa* publishing house (linked to KOR). Usually they printed by hand, day and night, working in shifts. The shipyard's presses had been dismantled and locked up by the yard manager, and would only be made available during the final days. At the *Lenin* shipyard something like 40,000 copies of each number of *Solidarnosc* were produced. There was another printing press, with more equipment, at the

Paris Commune shipyard in Gdynia. The strikers there had shown more foresight. On the first day they had asked the press manager to give them the key. But he refused. Much good it did him! The workers broke into the printshop, and gave the staff five minutes to get out. The staff, on the other hand, being hostile to the strikers, had used those five minutes to remove key parts from each machine. "Next time," said Pawel on 28 August, "we won't be such idiots. We will go straight into the printshop, without warning, and we'll say: 'Hands on the table', and we'll take negotiations from there." The printing machinery was carefully guarded by the stewards, but it was to take three days before the machines were operational. They appealed over the broadcast system for anybody who knew about printing presses to offer their services, but the only person to come forward was an electrician who had seen a printing press operate one time. The offset machine was the first to be repaired, followed by the typesetter. Finally, in addition to these two machines, the workers had a photocopier capable of turning out large numbers of copies. This meant that they could produce between 60,000 and 80,000 copies of each leaflet. There were plentiful supplies of ink and paper stored at the shipyard. Half of the printing work was done by workers from the shipyard, and half by volunteers. In the final days a qualified printer arrived, enabling them to increase their production to something like 100,000 copies. This output was mainly for the Inter-Enterprise Strike Committee; the rest being allocated to the *Paris Commune* yard, the town, and the region. Transporting all these leaflets was not without its problems. The method chosen to evade police controls consisted of making up large numbers of small packages and sharing them out among many people. This would guarantee that they could not all be seized. One time, the strike committee, while monitoring the militia radio, learned that anti-riot units from the Goledzinov training school were preparing to shut down the printshop. Pawel explained to me why their action was called off: "they saw that we were preparing to defend ourselves. They were tapping our telephone, and knew exactly what we were doing. Also, they obviously had a number of informers in the shipyard. They were afraid. We knew this by listening to their radio, because this was the reason that they gave for calling off the operation."

The strikers had many other forms of expression: slogans on the walls, poems, and wall paintings in the shipyards. There were few posters, presumably due to lack of materials, and these were all small, printed on blue Bristol board. In the windows of the Inter-Enterprise Strike Committee office the strikers could admire a mock-up of the proposed monument to the victims of 1970, prepared by Bogdan Pietruszka and Wieslaw Szyszlak. A large mock-up model, about a metre high, stood in the conference hall. There were also drawings by an anonymous artist, showing the fist of a worker raised above the coastline, and the by now famous, *Solidarnosc* logo designed by Jerzy Janiszewski. History also provided inspiration. Occasionally combined with a spirit of mockery: the communist slogan of the post-War referendum — '3 × YES' — was transformed into '21 × YES'; sometimes with respect: Czestochowa's black Madonna was to become 'Our Lady of the Strike'. This was a naive painting, showing the virgin on a pillar to the left of Gate No. 3. This image was sometimes combined with the Polish national flags that draped the shipyard walls. Sometimes things also went to excess: at the beginning of the strike two enormous eagles decked with crowns (symbol of Poland before partition) appeared one day between Gate No. 3 and the construction office. They had been built by two shipyard workers, out of plywood. They had painted them silver, on a red background, and, having decked them with flowers, stuck them up, on poles. The Inter-Enterprise Strike Committee, fearful of a political provocation, said that the crowns had to be removed. Another time, a man came to present a proposed design to the members of the praesidium. His drawing showed the shipyard, with its cranes and scaffolding, and on the slipway a new ship named Lech Walesa!

The decorations on Gate No. 1 looked more like a Corpus Christi festival than a May Day celebration. There was a makeshift altar, and under a heap of floral decorations, Catholic banners and Polish national flags, there was a picture of the Czestochowa Madonna, a portrait of Pope John Paul II, and, rounding it all off, a banner: 'Proletarians of the World, Unite!' Placards hanging from the gates and from the top of the perimeter wall summed up the aspirations of the movement: 'Stick together', 'The people are with us', 'Freedom for the political prisoners', 'Fight on', 'Thank you', 'God is with us', etc.

Dozens of poems were arriving every day on the delegates'
tables, some of them anonymous, and some signed by B.
Rawicz. Some captured the atmosphere of the strike, some
summed up the demands, and some made fun of the government. There was even an outline for a Hymn of the Free
Union. Among the most popular were those which spoke of the
future. This one, for example, which was read from the platform on several occasions. It was addressed to 'my daughter':

I have no time for you
Your mother cannot see you either
But stay very patient
You will know all that is happening.

They will talk to you of these days
Full of hope, of discussion,
Of these sleepless nights
Of our hearts that beat so strong

Of these people who for the first time
Have felt at home
Who are fighting together today
For the future, for your tomorrow.

Don't be sad. Await with patience
The moment when you will return to our arms
Into our home, which was not really a home
Because there was no true happiness in it.

5. Between God and the Devil

At five o'clock every evening, between 2,000 and 3,000 workers gathered around the shipyard gate for a religious service. Every Sunday an enormous crowd gathered to celebrate mass. Meditation, simplicity. Around a makeshift altar they sang old hymns, asking God to give them more strength. From both sides of the gate, the strikers and their families prayed for victory and for support from the whole of Poland. The daily service was sacrosanct. It was a public display of that religious freedom that had been part of the workers' demands. People went there as a matter of course. Many also did not go, but did not see the service as something abnormal. There was a mutual tolerance, one of the moral and political forces binding the strike together. Those who believed in God found in these services the strength to go on fighting; those who did not saw in them the proof of the free expression of one's convictions. Thus they represented two ways of living out respective truths, outside the ruling ideology.

The support given by the Church, and the Pope's letter to Cardinal Wyszynski, were much appreciated. They were seen as an unconditional support for the strike, at a time when the Bishop of Gdansk (for example on Sunday 24 August) was putting forward far more moderate positions. Of course, he hoped for victory, but he also warned against disorder. A young delegate explained to me at length the role which, in his opinion, religion had played in this strike: "I do not believe in God. I have my own personal point of view... I do not think that the workers here want to give the Church a political role. Rather it is a moral support, an individual question." We were walking peacefully in the shipyard. The sun was shining again after two days of rain. It was a gentle evening. Here and there men were sleeping on the grass, or chatting in small groups under the scaffolding. The hull of a large cargo ship towered over us. Enormous cranes, their arms swinging, stood out across the sky. As we went over the bridge, a group of workers greeted us. "Here, you see, people are calm and relaxed They are guarding their machines and their workplaces." The scene was perfect. You had the impression of a revolution that was honest and sure of itself.

The delegates that I was to interview in the days to come confirmed this point of view as regards religion. While they believed that the new union would play an important role, the same did not go for the Church. They simply wanted everyone to be able to think, and believe, according to conscience. "We are very happy with the bishop's statement, and that is that," explained a delegate from the repair yard. I got the same answer from two women delegates from the food industry — a 100 per cent female workforce: "The Church can help us in all sorts of circumstances." "Do you think that religious leaders should one day be involved in the government?" "No! No!" They were categorical. Government was a matter for the workers, not for the Church. "You know, Poles are very religious, but this has no bearing on our rights."

Cardinal Wyszynski's letter of 22 August, advising moderation in the strikes, was received — unlike his former contributions — badly. It had no influence on the strikers' determination. Fortunately for the episcopate, they were able to get out of it by arguing that some sentences had been left out by the official Press. "Well, if the cardinal himself is being censored, then it's a different story..."

Nonetheless, this contrast between the undeniably working class character of the struggle, and the religious devotion of the strikers, with the very public presence of religion in their movement, requires further examination. It was a source of amazement for people in the West, and it fascinated the Press. It also worried those people for whom a working-class struggle that was dominated by religious ideology would inevitably, in the long term, lead up reactionary paths. One was reminded of the power of the Shi'ite hierarchy in Iran, and the strength of Islam.

For my part, I believe that the Polish experience provides another opportunity for us not to make that same familiar mistake — that of seeing ideologies as the motor of history, rather than the social forces which carry them. If one were to limit oneself to appearances, one could as well show that the people of Poland were anti-communist in the strict sense of the term. All the symbols of the workers' movement were hated. The *Internationale*, for example. When the *Internationale* was played at the end of Gierek's speech (following in the footsteps of Bierut and Gomulka), the crowd of strikers immediately broke into the national anthem, and an old hymn entitled 'God Save Poland'. Instead of the red flags, which traditionally decorate occupied factories in Western Europe, in this case there were the red and white, and blue and white flags of Poland and the Virgin Mary respectively. On the anniversary of the October Revolution, supposedly a day of celebration of 'Polish-Soviet friendship', only official buildings in Gdansk flew the red flag. Elsewhere there was a vast display of national colours, and the colours of the Virgin.

One could cite many more examples. From official language (whatever happened to 'comrade'!) to everyday life, everything that evoked communism — in other words, totalitarianism, as people saw it — was rejected. A superficial sensitivity became all the more strong as society as a whole mobilised against the power that represented that kind of socialism.

But at the same time you could have asked any striking worker, or any Solidarity trade unionist what they wanted, what they were hoping for, and they would describe to you a democratic society where everybody would be able to control the fruits of their labour, could live, think and believe as they wanted. They shared a concern for the future which was often more moral than political, but which was based on hope, generosity, equality, an ideal they had cherished for years, and which found expression in the full force of this ongoing revolution.

For many the Catholic faith was seen as the force which had preserved this conviction. The Church represented a refuge. To justify it, they cited Poland's history. A Catholic writer, Bogdan Cywinski, described in his *Genealogies of the Unconquered*, a widely-read historical novel, the period when, under the Tsarist occupation (two centuries), a united resistance front was possible, thanks to the Church. Believers and non-believers had fought side by side, despite the brutal repression. This had contributed to the image of the Church, and the story's allusion to the present day was obvious.

The theologian Stanislawa Grabska, vice president of the Catholic Intellectuals Club in Warsaw, explained to me how the interaction between faith and history had operated in the Gdansk strike: "During these days of the strike, religion played the same role that it should have in life. Either you treat it as something separate, as a rite which takes place in churches once a week on Sundays, or you see it as a factor involving the whole of human life. In that case it is as important in family life as it is in political and social life. It forms a whole. And if religion is that whole, then it has a part to play in political action, and in strikes. People need it in the course of their everyday lives."

She went on: "In Poland this conviction is grafted onto our own special history. For centuries the Church has been the sole organisation through which the Polish nation could hope to survive. In the 19th century, when social action was starting, in which the idea was to 'make people aware' — as is currently happening in Latin America — a part of the Catholic intelligentsia began to realise their responsibilities. A fair number of people began to meet in religious organisations to work in the community. While in the West, this was the century of dechristianisation, in Poland, the Church was extending its influence. It was the only officially recognised structure in which one could find oneself as a Pole and as a Christian, and could undertake political or cultural activity. A lot of things were done via the Church. During the wars and during uprisings people would hide in churches and would plot within the walls of convents and monasteries..."

This idealised view of the Catholic religion and the history of the Polish Church was very widespread. It was far too crude, it underplayed the existence of the first working-class organisations, but it had the advantage of stressing the solid bond that existed in Poland between nationalist sentiment and the religious institutions. It is in this bond, reinforced by the ups and downs of the nationalist struggle in the course of more than a century, that one must look to find one of the deepest reasons for the hold of religion. The Church, or alternatively the Catholic faith, has consistently taken the place of social and political alternatives as they came and went throughout Poland's long and tormented history. This has been its tradition, admittedly with its obscurantist, retrograde and reactionary side, but also with aspects that gave to a people without territory the strength to endure the partitions, the invasions, and the failure of their own insurrections.

In the 19th century, as other bourgeoisies were redrawing their frontiers in Central and Western Europe, and unifying their nations, the Polish bourgeoisie was making a very comfortable accommodation with the partition of Poland under Tsarist rule. "Since the majority of the bourgeoisie were foreign (having settled in Poland at the start of the 19th century), it was always hostile to the idea of national independence," noted Rosa Luxemburg.[7] "All the more so since, in the 1820s and 1830s, Polish industry had been built around export trade, before an internal market had even been created. The kingdom's bourgeoisie, rather than welcoming a national reunificiation with Galicia and the Principality, always sought their support in the East, since the massive export of their textiles to Russia was a key factor in the growth of Polish capitalism. The abolition of custom tariffs reinforced these pro-Russian tendencies still further (...) The Italian and German bourgeoisies owed their growth to the development of an independent national state, whereas the Polish bourgeoisie drew their profits from partition and the occupation of the country. These very particular conditions of capitalist development were to determine the development of Polish nationalism, which — instead of, as elsewhere, drawing strength from progress — became an ideology that was historically backward." The rising of the 'Gentlemen of the Kingdom' in January 1863 was crushed, as were to be those in the Ukraine, Polodie and Lithuania. With the support of Bismarck, the Tsar drowned them in blood, while at the same time abolishing slavery and enfranchising the peasantry. From 1871 onwards, he attempted to assimilate the Polish people into Russia, by centralising the administration. The Russian language was to replace Polish, which was forbidden in schools in 1885, and in religious teaching in 1892.

At the same time, the industrialisation of the country gave rise to a very concentrated working class, notably in textiles (the Lodz spinning mills) and the coal mines (the Dombrowa basin). The first risings of this working class (for example in Lodz in 1892) found it face to face with an employing class which was foreign, and which managed from its offices in St Petersburg.

Thus while the Polish ruling classes, carried away with economic expansion, were seeking to carve themselves a niche within the Russian Empire, the young proletariat from the countryside was organising its first struggles, and within all this the Church stood as the guardian of national values, of the Polish language, and of culture. As Adam Mickiewicz wrote at the start of the 19th century, in his *Book of the Polish Pilgrims*, God was their only hope: "In the war for faith and freedom, oh Lord, deliver us; grant us the general war for the freedom of our people, Lord." And the emerging workers' movement was still too weak to constitute an alternative to the national bourgeoisie.

After the setback of 1863, nationalism saw itself as wiser, and more realistic. It no longer called for uprisings. On the contrary, insofar as it was now supported by the ruling bourgeoisie, it advised compromise and the acceptance of a *status quo* with the Russian empire. Romanticism was succeeded by 'positivism', and the Polish people drew back en masse from political action. In the face of an awakening working class, with its early trade unions, this nationalism also provided a means of control and division. It spread the worst of poisons: hatred, and in particular anti-semitism. The mass arrival of Lithuanian Jews (the 'Litwaks'), and the assassination of Tsar Alexander II by the 'populists' was a pretext. Although the Church formally condemned the Warsaw pogroms in 1881, a fair proportion of the Catholic clergy were to support actively the first openly anti-semitic weekly founded by Jelenski in 1883. This nationalism also produced its own ideologues: Roman Dmowski, who founded the National Democratic Party in 1896, and Josef Pilsudski, who, in 1893, joined the Socialist Party (PPS), which had been founded in Paris the preceding year. The former, at this time, was bound up with positive realism — i.e. a temporary reconciliation with Russia — and was to be the principal ideologue of the nationalist, anti-semitic extreme Right up until the Second World War. The latter, violently anti-Russian, claimed to be inspired by the Romantic tradition, and, having very soon quit the Socialist Party, was to profit from its support in order to forge his image as a great national liberator.

After the victory of the Russian Revolution and considering the key role of the Lodz proletariat in the 1905 revolution, one might have expected a radical change in popular awareness, a dissociation from this nationalist, anti-semitic and religious ascendancy. However, yet again, the movement which might have brought to reality both the hopes of a national liberation and hopes for social liberation, failed. Or, more precisely, was proved bankrupt. At that time the Polish workers' movement consisted of three political parties: the Socialist Party, a reformist party, was to prioritise the struggle for national independence, and, in November 1918, contributed to Pilsudski's victory; the Socialist Left was made up of Rosa Luxemburg's SDKPL, established in 1893, and the Left Socialist party (PPS-Lewica), which had emerged in 1903 from a split in the Socialist Party. In December 1918 these two groups merged and set up the Polish Communist Party. The positions of this revolutionary Left, which identified with the Russian Revolution, were diametrically opposed to those of the Socialist Party: "They were convinced," wrote a historian, "that capitalist Europe was racing at breakneck speed towards the abyss," at a time when "the proletariat sought to grasp its historical heritage, even though it still had more than one enemy to defeat, and more than one illusion within its own ranks to bury." The first among these illusions was the "false tinsel of parliamentarism and bourgeois democracy", along with "slogans relating to the creation of new bourgeois states", since these states were not capable of doing away either with imperialism, or with national oppression. The socialist Left, with its ideas on Poland's independence, was completely isolated and had not succeeded in winning the majority of the working class, let alone other strata of society. The national question and the question of relations with the Russian Revolution were to dominate the political life of those years, while the test of events was unfortunately to strengthen the positions of right-wing Social Democrats within the working class.

The newly-formed Communist Party wrongly allowed itself to be carried away with the enthusiasm that accompanied the constitution of an independent Poland after two centuries of foreign occupation. The growth of the German revolution and the development of workers' councils in the Dombrowa basin, in Lodz and Warsaw, might have hastened the process of social emancipation. But the 'leftist' policies of the young Communist party, and the mistakes made by the Bolshevik leadership at the time of the Russo-Polish war in 1920 proved a definite setback. The result was that Pilsudski allied himself with feudal leaders in the Ukraine, and joined up with the White armies which were seeking to crush the new Soviet revolution. After a number of defeats, the Red Army, led by Trotsky, launched a counter-offensive and defeated the Polish armies at Kiev. The counter-revolution had been checked, and, carried away with their victory, the Russian revolutionaries imagined that this would enable them to liberate the whole of Poland. They marched on Warsaw. They expected to be welcomed with open arms by an enthusiastic proletariat — a terrible mistake. Pilsudski drove the Red Army back to the banks of the Vistula, and mobilised the whole Polish nation against the 'Judeo-Bolshevik plot'. The new Communist Party stood alone in justifying Soviet policy — a policy which, it should be stressed, had not been unanimously agreed within the Bolshevik Party. Trotsky and Radek had fought Lenin over this.[8]

This mistake left a deep mark in the memory of the Polish people. Combined with the defeats of the Hungarian revolution (1919) and the German revolution (1923), it was to isolate the Communist Party, and the Party was banned.

After Pilsudski's coup d'etat in 1926, it appeared that in the short term, any revolutionary alternative for the Polish working class was out of the question. It was sapped by the nationalism and anti-semitism which the Catholic Church tacitly supported. The period of Sanacja rule, followed by the colonels who succeeded Pilsudski, opened the door to Fascism. Stanislawa Grabska, who had lived through that period in Lwow, summoned up the attitude of the Church: "The Church had always been too fearful of communism. Its position in relation to Left movements was often less favourable than one might have desired. The majority of priests were linked, not to the government, but to the nationalist and fascist movements, particularly the Endecia (Dmowski's party, the spearhead of anti-semitism). There were also some good positions put forward, with a number of progressive bishops very close to the people. The bishop of Cracow, for example, Adam Stefan Sapieha. At Lwow there was also the Catholic Armenian bishop. He had been 'Polishised' and was very popular. A few years before the War there was a workers' rising, rather like the

Gdansk rioting in 1970. Riots, with the police shooting at workers, arrests etc. Those days were to remain engraved on everybody's memory. My father was a university teacher. He said to my mother: 'You know, if I go to see the Catholic bishop, he will do nothing, because he is too fearful of communism. But if I go to see this Armenian, he will take the side of the workers, and will influence the other.' And that is in fact what happened. The two bishops made a joint appeal to the government in support of the workers. During the war, all those who were of the Right and all the priests linked to the nationalists underwent something of a crisis of conscience in the struggle against Fascism and against the Germans. This explains why it is that people have now forgotten the position taken by the Church in the inter-war period."

At this point I raised the controversial question of anti-semitism. "There again, you can't talk about an attitude of the Church in general. It was different from one person to another. There were, of course, many anti-semitic priests, but one could not say that all priests were anti-semitic. The struggle against the Jews had its foundations in an economic problem. In the villages, almost all the small traders were Jews. Therefore all peasant movements against private merchants and in favour of cooperatives, tended in the countryside to come up against Jewish merchants. This favoured anti-semitism. In a given school, if the priest was a member of the Endecia or some other nationalist group, he was anti-Jewish. If not, he wasn't. At Lwow I did not experience anti-semitism as a Church matter. I never heard sermons hostile to the Jews. This was principally the result of action undertaken by nationalist youth, who were provoking riots and pogroms at the universities. My father rejected all that. He was linked to the WICI, the Association of Peasant Youth, which was close to the Peasant Party. These people were more or less of the Left. As a teacher he had set up a section of WICI in the University, and when he held political meetings, Endecia gangs tried to stop them. The young people in WICI were not anti-semitic, nor was the bishop of Lwow."
However, we should add that the attitude of the clergy towards this movement of rural youth and its popular universities was in general hostile. The clergy "fought by every possible means against the WICI, inasmuch as it was an autonomous, radical Catholic peasant organisation which was not willing to sub-

ordinate itself either to an organ of the hierarchy, or to Catholic Action, or to the authority of the priests. As a general rule the WICI circle, with a few small exceptions, encountered a thousand difficulties in the course of its educational and cultural work. It was up against the illwill of the local priesthood." In short, the majority of the Catholic clergy were less sympathetic to WICI than to the Fascist and anti-semitic special pleading of the priest-deputies who held sway in the Sejm. A good example was the well-known Abbot Trzeciak, who used the Catholic daily *Maly Dziennik* to justify Hitler's racist policies, basing himself on papal encyclicals.

Thus, between the two wars, at a time when Poland was torn by national hatreds, was a plaything of the international powers, and where 60 per cent of the economically active population lived in the countryside, the Catholic hierarchy supported the swing to the right in Polish society. It benefited from the shortcomings and incapacities of a workers' movement that was not capable of embodying people's hopes for social and national liberation. The progressive currents were in a minority, and were only to show their real strength under the Occupation.

"During the war," concluded Stanlislawa Grabska, "the Church played an important role in the defence of Jews. I was a member of the army, and we used to make counterfeit papers for people. That was my job. I was able to obtain many fake baptism certificates from priests for Jews. The clergy became massively involved in the Resistance movement, and saved a lot of Jews. The whole Polish nation was by now in the same boat, and everyone did all they could to help Jews. At Lwow it was the Ukrainians who persecuted Jews and Poles alike, because they were working with Germans. They saw themselves as enemies of Poland. In Warsaw many Catholics helped the Jews, although obviously they were also afraid. But then this was the case in every country..."

Then came the war, the Liberation and Stalinism. For the third time in a century, the hopes of freedom and independence which had fired the people of Poland were to be betrayed, led astray and ridiculed. And if, 35 years later, the working class once again were to rise up, flying the banner of the Czesto-chowa Black Madonna from the factory roofs, this was because those banners still symbolised the endurance, the purity and the self-sacrifice that were necessary to pave the way. One might regret this fact. One might say that the Church defends retrograde values. One might also stress its traditionalism, particularly strong in Poland.

All this is true, but one cannot forget that the main responsibility for this situation lies with the regime imposed by Stalin after the war, with its methods of government and its destructiveness. To be sure, this phenomenon was not peculiar to Poland — it was characteristic of many so-called socialist countries — but in Poland it took on all the aspects of a caricature. To be sure, Stalinism destroyed the foundations of capitalist domination in those countries, but only in order to introduce at once the worst forms of bureaucratic terror. Stalinism installed a system of political domination, which, in the absence of solid internal social roots, sought to preserve its absolutism by any means available. A nation cannot live for 35 years under a regime like this without looking for an ideal to oppose it, even if this ideal only takes the form of a hope.

The only social force which could endanger this dictatorship was of course the force which produced the country's wealth. Whatever the attempts to divide it, to gag it, to control it, it repeatedly rebuilt its strength and its solidarity. The practical demonstrations of this fact lie in Poland's past and present. But at the ideological level, the cultural domination of the working class by bureaucratic power was bound to breed false consciousness, was bound to thrust the people back into the arms of the Church and its myths. The history of Poland as we have briefly summarised it was an ideal and fertile soil for such a process. It had produced a collective memory which often identified the ruling regime with a foreign power which, in addition, ruled over the same territory as had the tsars before them — this time as secular oppressors. To this was added the policy of Stalinism, which, by taking a short-term view, tended in the long term to bring about results that were the exact opposite of what had been intended. Examples include the following:

Stalinism began by destroying the revolutionary tradition of the Polish working class vanguard. This was not a recent development. It had begun in the 1930s with the struggle against 'Luxemburgism' and the dissolution, in 1938, of the Polish Communist Party by the Communist International.

After the war, the best elements of the workers' movement, those that had not been killed by the Nazis, were either bought off by the regime, or were deported to camps where they were got rid of. The Christian and Socialist militants who had been the working-class lynchpin of the Resistance in Poland and who had led the Warsaw rising were at first abandoned to the occupier. In 1944 the Red Army stood with folded arms and watched the spectacle from the other bank of the Vistula, as the capital fought its lone 64-day battle. After the war, it was to take several years of social tension and civil war for this opposition force to be brought within the Party monolith. The slightest dissent would be stifled. This happened regularly: in 1949-50, at the time of the trials; in 1957-58 against the October Left; in 1964-65 among the youth of the Party; in 1968-69, against the intellectuals; in 1970-71, and so on. The worst of arguments were mustered to help in this process — from 'revisionism' to anti-semitism — then taken up by the regime. Particular attention was paid to anything which might have emerged from within the Party itself, to those who might try to take literally the revolutionary ideas of Marxism-Leninism which had been neutralised by the regime. The language and concepts of Marxism were changing meaning. They now bore the mark of a totalitarian power. A song that had by now become dry, boring and outdated. These concepts were learned at school as the vehicle of a lie. They were practised like a second language, the language of official life, life without importance or committment. History was falsified and stolen from a people who feel their history in their bones. Even the flags of the pre-war trade unions have been taken away from the labour exchanges and hung up in dusty deserted museums.

The list is long. So it is not surprising, in such conditions, that the words which, in Western Europe, express the hopes of a left-wing movement, are here kicked in the gutter, trampled underfoot by a working class which can at last shout aloud what it thinks and what it wants. Where is it supposed to go in search of another language, other symbols and other heroes? It will go to what survives in its memory. To that tradition which bureaucratic domination has not been able to kill. To that culture which, despite everything, has remained alive. One sole institution has kept sufficient strength and sufficient tradition for this — the Church. The labour movement had been undermined from within by Stalinism. Stalinism had also attacked the Church, head-on, thereby building its martyred image, keeping it away from power and from the ruling strata. The Church also profited from its lay presence within the newly proletarianised rural masses.

Pilsudksi became a hero of national independence, a man who was able to speak both for and from the people. He became something of a legend. People would hide away the old medals made and given in the pre-war years, which the UB (the political police) regularly confiscated on their searches. The regime removed his name from school books, from roads and streets, and people had to celebrate his 11 November anniversary in secret.[9] Every possible opportunity was taken to raise the question of the Katyn massacre, a thorn in the side of Big Brother Russia. Pilgrimages to Czestochowa, and collective and individual prayer were all a way of saying No. And in October 1980, Lech Walesa, after a rapturous welcome from the working class of Cracow, read out the sermon of Kosciuszko, a Polish national hero, leader of the 1794 uprising against the Russian occupation. In all that, the realities of history really had little importance. You could discuss for hours with someone like Adam Michnik, about the history of this Pilsudski whose photograph stood on his desk. Being a clear-sighted historian, he would accept many criticisms of the man — but that portrait would still stay there. Perhaps as a means to provoke those who have killed history.

Naivety? Maybe. But we have to understand this complex relationship between the oppressed and their ideology, this theatre in which the oppressor has stolen the langauge of the oppressed, and where the oppressed speak the language of their masters of yesteryear. This interplay produces confusion. It leaves you with a picture of two seemingly irreconcilable camps: state and society.

However, our analysis must not limit itself to appearances. On the contrary, it must trace the real social forces which, when they are stripped bare by crisis, reveal the basic cleavages and splits within each of these camps. Thus, for example, the State may be assimilated to the Party and all the associations which it controls as a means to subjugate the working class. However, it also draws its legitimacy from within that class, and when the class takes matters into its own hands, it shakes the Party from within. On each occasion it gives rise to reformist currents. The Church, on the other hand, is seen by many as an institution expressing a certain basic level of conflict with the regime. They see the Catholic faith as embodying free, independent, incorruptible thought. In fact relations between the Catholic hierarchy and the State are far more complex; they swing between compromise and mutual rejection. They may also turn the Church into a means of domination, one of the elements stabilising the regime.

In short, when the State feels its power to be threatened, it finds an ally in the Catholic hierarchy, which preaches moderation, responsibility and national unity. In return, the Church is given wider freedom of action and expression. This was the case in the immediate post-war years, up to 1947, and, to a lesser degree, after the 1950 agreement. The support and collaboration of the Church was indispensable in those periods: first for the task of shifting something like five million Poles to the west of Poland, and then, at the beginning of the 1950s, during the unpopular process of agrarian collectivisation. On the basis of the agreement signed with the government in April 1950, the Church counselled its faithful in loyalty towards the authorities and the system. It refrained from any form of extra-religious activity.

After October 1956, the Church, like the rest of society, supported Gomulka. The new Secretary General released the Cardinal Primate, Wyszynski, who had been imprisoned since 1953; reintroduced for a while religious teaching in schools; and permitted the nomination of bishops by Rome. A group of Catholic deputies — the *Znak* — entered the Sejm. "At the same time," as A. Michnik has noted, "the public declarations of the episcopacy during the first year that followed October 1956 were notable for their apoliticism, for their moderation, and even a certain benevolence towards the regime. The episcopate's public statements were largely appeals to the faithful to bring up their youth in a Catholic manner, along with attacks on abortion. None of these statements was anti-government in character."

In the wake of the 1970-71 riots, Gierek began his rule by re-stabilising relations with the Catholic Church. This was highlighted in a spectacular manner by the meeting on 3 March 1971 between Cardinal Wyszynski and Jaroszewicz, the new

Prime Minister. In September 1976, after the risings at Ursus and Radom, the episcopate issued a note in response to Gierek's appeal for solidarity from all Poles in the face of the country's economic problems. Then, at the time of the August 1980 strikes, as the strikes were expanding the possibilities of religious expression (for example the broadcast of the Sunday Mass), the episcopate once again called for calm and a sense of national responsibility. Thus, every time the working class has an opportunity to free itself from its oppression, the Catholic hierarchy preaches 'historic compromise'.

But in 'normal' periods, it carries on a daily guerilla warfare with the regime, supporting democratic demands. It features as a power of resistance, which, furthermore, possesses material means and an infrastructure which is independent of the State. At the present time there are 20,000 priests, of whom 2,500 are monks, and 28,000 nuns, spread over 27 dioceses, which are overseen by four archdioceses (Warsaw, Poznan, Cracow and Wroclaw). The Church provides teaching at the Catholic University of Lublin, in the Theological Academy of Warsaw, and in numerous seminaries. In addition to parish publications, it exercises direct influence over a current affairs weekly, *Tygodnik Powszechny*, and two monthly magazines, *Znak* and *Wiez*, which have their own publishing house.

It is undeniable that, particularly in the last eight years, this potential of the Catholic Church has guaranteed an effective defence of democratic freedoms. The freedom of worship, for example: there is an endless list of conflicts and negotiations with the authorities over questions like the building of churches, freedom of teaching, and institutional autonomy. Freedom of expression: protests against the repression in 1968; condemnation of the 1976 Constitution which institutionalised the leading role of the Party; support for the 1976 strikers in the face of repression; aid and defence of the democratic opposition.

While it is true that the public statements of the episcopacy have always been moderate, a large section of the clergy, particularly in the period since 1976, began to get involved on the side of the workers and the opposition. Parish priests, as well as certain bishops, condemned the repression in their sermons, while others became personally involved in KOR and ROBCIO

(Movement for Human and Civil Rights).

When the new Constitution was voted in, in February 1976, the Catholic intellectuals, members of the intellectual clubs which had been formed in 1956, broke with the *Znak* parliamentary group. This latter changed its name. They pursued their increasingly radical activities within an extra-parliamentary framework, in liaison with KOR and within the 'Experience and Future' (DiP) group, alongside critical Party intellectuals. A well-known abbot, Jan Zieja, one-time Chaplain to the Armed Forces, and hero of the Warsaw Rising, signed the founding statement of KOR. Similarly, the Pope's visit in June 1979 was to be more significant than a simple affirmation of religion. It was the first big demonstration in a long time of the independence of Polish society, a collective realisation which prefigured the unity and discipline which were to be seen in the strikes of Summer 1980.

This relative independence of the Catholic Church has always embarrassed the regime. It bears witness to the deep religious feelings of a people whom the regime has attempted in vain to secularise. Thus the bureaucracy itself set up, in the post-war period, its own 'progressive' Catholic organisations. The most important of these, PAX, was entrusted to an ex-fascist, Boleslaw Piasecki. This episode is very significant for anyone seeking to understand the Church's prestige in Poland today.

Before the war, Piasecki had been one of the leaders of ONR-Falanga, a paramilitary Nazi organisation linked to National Democracy. In 1939 he had been involved in an attempted alliance with the occupying Wehrmacht, but Hitler had other ideas. Piasecki was arrested — and then released after the personal intervention of Mussolini. He then threw himself into the resistance against both Russians and Germans, in order to revive 'imperial Poland'. Piasecki was an anti-semite, and also took arms against the Soviet partisans. In November 1944 he was arrested by the Soviet secret police, and faced the death penalty. In an attempt to save his life, he offered his services to the head of the secret police in Poland, whose principal concern was how to neutralise the influence of the Church. He drew up a memorandum proposing the establishment of a pro-communist Catholic association. A deal was struck, and on 25 November 1945 this pre-war fascist reappeared in Warsaw as the editor of a 'left-wing' Catholic weekly. In 1949 he set up PAX, at a time when Bierut was about to lock up Cardinal Wyszynski.

PAK sent its deputies to the Sejm, and also set up a commercial empire selling religious artefacts. Its 'United Economic Establishments' comprised a network of 39 enterprises, with 18 branches, 48 shops and a number of newspapers. It had a monopoly of the production of religious goods, but also of transistor radios and washing powder. It made fabulous profits. Piasecki became 'the millionaire of Polish socialism' and served equally zealously the successive governing factions. For example, in 1968 he was able to put his pre-war experience to good use, as the principal ideologue of Moczar's anti-semitic campaign. PAX's newspapers spat out their hatred. When he died at the end of the 1970s, he left behind him a powerful Catholic-Stalinist propaganda machine, which had never been recognised by Rome. His impact among the clergy was not very great, and the majority of progressive intellectuals who had joined it in 1949 were to leave it between 1956 and 1958. But its continued existence and its industrial strength made it an important factor in the situation, a sort of official counter-Church, which controlled selection of the personnel of the Church itself.

Thus, when one combines the history of the Polish nation and the place of Catholicism within it, with, on the one hand, the Stalinist forms of domination of the working class (in the shape of its religious policies), and, on the other hand, the simultaneously moderate and critical attitude of the episcopate during the past 30 years, one can begin to understand why the Catholic Church has maintained, or rather extended, its influence. To this must be added Vatican policies in Rome, which, with the surprise election of Cardinal Wojtyla as Pope, had added a brilliant touch.

But these factors alone are not sufficient to define the character of this Church. Religious sentiment in Poland has other specific characteristics in addition. We have to distinguish different types of Catholicism, not only as regards dogma, but also in relation to the secularisation of society in the past 50 years. The counter-Reformation had engendered two opposing conceptions. In a country like France, the secularisation of society and the rise of the bourgeoisie from the 17th century onwards turned religion into an individual affair. It became privatised, internalised, and intimate. It became a question of personal conscience: one was baptised, one might believe in God, but the numbers of practising Christians was diminishing. This was what Emile Poulat has called 'bourgeois Catholicism', as opposed to the 'intransigent Catholicism' of Roman inspiration: "Previously, religion had been principally a community phenomenon, and it is this community conception which has continued to prevail within Roman doctrine, where religion is a social fact: in the end it is of little importance what one does or does not believe, as long as society itself remains a society that is institutionally and structurally Christian." Historic circumstance in Poland has meant that this community model of christianity has predominated. Catholicism still has deep roots among the people, because it offers a focal point of resistance against national and social oppression; it offers a structure whose moral values protect individuals against the lie organised by the ruling classes. The 19th and 20th centuries were period of christianisation, which saw the creation and implantation of a religious sentiment along Roman lines. It did not identify with the ruling class, a class which privileged individual conscience. A comparison with other countries of Eastern Europe led a Polish sociologist to the following conclusions: "In Poland, throughout the 19th century and the early 20th century, the Catholic Church pursued its activities with a far lesser degree of support from the lay powers (...); that was true not only for the political powers as such, but also for the important economic strata. Thus the largest industrial concentration in Poland — Silesia — was at that time under the domination of German capital, which preferred Protestants to Catholics." This same idea was pursued by Bogdan Cywinski in his book *Genealogies of the Unconquered*, where he places the Polish Church within the tradition of the 'Julian Church' (from the name of a Roman emperor who fought against Christianity). "Julianism is defined by a divergence between the lay and spiritual powers, rather than a cooperation. The Church becomes an opposition. It is stripped of all political power, but on the other hand it possesses a moral authority, and there resides its strength. This could perhaps be seen as a general norm defining the social situation of the Church within the State: its moral authority within society is inversely proportional to its participation in political power (...) The fundamental characteristic of the Julian Church is precisely its moral authority.''

This 'Julian' communitarian Catholicism spread its influence to all the dominated classes in society, including the nascent working class. Traditions were established and passed down from generation to generation, with the family acting as one of its principal supports. Thus, for 35 years, the Communist Party has faced two complementary phenomena: a Church which is strongly implanted among the people, and a form of religion in which community values are privileged. The Party's religious policies and its forms of domination over society, far from tending to reduce this Catholic influence, were, despite themselves, to feed it and give it new life.

This was because Stalinist domination established and perpetuated itself via an attempt to atomise the labouring classes by all means possible: division, competitiveness and inequalities in work; social and geographical mobility; destruction of the traditional forms of association; alcoholism; corruption; lies; individualism etc. Faced with this decomposition of society, the Church, which had itself been thrust into the ranks of the oppressed, became a factor for regeneration. It worked to rebuild the fabric of society. And its communitarian concepts were an important factor in its success.

This is a crucial point. It enables us to avoid the traditional explanations which do not always correspond to reality. Thus, for example, it is customary to establish a relationship of cause and effect between the cultural level and the degree of secularisation of a society; or, again, between the diminution of religious belief, and urbanisation and industrial development. Sociological inquiries that have been undertaken in Poland do, admittedly, reveal a certain tendency in this direction (92.2 per cent believers in the countryside; 80.9 per cent in the towns). But these figures are much higher than those observed in, for example, Yugoslavia.[10] This observation is all the more important nowadays, when the majority of the Polish proletariat is town-born.

Finally, the growth of Catholicism has been made possible by the regime's national policies. Pre-war Poland was a multinational country (several million Germans, Jews, Ukrainians etc). The new regime made determined and conscious efforts to 'Polishise' People's Poland. Several thousand Germans were deported from beyond the Oder-Neisse line; Jews who had not been exterminated by the Nazis were forced to emigrate. Gomulka was the great artisan of this 'national unification', first as minister for the territories won back after the war, and later, in the 1960s. The Galician Ukrainians, rejected by the USSR, were dispersed to different voivodies; the Jews suffered the anti-semitic campaign of 1968; as for the remaining Germans, Gomulka negotiated their emigration with Walter Ulbricht in 1963.

Thus, the hold of the Catholic Church over Polish society is the result of a number of complex factors, firmly anchored within the history of a battered country. The theologian Stanislawa Grabska outlined to me how, in return, these factors affected the clergy within the Catholic institutions. She explained: "Our traditions have been such as to turn our bishops to questions of politics and society. They defend human rights, and the rights of the nation. At the same time, this siege mentality situation has strengthened the traditionalist tendencies in the Church. In the West, when one is a progressive in social matters, one tends to be a progressive within the Church's internal debates also. One seeks to democratise the Church. In Poland, things are different. One looks to the Church for a bastion of support. One wants it to be a strong organisation. Take the situation of a parish. If the parish priest tries to democratise the parish, by involving lay people, or organising a commission to oversee economic matters, then, very soon, a proportion of those lay people will turn out to be members of the political police. And how is he to detect them? How is he to involve people without immediately coming under the influence of the government? The priest prefers to administer his finances all by himself. He knows that otherwise, sooner or later, he will come under the thumb of the State economy, which will demand its cut. He will be left with nothing. This is just an example, but it reveals a mentality which cultivates the idea that one must not allow oneself to be influenced by the State. People are suspicious. And this mentality can be found at all levels of the hierarchy.

"The Church of Poland is not dependent for its funds on the State or on big business. Aid from the Vatican is not very substantial. It is the faithful, ordinary workers who give. And they give a lot — sufficient, for example, to sustain the University of Lublin. In general, a priest lives better than an ordinary worker, than a doctor, or a teacher — simply because people give. This wealth is not ostentatious, it does not do harm to people. Everything depends upon the manner in which it is used. In each country the moral attitude of the priesthood tends to be the same as that of the country as a whole. If it turns out to be a bit better, well and good. When people are tempted by the consumer society, then that is also true for the clergy. And the same is true when a movement of social commitment emerges.

"I think that in Poland the temptations of a consumer society have been very strong — not so much as an actual possibility, but as a dream. At the same time, though, there has also been a level of social commitment, a vocation. When a large number of people have become involved in this social commitment, they find it possible to be active via the Church and they commit themselves with total idealism. This is what is happening today: a solidarity which goes beyond this humiliation of man by totalitarianism, which goes beyond one's own private well-being." Did this mean that the strength of the Solidarity union would now encourage democratic tendencies within the Church? Stanislawa Grabska thought not in the short term, although this is what she prays for. "In France the priests and intellectuals inter-relate with militants and a Left movement that is fairly atheist. Here, though, militants like Walesa and the others are among the most devoted of Christians, and practise a fairly traditional form of christianity. They are committed to a vision of religion which one could compare with that of orthodox christianity. For them, religion arises out of everyday life. It is something a little bit separate, which yields a blessing. For us, this means the holy mountain of Czestochowa, the Black Madonna, and the Church. The priest must be *within* everyday life. He only steps out of everyday life in order to say mass and to give the sacrament. Nothing more."

6. "Living with Dignity"

Right from the start, the seaboard strikers were actively supported by the democratic opposition movement. The activities and communiques of KSS-KOR were crucial in spreading the movement. The authorities obviously understood this, and on 20 August had 18 militants arrested in Warsaw, including Jacek Kuron, Adam Michnik, and Jan Litynski. The regime banned all official contact between the Inter-Enterprise Strike Committee and the KOR, and when a KOR delegate arrived at Gdansk, he was sent back to Warsaw. There were systematic police raids in all the major towns. These brought about total disarray among the opposition — for example, among the *Robotnik* editorial staff.

I was in Warsaw at the time of these early arrests, and I saw how effective they were. A large number of contacts were broken; the harassment stopped publication of a special edition of *Robotnik*, because the editorial staff who were still at liberty were unable to contact the people at the printing press. After two days, the prisoners were taken home — and then were re-arrested an hour later. One of them, Henryk Wujec, the founder and principal organiser of *Robotnik*, took advantage of this situation and escaped. He was free — but powerless: all his friends were either in prison or in hiding. Finally he returned peacefully to work, where he was literally kidnapped by the secret police. He was severely beaten, and was released on 1 September, covered with bruises.

So, the disarray was real, but it could not break the movement of support for the strikers. The hundreds of young people who for several months had been active with the opposition stepped up their efforts. One of them told me how he spent his days in a number of different apartments, using the telephone to gather and centralise information. Another suggested that I join him to go to Szczecin carrying leaflets. Finally, though, the trip was called off, when the leaflets did not materialise. All over the country a hive of underground activity was spontaneously organising actions of this sort, in a climate of uncertainty, rumour and false information. Western radio stations, in particular the BBC, were the only more or less reliable sources of information. The first time I came back from Gdansk, on 26 August, I had to fetch out my tape-recordings so that people could listen to them, so that they could read the leaflets, before they would believe me. Everything appeared so unbelievable! However, during the final week of August more and more people were travelling, and the information began to get through.

On 20 August, in Warsaw, and on 22 August in Poznan, several dozen noted intellectuals launched an appeal. The appeal supported the strikers, and demanded that the government recognise the Inter-Enterprise Strike Committee and open negotiations. They warned against a showdown: "Only imagination and reason can lead us to a consensus which will be to the benefit of our common national interest. History will not pardon anyone who attempts any different solution. We call for a commitment to the road of consensus. We appeal for reason and imagination to prevail, convinced as we are that, at this moment, there is no question more important in Poland today." The signatories included at least five members of the Academy of Science, including party members such as Adam Kersten. Others were organisers in the Society of Scientific Courses (TKN — better known as the 'Flying University'). The majority of important writers also signed, in particular Marian Brandys and Tadeusz Konwicki, historians such as Wladyslaw Bartoszewski, Bronislaw Geremek and Aleksander Giezystor, director of the History Institute of the University of Warsaw. Catholics and atheists were to be found side by side, communists and ex-communists, artists, socialists, sociologists, jurists etc. Two of these, Tadeusz Masowiecki and Bronislaw Geremek, came to Gdansk and delivered their appeal to the Inter-Enterprise Strike Committee. The former was an ex-Catholic deputy, director of the magazine *Wiez*, and the latter an eminent mediaeval historian, the author of several major works. They were warmly welcomed by the workers, who asked them to provide technical assistance. This request led to the formation, on 24 August, of the 'Commission of Experts', which was to assist the Inter-Enterprise Strike Commitee during negotiations. It included six people 'in permanent contact with other specialists throughout the country'. In addition to the two cited above, there were: Bogdan Cywinski, a member of the editorial board of the Catholic review *Znak*; the economist Tadeusz Kowalik; Jadwiga Staniszkis, a sociologist at the management training institute; the economist Wlademar Kuczynski; and Andrzej Wielowiejski, a member of the Catholic Intellectuals' Club. Later on, these experts, and the KOR organisers liberated by the victory of the seaboard workers, were to meet again. They were to identify with the emerging union; they would assist in its building, and would contribute to its discussions on programme and tactics. Thus, before going into the details of the negotiations and their results, I feel it is important to pause, to ask where these intellectuals came from, what path brought them to Gdansk, and, finally, what were the ideas that motivated them.

The intellectuals can be schematically divided into three groups, each with fairly different origins. The most radical among them had been organising KSS-KOR for the past four years, but they already had behind them 20 years of experience in the opposition movement. For the most part they were ex-communists. The other component, more moderate in character, emerged from the Catholic parliamentary group which had been formed after 1956, and represented the core of the Catholic Intellectuals' Clubs, in particular the one in Warsaw. Finally, there were also intellectuals who were still members of the Party, who had not broken with the 'revisionist' perspective of the October Left of 1956. Some of these had joined with Catholic intellectuals in an informal work collective, the DiP ('Experience and Future'), set up on the initiative of Stefan Bratkowski, one of the Party's most brilliant journalists, who had been thrown out of the Party some years previously.

Obviously these three groups were not the whole of the democratic opposition movement in Poland, and they themselves had a number of fairly different tendencies among them. In addition, one should mention the constellation of small nationalist groupings emerging from various splits within the ROBCIO (Movement for Human and Civil Rights), which had been set up in Spring 1977 by people like Moczulski and Czuma, who rejected the idea of socialism and called themselves 'unpolitical'.[11] However, their influence on the events which concern us was negligible, with the exception of the 'Young Poland' group, which was very active in Gdansk.[12] I think that the three currents that I have emphasised here are the most important, and any consideration of the future of the Polish 'thaw' must necessarily analyse their evolution. This evolution was, in effect, intimately tied to the experience of the Polish people under Stalinism. It represents in concentrated form the succession of attitudes.

The first current that concerns us emerged from the October Left, or rather from its extreme Left. While in 1956 the majority of Polish intellectuals supported the line embarked on by Gomulka, the latter turned against the majority of them, called them 'revisionists', and in May 1957 condemned the public expression of differences. A wave of repression followed. It was clear that any possibility of democratising society and reforming the Party from the top had been blocked. The coup de grace came ten years later, with the campaign against the 1968 student movement, the exile imposed on numbers of intellectuals, and particularly the practical demonstration offered by the tragic end of the 'Prague Spring' in neighbouring Czechoslovakia.

Within the young generation of 1956, a number of people were immediately sceptical and very quickly realised that the regime was not going to reform itself. These included Karol Modzelewski, the son of a communist minister, by then deceased. He was one of the leaders of Warsaw's student youth during the October days. He started a discussion group in the University, and began to express opinions that were openly critical in regard to the State and the Party. There was also the young Jacek Kuron, the son of an old Party cadre. He was 22 years old, and had already been expelled from the Communist Party in 1953. Readmitted in 1955, he took an active part in the discussions, and was also involved in running a young people's organisation: the 'Red Scouts'. This young generation of communists provided the base for the founding, in December 1956, of a Union of Revolutionary Youth, to replace the old official organisation which had died in the October convulsions. The manifesto of this Union aimed to 'revive the ethical rules of socialist humanism'. Gomulka considered it too radical, and in January 1957 merged it with the remains of the preceding organisation to form the ZMS (Union of Socialist Youth).

At the beginning of the 1960s, when the new Secretary General had definitively broken with the ideas of October, when he had purged every reforming element within his political staff, criticism still found a home among the intellectuals. It also involved young school students. A number of groupings tried to perpetuate the spirit of that failed revolution, and were persecuted by the regime. For example, there was the 'crazy group' of Leszek Kolakowski, which had emerged from the 1956 movement and was dissolved in 1962. Another small group, initiated by a 15-year old boy, Adam Michnik, operated in Warsaw schools. It was called 'the club for seekers after contradictions'. Its aim was to debate all subjects that had become, or were about to become, taboo. At the University Jacek Kuron and Karol Modzelewski were pursuing their activities as historians and beginning to systematise their critique. In addition, in March 1964, 34 scientific and literary notables wrote an open letter condemning the government's cultural policies.

From this ferment emerged a generation of intellectuals, of whom many are today in the leadership of KOR, or are experts aiding Solidarity. They broke definitively with any perspective aimed at democratising the Party — a perspective derived from the ideology of the XX Congress of the Soviet Communist Party and which had raised certain hopes in October 1956. The death of intellectual revisionism was announced by L. Kolakowski and K. Pomian on the occasion of an important meeting celebrating the tenth anniversary of Poland's October in Warsaw University. But the first document to systematise this self-criticism was an Open Letter called *A Revolutionary Socialist Manifesto* (Pluto, 1972), written by Kuron and Modzelewski in 1964-65. It was to bring their expulsion from the Party, and a three and a half years prison sentence following a trial conducted entirely behind closed doors.

This text was welcomed by the fast-growing extreme Left in Europe as an exceptional document, the first revolutionary Marxist analysis to have come out of the Soviet bloc since the annihilation of the Trotskyist Left opposition. It presented an original Marxist analysis of the Gomulka regime, and — perhaps a bit despite itself — formed part of the renaissance of revolutionary thinking in the West. It also penetrated other 'people's democracies', particularly Czechoslovakia, where the 'Student Parliament' of 1968 was to reprint it in several thousand copies. In Poland, however, its impact was to be more limited. By virtue of the repression, its readers were few and far between and were limited to a small fringe of student and school youth. The working class, having been betrayed in 1956-57, was demoralised. This isolation was not lessened by the events of March 1968, and was to have its effect on future developments. Kuron, Modzelewski, Michnik and many others were again sentenced to several years of imprisonment.

It was not until the mid-1970s that one saw the publication of the majority of the texts that were to determine the actions of KOR. Their authors, basically Kuron and Michnik, already had years of political experience behind them. That experience led them to a certain line of action which, this time, had a big impact on Polish society, but which appeared to make a break with the line contained in the Open Letter. The evolution of their ideas had been the fruit of various social and ideological influences. These included, of course, ten years of difficult struggles, of isolation and repression. The marginality of the student rising of 1968 forced them to engage in self-criticism, while the working class explosion of 1970-71 showed the strength which could be acquired by the working class. But all this thinking was being done by individuals who were either on the sidelines of society, or in prison. Dismissed by the regime's official intelligentsia and ignored by the working class, they also maintained a relationship of mutual suspicion with the Catholic intellectuals.

At the start of the 1970s the situation started to change. With the support of men like L. Kolakowski, or the noted writer A. Slominski, a number of intellectuals emerging from the Marxist Left joined in an enormous movement of self-questioning within the intelligentsia. This movement encompassed very different personalities, often of opposing viewpoints. Via these exchanges there began the renaissance of a liberal and humanist culture. Little by little the political thinking of these militants began to evolve, and at that time there were three principal influences.

First, there was the encounter with the Catholic intelligentsia, which had itself undergone an evolution. This was symbolised by the joint signing of two petitions: the *Letter of the*

15 in December 1974, protesting against the situation of Poles in Russia; and the *Letter of the 59*, a year later, against the revision of the Constitution. But more significantly, this evolution was to produce a common conception of social responsibility. "The notion of responsibility provides the common ground between the Christian and the lay Left," as A. Michnik has observed. It was to introduce a moral dimension into political thinking.

Then there was the influence of Western liberal analyses of 'totalitarianism' and of the opposition between State and society, in particular the works of R. Aron, H. Arendt, de Tocqueville and J.S. Mill. These were introduced into Poland via a number of journals, in particular *Res Publica* and *Aneks*[13], and encouraged a break with the dogmatism of Marxist theory as represented by official ideology. Finally there was the decisive and many-faceted role played by the journal *Kultura*. This was edited in Paris by Jerzy Giedroyc, a pre-war emigre. Established in 1947, it had published almost 400 issues, as well as several hundred books. In addition it produced many documents and 'historical notebooks' on the history of contemporary Poland, as well as publishing all the important writers in exile (C. Milosz, W. Gombrowicz, Hlasko, Kolakowski etc), and a number of those still living in Poland. The broad orientation of this journal was summed up by one of its producers, Constantin Jelenski: "From the start *Kultura* has been opposed to a return to capitalist society, and saw itself as promoting ideas of self management, cooperativism and trade unionism (...). So it is not surprising that from the start a relationship was established fairly quickly between *Kultura* and a number of Polish reformists, and that the magazine backed Gomulka to the hilt in 1956. (...) It broke with him definitively when he shut down the anti-establishment journal *Po Prostu*, in 1957, leaving other reformists still supporting him, for lack of a realistic alternative. *Kultura*'s immediate reaction to the anti-semitic campaign launched in Poland in 1967-68 under the guise of 'antizionism' was due to one of the most positive aspects of its politics." Namely, an "innovative anti-establishment attitude towards a communist Poland that was enslaved, and an exiled Poland that was set in its ways. The main common denominator between Gombrowicz and Milosz was precisely their denunciation of the stereotypes of Polish culture, which applies equally

(albeit interpreted in diametrically opposed manner) whether in
Poland or in exile. Another factor in common was that they
both began from a conception of a basic 'Polishness', which
Polish establishment culture was shamelessly doing away with,
by identifying, rather like a poor relation, with an idealised
West. (...) *Kultura*'s great merit was that from the start it had
reacted against the irrational hatred of Russians which is so
widespread in Poland, an achievement which is all the more
considerable when you think that out of the six people who
made up the original hard core of the magazine, four had been
deported to the USSR after the annexation of the Eastern part
of the country.''

Out of this intellectual ferment was born a new political
thinking, often very empirical, which is an elaboration of the
basic positions taken up in 1965. In my opinion it is crucial to
understand that evolution more precisely, in order to be able to
assess the present orientation of the KOR leadership.

The Open Letter was in effect a theoretical reflection on
the nature of the ruling system in Poland, and put forward the
general elements of a revolutionary socialist programme. It did
not concern itself with conjunctural analyses, although the
authors' arguments were underpinned by a detailed study of
the country's recent history. This was at once its strength and
its weakness. Its strength in that it formulated one of the best
Marxist analyses of a bureaucratic regime; its weakness
because it remained too general at the level of formulating
tasks for the opposition. Fifteen years later one was to see this
situation reversed: theoretical analysis was replaced by subjec-
tive considerations on 'totalitarianism', while at the same time
plans for action were being refined, were becoming more effective in the short term, and were embracing a far wider movement. This reversal was confirmed by a change in strategic
objectives. The slogan was no longer, as it had been in 1965, to
overthrow the power of the bureaucracy in order to establish
the power of 'councils of workers' delegates', but simply to
open 'democratic spaces'. Kuron himself detailed his own
evolution in an article published in 1976: ''My ideas on a
number of important points have changed profoundly during
the past 20 years. While I have remained faithful to the basic
values that I hope will come to prevail, my ideas have changed
on the best and most convenient methods to obtain our objec-

tives.'' Modzelewski went still further in an interview recorded in October 1980: "I think that revolution is not an end in itself, and that it is wrong to allow oneself to be guided by a value system to the extent of subordinating to it all values in general." Here he was alluding to Marxism, which, in his opinion, contained 'totalitarian elements' in its critique of capitalism. This evolution was not restricted to these two men (Modzelewski's contribution was in fact to remain marginal throughout the 1970s). One occasionally finds it expressed more clearly in the writings of Michnik and the philosopher Leszek Kolakowski, who, having broken with the 'revisionist perspective' exercised a powerful influence from his exile in London.

One could sum up the central idea of the Open Letter by this formula, which concluded one of its chapters: 'Revolution is inevitable'. At that time, its authors believed that bureaucratic society was characterised by an irreducible opposition between, on the one hand, a very restricted ruling class — the 'central political bureaucracy' — the owner of the social surplus product, and unrestrained by any social control; and, on the other hand, the working class and the peasantry. The bureaucracy was unable to relinquish even a fragment of its power, not even to the technocrats, because a 'general change of the system of management is impossible without a change in the relations of production'. During the phase when this new class was being created, it relied for its support in part on police terror, and in part on an emerging social base arising from the necessary industrialisation of the country. But it was soon to become isolated. It was to check the evolution of the productive forces which it had previously 'objectively' favoured in an earlier period. The system was thus afflicted by ongoing social and economic crisis. "Thus not only can the economic crisis not be overcome on the basis of present relations of production, but also the general social crisis cannot be overcome within the framework of present social relations, which merely aggravate the crisis whose solution will only be possible via the abolition of the present relations of production and social relations. *This development can only take place through revolution,*" the authors stressed. This situation 'forces the working class to take a stand against the system and the bureaucracy', since the working class is the only class capable of carrying out the anti-bureaucratic revolution.

This analysis had the advantage of describing the basic splits within society — for this it drew its inspiration from the writings of Trotsky[14] and Kollontai's Workers' Opposition — but its fault was that it was too schematic. This led it to predict a coming catastrophe for the bureaucracy in Poland and internationally. It underestimated the bureaucracy's margins of manoeuvre, and laid the ground for a perspective of rapid insurrection. Furthermore it described the bureaucracy as a ruling social class in the Marxist sense of the term. All these things had little consequence for the coherence of their exposition, but were to become decisive when it came to drawing up a line of practical action.

Historical experience confirmed this judgement. In 1968, at the time of the student struggles, the working class remained passive; in 1970 its revolt was limited to just a few centres, and further explosions were not to come for another six years. In short, the bureaucracy showed a greater capacity for adaptation than had been foreseen, while at the same time contradictions were sharpening within its system of domination. A number of experiences, in particular that of the Church, showed that limited democratic gains were possible.

In an article written at the start of the 1970s Leszek Kolakowski drew the lessons of experience and came to different conclusions from those contained in the Open Letter. He explained: "I reject the thesis — incidentally, a thesis in line with the Marxist tradition — whereby the specifically socialist form of servitude is incapable of being partially abolished or reduced by progressive reforms, but that it must be totally abolished once and for all. I find this thesis incorrect, and to defend it amounts to an ideology of defeatism rather than an appeal for revolution. My own convictions are based on four general principles: first, we are never in a position to define in advance the limits of flexibility of any given social organisation, and experience in no way proves that the model of despotic socialism is absolutely rigid; secondly, the rigidity of the system depends *in part* on the extent to which those who live under the system *are convinced of its rigidity*; thirdly, the thesis which I reject is based on the ideology of 'all or nothing', which is characteristic of those formed in the Marxist tradition; it has no grounding in historical experience; fourthly, bureaucratic socialist despotism is riddled with contradictory tendencies which it is incapable of synthesising in any sense, and which are relentlessly weakening its cohesion. These contradictions are tending to become more rather than less acute.'' Kolakowski called for a more subtle understanding of these mechanisms, and 'an active resistance movement, making use of the natural contradictions within the system'. While he still called for a democratic socialism, he also defined himself as a 'reformist', that is to say, one who had 'faith in the potential and efficacity of partial progressive measures, exercised within a long-term perspective'.[15] Thus his theses bore a strong resemblance to those of Social Democracy or Eurocommunism. However, despite its abilities to adapt, the bureaucracy does not have the same power of domination as the western bourgeoisie. In other words, an orientation which might, in capitalist countries like France, Italy and Spain, favour the perpetuation of the ruling class, might in societies ruled by the bureaucracy have (if carried by the working class) a profoundly destabilising effect. These ideas, as they were developed and specified by Kuron and Michnik, were to add to the effects of the social crisis and to give rise to a movement which, little by little, came to encompass all the oppressed layers of society, a movement which was to lead to Summer 1980.

This explains why this evolution cannot be described simply as a lapse from the revolutionary programme towards reformist ideas, and even less as a renaissance of the 'revisionist' orientation of the October Left. On the contrary, this evolution developed an original tactic, which was to prove its worth, notwithstanding a heterogeneous theoretical platform marked by a large degree of empiricism. It can be defined around five basic ideas. The first was already at the heart of the programme presented in the Open Letter. It stressed the central role of the working class in the struggle for democratic freedoms and against the bureaucracy. One might find this a curious observation, given Polish history and the Marxist tradition within it, but this was precisely the point rejected by Michnik in 1968.[16] In addition, a number of dissident theoreticians in the people's democracies — beginning with Rudolf Bahro — had denied this role to the working class. The Open Letter said: "Only the working class, because of its conditions of living, and working, feels it necessary to abolish the bureaucracy (...) Thus the revolution which will abolish the bureaucratic system is, in its nature, proletarian." Thirteen years later, Adam Michnik's view on this point was: "The essence of a new strategy for the Polish opposition is an increased understanding of the strength of the working class. (...) The pressure of this social group is the precondition *sine qua non* for an evolution of national life towards democratisation." The language had changed, but the idea remained. It was to provide the grounding for important initiatives like the establishment of the *Robotnik* newspaper and the setting up of the first *Constituent Committees of the Free Trade Unions* at Gdansk, Katowice and Szczecin.

This idea links directly to the second basic principle — which was also present in Kuron and Modzelewski's Open Letter: the independence of the democratic movement from the Party administration, the necessity of building autonomous organisations. In 1965 an assessment of the failed 'first anti-bureaucratic revolution' led the Open Letter's authors to criticise the opportunism of the October Left in relation to 'liberal bureaucracy, the principal anti-revolutionary force', and the 'technocratic tendency within the workers' councils'. And finally, in the absence of a class programme, one had witnessed merely a transfer of authority: "All that enormous authority which the Left militants had enjoyed in their various situations has been transferred to the new leadership. Thus the Left has contributed to the maintenance of bureaucratic power, and so has laid the ground for its own political death and the defeat of the revolution." Adam Michnik took up a similar line of critique and extended it to the whole of the Catholic parliamentary group (*Znak*). He concluded that it was necessary to build an autonomous social movement, starting 'from the base', no longer placing one's hopes in the bureaucracy reforming itself from the top. This social organisation would have to be independent of the State and the Party.

The first concrete sign of action on this new perspective was contained in the *Letter of the 15* published in 1975, protesting against the planned amendment of the Constitution. Included among its demands was the following remark: "As one saw in 1956 and in 1970, any attempt to defend the interests of the workers may lead to serious and bloody disorders (given the monopoly of political power held by the Party). The way to remedy this situation is the free election by workers of their own representative bodies, independent of both State and Party. The right to strike must also be guaranteed."

Thus the policies of the new opposition were taking up two of the basic principles of the Open Letter — even if this continuity was not explicitly recognised: the role of the working class, and the necessary independence of the movement. However, it was to articulate them within a different strategic perspective.

Kuron and Modzelewski in 1965 were writing of a working class that would overthrow the 'central political bureaucracy'. But the new opposition was more modest. Michnik wrote: "The dilemma of Left movements in the 20th century — 'reform or revolution' — is not a dilemma for the Polish opposition. To propose a revolutionary overthrow of the Party dictatorship, and to organise to that end, would be as unrealistic as it is dangerous: one cannot hope for an overthrow of the regime for so long as the political structure of the USSR remains what it is (...) *In my opinion, the only path for the dissidents of the Eastern countries is that of a constant struggle for reforms, to bring about a development which will extend civil liberties and will guarantee the respect of human rights.* The Polish example shows that pressures brought to bear on the regime can bring considerable concessions." This position was characteristic of all the opposition's texts, including those of Kuron, who was one of their main authors. It was based on what one might call the fourth 'postulate' underlying this strategy: Poland's geopolitical position. In 1965 the writers' response to the argument about the danger of Soviet military intervention was that of proletarian self-defence. Ten years later they considered at length the interplay of interests at stake should it come to that. Michnik argued: "An analysis of the totality of Polish-Soviet relations reveals a certain community of interest between the political leadership of the USSR, the political leadership of Poland, and the Polish opposition. For all three, Soviet military intervention in Poland would have been, and will remain, catastrophic. For the democratic opposition movement, it goes without saying that its sense of responsibility and its patriotism are such that it resolutely opposes any such eventuality. For the rulers of Poland, the effect of a Soviet military intervention would be to reduce their role to that purely of guardians of the Soviet empire, compared with the present situation where they govern a country of 34,000,000 people. As for the Soviet rulers, the memory of the international consequences of their interventions in Hungary and Czechoslovakia are still fresh in their minds. They also remember the determination shown by Polish workers in December 1970 and June 1976. Furthermore, if one takes into account the traditional anti-Russian attitude of the Poles and their willingness to embark on desperate battles, one might conclude that, for the Soviets, a decision to intervene militarily in Poland would effectively mean declaring war on it.'' Thus everyone had an interest in avoiding the 'national massacre' which would ensue. ''This configuration of common interests lays the ground for a possible framework of compromise. I do not claim that Soviet intervention in Poland is unimaginable. On the contrary: I think that it could become inevitable if the powers-that-be in Moscow and Warsaw on the one hand, and the people of Poland on the other, were to lose their sense of reality, their restraint and their good sense. Thus the Polish democratic opposition movement has to accept that social transformation in Poland must, at least in its first phase, take place within the framework of the 'Brezhnev doctrine'. (...) The basic difference between today's opposition movement and its predecessors is the conviction that such a programme of evolution must address itself, not to the totalitarian regime, but to independent public opinion. Instead of suggesting to the regime means of 'improving itself', this programme must provide society with indications of 'how to act'. For the regime there are no clearer marching orders than those deriving directly from rank and file pressure.''

Finally, these principles provided the basis for a terrain of united action that encompassed the whole of society — in other words, the working class, the peasantry and the intellectuals, but also the Church and certain 'empirical' tendencies within the Party. What created this unity was opposition to the 'totalitarian regime', the struggle for human rights and for a social renaissance. It brought together all those who, in the words of Kolakowski, hoped one day to 'live in dignity'. As Kuron put it: ''In my opinion the political opposition movement comprises the individuals who have been actively and determinedly resisting the totalitarian system, and who have fought for the independence of nation from State. I do not include those who have fought exclusively for national independence without at the same time fighting against the totalitarian system." This was no longer, as in 1965, an opposition to be built on a class basis (which at the time had led Kuron and Modzelewski to propose the formation of a new workers' party, and to outline a policy of class alliance). Rather it was to be a social opposition. This involved the establishment of a Committee of Social Self Defence (the new name for KOR, as from 1977), which was to boost the development of various autonomous social movements. Later on we shall examine the extent to which this orientation was to become a reality. But I would first like to stress the fact that it coincided, on more than one point, with the orientation to which certain Catholic intellectuals had been led through their own process of development. Andrzej Wielowiejski, the General Secretary of the Warsaw Catholic Intellectuals' Club, identified four differing attitudes within Polish Catholicism. The first, which he described as 'individualist-passive' was harmless and was therefore accepted by the regime. The second was an 'active attitude of adaptation', and was practised by pro-government associations such as PAX, ChSS and ODDiSS (neo-*Znak*). These "are only able to exist by virtue of their lack of credibility, which strips them of any active social weight. This is related to the fact that they operate on the fringes of Church life". The third attitude was "strictly ecclesiastical; it recognises a certain correctness in the social commitment of Catholics, and is reticent in regard to cooperation with the government", but it also draws the line at "the formulation by Catholics and by the Church of their own political and social aspirations". Thus it comprised 'active and devoted priests', alongside 'Catholics of a more conservative or classically authoritarian mould'. Finally, there was the 'democratic and democratising attitude', which started from the idea that "the future of Christianity and the Church of Poland depends on an extension of civil liberties and the evolution of a political system, rather than an agreement between Church and State". Wielowiejski identified this attitude with the development of certain episcopal positions during the 1970s, and with the orientation of the Catholic intellectuals of the Clubs of Catholic Intellectuals — most of whom were to support the strikes of 1980. This was the only group that really polarised

Catholic youth. At their head was a symbolic personality: Tadeusz Mazowiecki, chief editor of the monthly magazine *Wiez*, later to become editor of Solidarity's national weekly. An ex-PAX militant, he had broken with the organisation in 1955-56.[17] In 1961 he had been elected as a *Znak* deputy, and was a driving force behind the Catholic Intellectuals' Clubs in Warsaw. At the beginning these clubs gathered people of very different origins. The first president had even been an ex-Christian Democrat of openly anti-communist views. But little by little, two principal tendencies emerged. One was led by the president of the Poznan club, Janusz Zablocki, also an ex-member of PAX, who was soon to set up a rival documentation centre to *Wiez*, the ODDiSS. The other tendency centred on Mazowiecki. Their disagreements first became apparent on the question of attitudes to the regime, with the latter considering the former to be opportunist. In 1968 the break was more clear. Zablocki and his more nationalistically-inspired friends tended to identify with the demagogy of General Moczar, whereas the Mazowiecki group issued a clear condemnation of the repression of intellectuals. However, given the lack of room for manoeuvre available to either tendency, they co-existed until 1975-76 — although a number of conflicts were to stir up tensions. For example, when the Polish United Workers' Party refused to allow *Znak* to elect Mazowiecki as a deputy, Zablocki's supporters complied and replaced him with one of their own.

In 1975 the Party's attempt to amend the Constitution created a great upheaval in Polish society. The Church came out in open condemnation, and numerous intellectuals — including a number of Catholics — signed petitions, in particular the famous *Letter of the 59* cited above. When the proposal came before the Sejm for voting in February 1976, four of the five *Znak* deputies approved the text. These were all friends of Zablocki. The only one to abstain was Stanislaw Stomma, a Catholic jurist, a member of the editorial board of the Cracow weekly *Tigodnik Powszedny*, and a deputy since 1957. He resigned. He was supported by intellectuals close to Mazowiecki who were themselves involved with those who were soon to form the KOR, in a campaign of protest against the new Constitution.

The break was definitive. The ODDiSS deputies retreated

into a position which was to become less and less critical of Gierek, while the Catholic Club intellectuals were becoming radicalised and were becoming increasingly involved in the democratic opposition movement. They received cautious support from the episcopate, and encountered widespread sympathy among the younger priests.

However, the Catholic Intellectuals' Clubs did not define themselves as political organisations. Their initiators described them as groupings for theological, biblical, social and economic education. Their objective was to train active people within the Church and within society. Their initial activities began with children, via a family section. Always great defenders of the family, they encouraged parents to undertake a Catholic upbringing, and seconded priests to teach the catechism. They readily compared their methods with those of the boy scouts, in that they organised camping holidays, excursions, and conferences. The adults met together regularly, to study history, theology and morality. Particular attention was paid to the struggle against anti-semitism. The young people of the Warsaw club, for example, provided volunteers to see to the upkeep of the region's old Jewish cemeteries. Without being actually integrated into the Church, they maintained a good working relationship with the chaplaincies. One Catholic Intellectuals' Clubs officer in Warsaw estimated that there were around 2,000 members in that town, and a further several hundred in each of the towns of Torun, Poznan, Wroclaw and Cracow. In addition, particularly in Lublin, there were many 'contacts' in situations where the authorities had not authorised the creation of clubs.

The political and social commitment of the militants in these clubs operated principally at the moral level. As they put it, they had to choose between truth and untruth, and had chosen the former because the latter was how the regime operated. If they had a 'strategy' it might be summed up in one word: dialogue. In other words, as Mazowiecki wrote in 1970, 'an effort to uncover something like another dimension of things where one might find oneself. (...) It's a method of existence which carves itself a path within societies which may be wholly different at the ideological level'. In the post-war period too, 'our approach to socialism took as its starting point its moral motivations and its tradition of social revolt or, in other words, the social question as it became transformed into an idea of social reconstruction. We also realised that the paths of socialism could evolve in such a manner that it would create openings at the level of personal values.' In more general terms, the clubs' intellectuals sought to retrieve the values that had guided their predecessors in their struggles against their various oppressors at the time of the partitions. They aimed to rebuild a national cohesion via an encounter between the 'unconquered' of the lay Left and the Christian 'unconquered'. In this they drew a lot of inspiration from the work of the historian Bogdan Cywinski, who ended his book, *Genealogies of the Unconquered* on this hopeful note: "The up-to-date element in this heritage is the ideals with which the radical unconquered identified themselves, which, with an intuition of ethics, had linked the question of real social progress with a set of values, such as the necessity of social commitment, the respect of human beings and their opinions, a democracy which is never static but is a process of struggle between ideological inertia and social conscience; the ability to analyse one's own opinions in a creative manner and honestly to correct them; and finally, a proud nonconformism, an indispensable precondition for developing a sense of moral responsibility for society's future. The most eager hope of any Catholic thinking on these problems would be that in the propagation and defence of these values, all their followers could find in the Polish Church an ally and a source of Christian inspiration. (...) As we consider our contemporary Christian attitudes regarding our mission, and as we think about our ethic of social action, we must find space for an understanding for this ideological and moral tradition, the recognition of these real ethical values, and a respect for the memory of those who have paid witness to it. This will enable us to take a fundamental step in the honest dialogue between believers and non-believers in Poland. This step will enable us to bridge the divide, which we have inherited from the last century, and which is so outdated and mistaken today — a divide which has separated from the Church an important and precious section of the unconquered Polish intelligentsia."

This type of moral and social commitment obviously meant that these Catholic intellectuals would involve themselves in questions of human rights. There they encountered ex-communists, socialists, and young people — in short, the social movement which was moving to the side of the working class at the time of the 1976 strikes. Out of this movement was born a unity of action and collaboration which gave rise to a number of actions, in particular the important hunger strike of July 1977, held in a church in the centre of Warsaw, in support of the KOR militants who had been imprisoned.

The third element, which was equally significant among these intellectuals who were to join the Gdansk Inter-Enterprise Strike Committee and later Solidarity, was made up of people many of whom had been expelled from the Polish United Workers' Party. In November 1978 they had organised a gathering of a hundred or so sociologists, economists, journalists, writers and film directors, including a number of household names. Among them were many Party members, but also many Catholics. Grouped under the title 'Experience and Future' (DiP), they planned to carry out an inquiry into the truth of the Polish situation. Despite police harassment, they ended by producing a report based on written answers to a questionnaire, completed by around 50 people. Their report was entitled: 'Report on the State of the Republic'.* It was published in the course of 1979 by the unofficial *Nowa* publishing house. In 100 tightly packed pages it drew a clear and stark picture of the Polish society under the management of Gierek's team. In their introductory remarks the authors detailed their aims: "Both the 'Experience and the Future' editorial team and the poll itself were born of the conviction that the crisis our country is experiencing affects many basic areas of communal life and indeed is creating a highly alarming situation that will inevitably grow even worse. The hope that with the passage of time the symptoms of crisis would gradually give way to a readjustment and improvement in the methods of government and management did not materialize. The situation is exacerbated, on the other hand, by the ever more acute contradiction between the mounting tasks created by the development of an industrial society and the increasing complexity of public life, and on the other hand, by the ever more glaring inefficiency of the entire system of social interaction. In recent years we have witnessed a telling illustration of this con-

* Published with 'Which Way Out?' in *Poland: The State of the Republic* (Pluto Press 1981)

122

tradiction, when at the beginning of the seventies, unques-
tionable, objective, and fruitful economic, technical, and
cultural progress, instead of quickening and consolidating improvements (as had been anticipated), only revealed even
greater weaknesses and flaws in the system, thereby deepening
the general sense of frustration.

"The more or less clearly perceived dimensions of the crisis
and their repeatedly dashed expectations and hopes have left in
the minds of Poles lasting traces, reflected in the bitter conviction that radical changes in the way the social and political
order functions are absolutely necessary and at the same time
futile. Furthermore, resigned acceptance of this state of affairs
leads to a variety of extreme and even contradictory attitudes,
ranging from conformity and defense of the status quo, through
various forms of escape into private life, to vacuous, hate-filled
rebellion. Despite the quite different moral qualifications we
can attribute to these attitudes, they have one trait in common:
they all lead to disbelief in the meaning of any effort, to
apathy, and to the paralysis of any constructive social
thinking." In a later document entitled '*Which Way Out?*' they
put forward a number of proposed solutions. These were summed up in a letter to the Gdansk strikers on 22 August 1980.
The analysis contained within these documents had tremendous repercussions within the opposition movement. They
were often cited, and were to prove extremely useful during the
Gdansk negotiations. They provided the underpinning for
many of the demands.

However, the 'strategic perspective' which inspired the
authors of these reports remained extremely timid. It could be
described as 'neo-revisionist', with reference to the perspective
of the 1956 October Left. Stefan Bratkowski, a communist
journalist and the prime mover of that group, explained it
clearly on 19 October 1979, on the occasion of a meeting of the
rank and file Party organisation of the Warsaw section of the
Union of Polish Writers: "he described DiP philosophy as a
'culture of negotiations' ". As he explained to the Party
militants meeting on that day, the majority of whom had un-
doubtedly been involved in the inquiry: "In my opinion our
negotiations must not consist of injurious and malevolent
polemic, in reservations, in accusation or in a series of
demands drawn up with aggressive intent. The ability to

negotiate means the ability to be able to understand the basic interests of your partner. People say that the *Report* is bold in its diagnosis but timid in its conclusions. This is a misunderstanding: the thought process is one and the same — a respect for the realities of the situation. It is for this reason that the political conclusions of the *Report* do not go beyond the framework of the postulates already contained within our Party's documents." The *Report*, just like the 1956 reformers, called on the militants' good conscience. "We are three million, three million adults. Not all of us are entirely frank, some have a tendency to forget that the Party card is not a passport to an easy well-being, that belonging to the Party is not synonymous with fighting for cushy numbers: some are tired, disillusioned, discouraged, dormant and demoralised by the present stagnation. But nonetheless we make up a potential of three million people, living with a sense of their own dignity. I think that we should take this into account today (...). Even if this might appear naive and infantile, we have to find again the strength and the determination of our youth." This line of thinking was clearly in the opposite camp to the 'movement from below' advocated by the KOR leadership. It was even capable of positive acceptance by the liberal wing of the bureaucracy. In the general rumbling, men such as Rakowski, editor of *Polityka*, or Olszowski, soon to return to the politburo, used their authority to provide cover for this initiative. The split as regards prospects for action was highlighted by the economist Edward Lipinski when, in the name of KOR, he wrote the postscript to the first edition of the *Report* published by *Nowa*. "As regards changes that are possible in the immediate term, the authors of the *Report* situate their proposals within a framework of the political system currently applying in Eastern Europe. Whatever formulas they propose, they nonetheless argue for the maintenance of existing relations with the Soviet Union, and for a recognition of the 'leading' role of the Communist Party. These two points mark the fundamental differences between us: we, the democratic opposition movement, argue for national sovereignty and political pluralism as the main objectives of our activity. While our sense of responsibility in the present situation may on occasion lead us to moderate and compromise, it will never lead us to go back on our fundamental principles."

It is not in fact possible to locate the three tendencies that I have outlined (KOR, the Catholic Intellectuals' Clubs, and Experience and Future) at exactly the same level. But each in their own manner expressed the radicalisation that was under way within Polish society since the dramatic intervention (and the victory) of the working class in June-July 1976. At the social level, this class was henceforth to hold the initiative and to stimulate a movement within society as a whole. The working class was by then a majority of the economically active population (with no more than 8 million industrial workers). It was concentrated in large workplaces, it was young, not jaded by painful political experiences, and it had produced its own leadership, which, for the most part, was tied to the KSS-KOR. In addition, it had provided the latter with a central position within the democratic opposition. It was thus natural that the KOR's political positions were to both guide and inspire the Gdansk negotiators. Even though key KOR members were in prison at the particular time, men and women like Andrzej Gwiazda, Bogdan Borusewicz and Anna Walentynowicz were capable of effectively representing their own viewpoint within the Inter-Enterprise Strike Committee. This viewpoint frequently coincided with that of the Catholic intellectuals who, under the presidency of Tadeusz Mazowiecki, were organised in the commission of experts. However, the Catholic intellectuals too often showed a tendency to moderate the demands of the workers, and in this they were to find an echo in a section of the Inter-Enterprise Strike Committee, in particular with Lech Walesa. Within this overall framework, the DiP's contributions were mainly technical, taking the same broad line as Mazowiecki's.

An initial assessment would have to start from the predominance of the KOR position, and from the fact that the five general principles outlined above had tremendous effect during the period between the 1976 strikes and those of Summer 1980. This impression is confirmed by looking at their effect on the opposition movements in other 'people's democracies'. However, as I have already stressed, this overall orientation was based on a heterogeneous theoretical foundation. This fact left a number of grey areas, whose practical consequences may have been secondary before August, but which could prove more serious subsequently.

The first ambiguity relates to the claimed divergence of the majority of KOR intellectuals from Marxism, a divergence which may well be real. It was the subject of a philosophical treatise published by Kolakowski in exile, and quoted by many authorities.[18] My point here is not to discuss the validity or otherwise of the analyses provided by Marx or Lenin. I simply want to observe that a number of these critics showed an annoying tendency to confuse Marxist theory with the Stalinist falsifications disseminated by the regime. This is all the more surprising in that this confusion breaks with what had been the most vital element in the tradition of the October Left, and with Kuron and Modzelewski's Open Letter, as well as Kolakowski's writings at that time, had developed brilliantly. Michnik gives an implicit explanation of this divergence, by identifying language with power; but this explanation resides in the realm of fantasy. Is it really the case that the power of language is greater than the power of social classes and strata, and, in this instance, the power of a wing of the bureaucracy which was able to manipulate the hopes of the working class? This leads me to stress one notable difference, at the ideological level, between the processes operating in 1955-57 and those of 1976-80: 1956 saw the publication of a mass of texts arguing within the revolutionary tradition of Marxism; but such texts were rare in 1980. I have already dwelt on this problem in the previous chapter by stressing the ideological weight of the Church and the falsification of Stalinism. I will now examine it from another point of view.

The ideological confusion shown by the best opposition intellectuals, by those whom the workers correctly recognised as courageous allies, could, in a period when social tension unavoidably raises the question of power, have effects that were the opposite of those expected. They could prove harmful to tactical clear-sightedness, and in particular might foster illusions in a possibility of a *long term* peaceful coexistence between an independently organised working class and a totalitarian state power linked to the Soviet bureaucracy. This illusion existed at a mass level, and the moderating tactics of the Church and the tactics of the 'neo-revisionist' tendencies in the Party relied on it. Historical experience has already shown amply and tragically that neither the Catholic hierarchy nor the liberal wing of the bureaucracy have any intention of questioning the monolith of bureaucratic power. In the course of the social crises in question, these two distinct forces have transformed themselves from factors of instability into agents for a restabilisation of the regime.

My second observation concerns the question of unity of action. In focussing on the struggle for democratic rights and freedoms as a basis for rallying the opposition and organising its activities, the KOR leadership found itself on common ground with Catholic intellectuals and a section of the clergy. They had broken, correctly, with the sectarian and dogmatic traditions which for a long time had paralysed the opposition. But in making the transition to seeing the whole of 'society' — in other words, all forces other than the totalitarian regime — as a potentially united opposition, there is a step which might once again paralyse working class action. After August this question was to prove decisive. It was no longer a matter simply of maintaining and extending the freedoms that had been won, but of fighting for a profound transformation of society; of giving the working class the means by which it could itself control and direct its own affairs.

Curiously, this weakness was already present in embryo in the Open Letter. At that time Kuron and Modzelewski saw the technocracy only as a destabilising element, since 'central bureaucratic power' would be incapable and unwilling to hand over to it any part of its power. At the end of the 1970s I believe that the same mistake was made in relation to the Church. This can doubtless be explained by the tactical about-turn made by the episcopate in that period. However, in my opinion it is one thing to seek to organise the mass of the Catholic population, to ally with radical intellectuals, to fight for freedom of religious expression, but it is another thing not to see that, basically, the Catholic hierarchy was refusing to bring into question the dominant power of the bureaucracy. Now, this power was to blame for most of Poland's ills. Its interests were opposed to those of the workers. By trying too hard to maintain unity with the Church, the independent workers' movement risks repeating the mistakes of 1956 and supporting a policy which, in fact, is looking to save and preserve the existing power structure.

My third observation relates to the socialist project itself. Until the early 1970s the majority of Polish radical intellectuals

identified with a perspective of 'democratic socialism'. Kuron
was still prepared to support an idea of socialism which linked
workers' councils, the independent trade unions, and parliamentary democracy. However, the absence of a deeper discussion of these questions seems to me to be a source of confusion
in the reform projects that were put forward after August 1980,
in particular in the realm of economics.

These reservations relate to the strictly political aspect of
the KOR leadership's orientation. They in no way altered that
leadership's remarkable demonstration of clearsightedness and
effectiveness during the past five years. However, they are indispensable if one is to stand back and understand the process
of social mobilisation that was initiated by seaboard strikes.
Future historians of the 1970s in Poland should not reduce the
movement that was polarised by the KOR simply to these
political discussions. The correct starting point would be the
level of social awareness that they revealed, which grew after
the defeats of 1968 and 1970. KOR had worked to rebuild the
identity of a people whom bureaucratic power had sought to
disperse across the country. To that end the State crushed any
conscious appreciation of Poland's true situation, developed
hypocrisy and dissimulation, and discouraged dialogue. A DiP
intellectual wrote: "In Poland we have apparent economic
plans and we have an apparent fulfilment — even an over-
fulfillment — of those economic plans. We have apparent successes in industry, culture, science and education... We have
apparent minutes of apparent debates, apparent votes and apparent elections, the apparent preoccupation of the authorities
for the well-being of the citizenry, and all the apparent
appearances of government and socialism... We have an apparent freedom of choice, an apparent modernity and progress; we have apparent — and solemn — opening ceremonies
for building projects that have apparently been completed; we
have the apparent struggle against social ills; the apparent
satisfaction of all citizens, etc. The game of appearances is
practised on such a large scale that nobody — and this includes
the highest authorities in the land — any longer knows what is
real and what is not."

It was this 'game of appearances' which provided the first
spur to the development of KOR. Not in the sense of discussions, but by engaging in a different form of social practice, a

constant and ongoing struggle, based on dignity, honesty and a transparency of social relations. KOR started to act, refusing to accept the comfort of this 'double life' into which many people had settled. In that respect the KOR leadership are the real source of inspiration behind the great liberation movement under way in Poland since August 1980.[19]

7. With Whom Are We Talking?

It takes two to negotiate. Gierek's first reaction was to ignore the Inter-Enterprise Strike Committee. He hoped to divide it, by using the same tactic that had been used in previous strikes: satisfy the most immediate demands, and once the working class has gone back to work, repress the 'ringleaders'. His speech on the evening of Monday 18 August was not exactly notable for its imagination. At most it revealed that he had underestimated the extent to which the balance of power had already swung towards the workers. Gierek attempted to win back their confidence: "I would say frankly that some mistakes have been made in our political economy. In this field, practice does not correspond to the orientation intended after 1970. We should return to the line of the VI Congress", that of 1971. This realisation had come a bit late. Gierek's statements were met with the indifference they deserved, given that they were there only as the trimming around the real substance of his speech — a denunciation of the 'irresponsible individuals, the anarchist and anti-socialist elements' who were aiming to 'exploit the situation', not realising that there are 'limits beyond which one cannot go': namely the preservation of Poland's constitutional unity, and the country's 'foundations of political and social order'.

Gierek's arguments were zealously illustrated every day by the 7.30 evening TV news. This revealed the 'enormous wastage' being caused by 'certain' work stoppages. On 19 August, for example, we learned that 34 ships were held up in the Bay of Gdansk, and that 75,000 lemons were rotting in the hold of one of them. Ah, those lemons... They were a joke the length and breadth of Poland! Because nobody believed this televised garbage, and everybody — even the news readers — knew that the 'news' lied. This was the rule under this regime. "At Szczecin 5,000 dollars a day are being lost for each of the hundred ships blockaded there... What a shame!" sighed the duty journalist. The television also showed 'debates' between workers and sociologists, condemning the strikes, appealing for patriotism, and making a few half-hearted criticisms of the state of the economy. All this was crude, stupid, and it fooled nobody.

Meanwhile, the police began to act on Gierek's orders: a large number of repressive initiatives against anyone who helped the strikers, or against the strikers themselves. In the Gdansk region many delegates were arrested and detained for several hours; the militants transporting leaflets from one factory to another were pursued by the militia. Systematic roadblocks were set up on all major roads. They were also set up in the area surrounding the *Lenin* yard, but the large number of people moving in the area continued to increase, so that searches were soon limited to vehicles alone. On 18 and 19 August increasingly precise rumours indicated the existence of troop manoeuvres in the region. A Western journalist told how he had seen unusual convoys in the area, while in Warsaw, several hours before his arrest, Jacek Kuron was to observe and condemn an extraordinary mobilisation of the forces of repression. However, the development of events forced the militia to show more restraint. For most of the time they remained discreetly deployed in the streets of the Three Towns, and a number of anecdotes bore witness to their fear in the face of a movement too great for them to control; in fact a number of militiamen went out of their way to let the strikers know that they were well-disposed to them.

Thus Gierek's much-vaunted 'firmness' had little effect. In fact, he was seeing his own power melt away, as he lost his grip on a society which was rallying to the side of the seaboard strikers. The week of 17-24 August represented a point of no return which forced a change of attitude onto the Secretary General.

On Sunday 17 August he named a negotiating commission under the leadership of Tadeusz Pyka, vice-president of the Council of Ministers. The commission arrived in Gdansk on Monday afternoon, surrounded by an impressive team of aides. But it did not proceed to the shipyard. Rather, it chose to meet immediately the local Party hierarchy. Jablonski, President of the Republic, was also present, along with Kania, the Central Committee secretary in charge of the army and police.

They tried to rally the ranks of the Party faithful in order to put into effect the policies which Gierek had outlined on television — not to recognise the Inter-Enterprise Strike Committee, and simply to negotiate enterprise by enterprise. The Pyka commission settled itself into the government building and waited. Only 17 out of the 253 enterprises on strike made contact. These were often represented by Party secretaries or by members of management, and received only promises. Some of them signed partial agreements regarding conditions of work or wages, but when Pyka and his minions asked them to go back to work, the workers refused. The decision depended on the Inter-Enterprise Strike Committee.

Other attempts at division were equally fruitless. On 19 August, for example, a leaflet signed by the Presidents of the Three Towns appealed for the strikers to show responsibility. But this demagogy, despite being scattered from a flying aircraft, flew a trifle too low: "Leaving aside the discussions presently taking place in many enterprises," wrote the Presidents, "and leaving aside the demands that have been raised by the workers, and the question of their fulfilment, the town *must* live, in order that its inhabitants may live. In particular this means our children, our loved ones, and the sick in our hospitals. And for that the proper functioning of municipal services is essential, as well as those sectors of production and transportation on which we depend directly for the bread and milk in our shop windows and on our tables, for the basic foodstuffs and the everyday objects that we require."

On 21 August the Inter-Enterprise Strike Committee replied to the leaflet, firmly, and not without irony: "The striking workers are not breaking the unity of the Polish people, and are not launching an attack on the Polish State. If the authorities want to check this, let them come and visit the strikers, and let them study the resolutions of the Inter-Enterprise Strike Committee, representing the strikers. If they are looking for the truth, it is here that they will find it, and not in the provincial government's Council building. The workers of the shipyard where the Inter-Enterprise Strike Committee is in session guaranteed the full security of the government delegation during negotiations. The Inter-Enterprise Strike Committee offers the same guarantee."

By Thursday the strikes were still spreading, and the Pyka

commission's assessment was that the situation was disastrous. One Inter-Enterprise Strike Committee was set up at the town of Szczecin, and another at Elblag, a small industrial town not far from Gdansk. Gierek recalled Pyka and selected a new commission team. This arrived on Thursday afternoon, with vice Prime Minister Jagielski at its head. Its task remained the same: it was still to ignore the Inter-Enterprise Strike Committee, and to attempt negotiations, this time, at sectoral level. The minister announced as much on the local radio on the evening of his arrival: "Those demands which can be met, will be met forthwith; as regards those which seem to us impossible to meet, we will explain why they cannot be met." This policy was about as little effective as Pyka's: the first contacts with a number of small construction enterprises were less than conclusive. All this led to one conclusion: the only power representing the strikers was the Inter-Enterprise Strike Committee. Jagielski understood this very quickly, and on Friday 22nd took up a different position. He made a discreet contact with the Inter-Enterprise Strike Committee. He found a go-between in Dr Gruszczewski, a delegate from the Polytechnic and a member of the praesidium. But his conditions rather outran his means. In particular, his demand that Walesa, Walentynowicz and Gwiazda were to be expelled from the Inter-Enterprise Strike Committee! People still laugh about this in Gdansk. Finally, after negotiations with three of the praesidium delegates — Gruszczewski, Wisniewski and Przybylski — it was arranged that the government commission would meet the Inter-Enterprise Strike Committee on Saturday 23 August, inside the *Lenin* shipyard. When Jagielski arrived at eight o'clock that Saturday evening, in this den of 'anti-socialist elements', an enormous crowd was gathered. Calm and smiling. The crowd applauded Walesa as he welcomed the minister, who was tense as he got out of his minibus. They walked towards the conference hall. They crossed the hall slowly, under the smiling, inquisitive eyes of the assembled crowd. There was complete silence. The entire praesidium was assembled on the platform. Jagielski climbed the steps to the platform, under the gaze of a marble Lenin:

"Let the rest of the delegation pass... There's a lot of people."

The various government experts finally took up their positions on the rostrum.

"We welcome these gentlemen."

The people in the hall applauded, half-heartedly.

Jagielski (to Walesa): "Where should I put myself? Here... Yes?"

Walesa: "Yes. Just for a moment, because we're going to move to the other hall, over there."

Jagielski: "May I meet the members of the praesidium?"

Walesa: "Please do."

The minister shook their hands and introduced himself: "Jagielski... Deputy Prime Minister... Jagielski... Deputy Prime Minister..." Then Walesa suggested that they go into the adjoining room in order to begin discussions. Everything would be relayed and broadcast directly to the worker delegates, and to the factory as a whole. Jagielski accepted this, The hall exploded with joy, as the praesidium members and the government commission once again passed through the crowd. They applauded Walesa: "Leszek! Leszek!"

Negotiations began. The Deputy Prime Minister had nothing concrete to offer. As regards free trade unions? He hedged on this for almost an hour. As regards payment for time lost during the strike, out of the funds of the old union? He was not prepard to answer this question; he was not authorised.

As regards the reconnection of telephone communications with the rest of the country?

"As you know, this week there was a storm in Warsaw. The telephone system has been damaged..."

Laughter in the hall. For sure, the storm had not lasted for 12 days. For the Inter-Enterprise Strike Committee the re-establishment of communications was a precondition for any discussion, and since the minister had not budged on any of these demands, he left at midnight with nothing to show. Obviously he had not yet understood the meaning of what was happening in the yard, the fundamental questioning which was under way there, and the nascent strength there. But nobody was particularly worried at the failure of this first set of negotiations. As one delegates said to me, that evening: "They will be back... They can't do otherwise." In fact, the arrival of the minister was their first victory. He had finally recognised the Inter-Enterprise Strike Committee as a negotiating partner, even calling Walesa 'Mr Chairman', a mere 24 hours after he had been demanding his expulsion from the yard. But on the other hand, his contribution was seen, in an article in the *Solidarnosc* bulletin, as 'woolly, full of platitudes, with no concrete proposals, and, for the moment, not even authorised to make decisions'.

On Sunday 24 August, the meeting of the Polish United Workers Party Central Committee ratified the Gierek leadership's change of tactics. It approved the opening of negotiations with the Inter-Enterprise Strike Committee, and in his summing up the Secretary General made a number of new proposals. He suggested the holding of elections within the official unions, 'where the workers demand them', so that they might 'develop towards a true defence of the workers' interests (...). And there is no doubt that if they show themselves capable of a lasting authority, the representatives who have recently been chosen in a spontaneous manner in a number of firms will figure among those elected. Finally, he announced that there would shortly be a discussion in the Sejm, of a reform of trade union law. However, these changes in the Party's tactics still had the same aim: to block the workers' mobilisation by making a number of small concessions, which could later be taken back. To this end, the Central Committee proposed a number of reshuffles within the Party leadership and the government. Edward Babiuch, as chief scapegoat, was shuffled out of his post as Prime Minister, and off the Politburo. He was replaced by a reputedly reforming economist, Josef Pinkowski. The secretary of the central Trade Union Council, Jan Szydlak, and propaganda secretary Tadeusz Wrzaszczyk suffered the same fate, as did Tadeusz Pyka, who lost his position as substitute on the Politburo. Among those newly promoted, one man made a triumphal return: Stefan Olszowski. He had a double advantage: he appeared both as a reforming spirit, and he also had the trust of a section of the bureaucracy by virtue of his uncompromising past (in 1968-69 he was fairly close to General Moczar's 'partisans', and had been in charge of the Press, culture, and youth). Ousted from the Politburo on the occasion of the VIII Congress in February 1980, he had, on that occasion, proposed a whole series of economic reforms. He was, as Gierek put it, one of 'those comrades who for some time have been pointing to the defects of our situation, and whom we have chosen not to hear'. He returned to take over economic affairs.

Thus, a mere ten days after the strike had started in the *Lenin* shipyard, the scene was changing in Poland. The working-class mobilisation spread from Szczecin and Elblag to Silesia, Wroclaw and Warsaw, where the first committees were set up in order to prepare for strike action. A general strike was in the air. The regime was on the offensive, and made its first tactical retreats in the face of a working class which was advancing, democratically organised, united, and independent of State and Party, who recognised the situation for what it was.

The situation had a meaning that transcended the simple pattern of events. It marked a break. It opened a new phase in Poland's history: a phase characterised by a separation between the mass of the working class and the Polish United Workers Party, which, for 35 years, had claimed to represent and lead it. We were seeing the public acknowledgement of a defeat.

Furthermore, contrary to what had happened in previous strikes, the situation had thrown up two *separately organised* camps: the strike committees and the Party. From the workers' point of view this situation was described lyrically in the editorial of the 16th edition of *Solidarnosc* on 27 August, entitled: 'With whom are we talking?'. The strikers themselves described how they had been changing: "Gentlemen! You are no longer talking to those who, in December 1970, when you asked 'Will you help us', answered 'Yes, we will help you'. We are different now, most particularly because we are together and we are strong. We are different because, over 30 years, we have learned that promises have always remained an illusion. We are different, because we have understood that when you talked of improvements, you were in fact talking about exploitation." And how did they assess the regime's representatives? "With whom are we talking? There should be a clear answer on this. We are talking with the government commission, with a Deputy Prime Minister of Poland. Can there be anybody more qualified to negotiate? But in the negotiating hall we always get the same answer from our Deputy Prime Minister: 'I don't know... That's not my department... I haven't had time to study this...' (...) This is not a dialogue — it's a double monologue. The delegates' feelings are expressed as howls of laughter. (...) The atmosphere in this negotiating hall is totally different from a few days ago. Obviously a lot of things have changed. People are laughing, laughing more and more, and laughing more and more openly!'' There was no longer any 'credit of trust' accorded to these incompetents who were governing Poland. This was the radically new element in this split between the working class and the Polish United Workers Party.

To be sure, this Party had only very rarely succeeded in winning the enthusiasm of the Polish proletariat. Every time an opportunity appeared in which it could have won this confidence, it always muffed it. After the war, for example. At that time, with the victory of the Red Army over the Nazis, with the Liberation taking place, and with all the enthusiasm of the younger generations during the country's reconstruction, the Party might have been able to erase the negative memories of the previous 20 years (in particular the march on Warsaw in 1920, and the invasion of Poland by Stalin's armies in 1939, after the German-Soviet pact). But the Kremlin bureaucracy preferred to put into power a Party that was weak and with few roots, making use of the weight of international agreements (Yalta and Potsdam) and employing police terror (the physical elimination of the AK (National Army) leadership, deportations etc.). At the same time the Party was to profit from the impact of the first social reforms, and was to recruit a lot of young worker militants, giving them responsibilities and integrating them within the State bureaucracy. But in some regions, like Silesia, because the Party lacked any working-class roots whatsoever, it had to recruit a whole set of careerists whose activities under the Nazi occupation had been somewhat open to question.

In broad terms one can say that up until the middle of the 1950s the Polish United Workers Party succeeded in attracting a number of the most conscious elements of the working class, while repressing anyone who rebelled. And it was those militants who, inspired by the positions taken by the intellectuals, and by the revolt of the Poznan workers, had been the spearhead of the 'renewal' which brought Gomulka to power.[20] Those few months of Polish history had seen the new Secretary General, freed from Stalin's jails, embody a certain hope; the working class had enjoyed its first large-scale experience of democracy in the workers' councils; this was the only period in which the Polish United Workers' Party had even the possibility of winning and keeping the trust of the working class. And, as we know, it missed its chance.

Throughout the 1960s the Party's mistakes led to an increasing gulf between the Party apparatus and working-class activists. Many who had entertained hopes in Gomulka were expelled (when they personally engaged in active protest), and others withdrew on tiptoe. Often they remained Party members, but stripped of all responsibility. They were replaced by narrow-minded careerist bureaucrats, while uncompromising Stalinists (the 'Natolinians') regained their influence. Gomulka was to pay very dearly for this state of affairs. In effect, it left a void — the area which had been occupied by his supporters in the early months — which was then filled by the manoeuvrings of the various fractions of the apparatus, in particular that inspired by General Moczar. By 1968-70, Gomulka was a prisoner of this balancing act between political cliques, he was completely isolated and hated by those who had brought him to power. The violence of the December 1970 demonstrations came at the height of this resentment. Henceforth the gap between the workers and their party was to prove unbridgeable, with the former soon to set fire to the offices of the latter. Gierek was never able to reverse the trend. To be sure, people were pacified somewhat by a new economic policy emphasising industrial development and domestic consumption, but the events of 1976, the extension of the democratic opposition movement and the strikes of Summer 1980 only served to sharpen the antagonism between the workers and 'their' Party.

Did this mean that the Polish United Workers Party no longer had any power, that it was no longer recruiting workers, and that it was reduced to a band of narrow-minded functionaries? No, of course not. The phenomena we have described only came to the surface during periods of crisis. It depended on the political trust accorded by the leadership of the working-class. It depended on those groupings that we described at the start of this book: the existence in each enterprise of spontaneous, unorganised militants, who had the trust of the working class, and who took responsibility for its daily relations with the Party bureaucracy and the State. In 1956 these militants were still within the Party; they hoped to be able to

138

reform it, and they formed the backbone of the workers' councils. In 1975-80, for the most part, they no longer had official responsibilities, and often no longer even had their party cards. Many had been influenced by the opposition movement.

This state of affairs inevitably affected those who joined the Party, and also meant that, in difficult times, the Party's cohesion might be less than that required. Membership of this ruling party was less and less founded on ideological convictions, on the hope of building a better future of lessening inequalities in society. In 1977 Krzysztof Pomian produced a study of the motivations of Party members, in which he distinguished a number of differing attitudes. "First there are all those — and they are many — who joined the Party simply because they are asked to, and who either didn't have the courage to refuse, or who told themselves that it might prove useful." Obviously, when the wind changes direction, people like this are not very reliable. Then, among the truly voluntary members, Pomian picks out "the workers, and those who are in general found at the bottom levels of society. One important factor driving them to join the Party is the fact that it enables them to become somebody, to win a certain recognition in the enterprises where they work, and perhaps outside. In effect, a Party member belongs to a minority whose opinion is periodically sought by local — or even national — personalities, and who, for his part, has certain rights of self-expression." Finally, "the situation of those who have completed their secondary and higher education is a little different. This is the group from which the apparatus will draw its future members; it is also this group that will produce recruits who will later be invested with a certain amount of power, due to their real or imaginary abilities. Among these people, direct invitations are more rare. Quite simply, everybody knows that, to get ahead, to advance beyond a certain level of the hierarchy, one has to be a Party member. And if young people imagine that they might be able to escape from subordinate status while still keeping their independence of spirit, reality soon tells them otherwise." These varying motivations lead to a situation where "a bond of complicity is created between the apparatus and the Party membership, which allows the latter to satisfy their legitimate aspirations to social recognition, and allows the former to channel these aspirations and transform them into one of the bases of its power, by using them in order to submit the whole of society to a level of surveillance which otherwise would not be possible." But this bond can be broken when the consensus on which it is based shatters. "The Party is a very heterogeneous entity; it is fraught with contradictions, and criss-crossed with borders between different groupings. The principal dividing line, the one which is systematically concealed in official utterances, is still that between the apparatus and simple members." Out of something like three million members, Pomian estimates the apparatus at 270,000, and, furthermore, suggests that the Party "prefers to look for its implantation within the privileged strata of Polish society".

This analysis defines precisely the importance of the crisis which had been sparked off by the seaboard strikes. Namely, the fact that, unlike the ruling parties in bourgeois societies, the Polish United Workers Party has no legitimacy other than that of representing and 'guiding' the working class. In Western Europe, politicians like Mitterrand or Schmidt obviously represent themselves as having been elected by the voters as a whole, but if their working class rejects them, they still retain that essential element — the support of their respective bourgeoisies, which hold the economic, financial and cultural power. They. can make use of them in a thousand ways in order to restore a given situation. The European bourgeoisies have time and again shown their abilities in this regard. However, the bureaucrats who hold power in the East do not have the same margins of manoeuvre. Their only safety net is an external force — the USSR — although, in certain situations, they may find an internal ally in the Church.

The process which began on 23 August in Gdansk was precisely this process of isolation of the Party apparatus. It began to lose its means of governing. It had no choice but to retreat. The process was still only beginning — it was to become clearer in the months that followed — but one could already make out its broad lines. The principal factor of this crisis was the self-organisation of the workers. However, it remained limited to the regions on strike — that is, to something like one million men and women. It was underpinned by a general level of sympathy throughout Poland, which was to be confirmed by the mass recruitment into the new Solidarity union in September. The strength of this working class organisation lay partly in its democratic rules, but also in its awareness of its own autonomy. In this regard, the reactions to Gierek's various speeches were very clear. On Monday 19 August, in the evening, in the Inter-Enterprise Strike Committee hall, one could hardly hear the Secretary General speak. People were laughing at him. The government reshuffle on 24 August produced the same effect. On that day I was in front of Gate No. 2 when the radio was broadcasting Gierek's final speech as Secretary General. Night had already fallen, and three or four thousand people were standing and listening. From time to time somebody made a comment. People were amused. Sometimes the transmission was a bit rough. Walesa picked up the microphone at one point and said: "He's gone on strike too!" Everyone cheered. But nobody believed that this reshuffle would change anything. A delegate from the *North* shipyard explained the situation to me the following day: "You know, it's like fishing. You throw out your hook with a bit of bait, and you wait. Gierek takes us for stupid fishes. He's wrong. In our factory we discussed his speech, department by department, and our opinion is unanimous. The speech, with the reshuffle etc, is just wind! It will change nothing." A woman worker from a fish canning factory agreed: "I think that the government will have to accept our demands. We might make one or two compromises, but not on the basic issues. The important point is the free trade union. The new Prime Minister? We don't even know him. What's important is what's going on here." I had the same response from an electrical construction factory employing 1,500 workers: "We quickly called together a meeting yesterday evening. Our point of view is that the government commission should come here. They're playing for time too much." Sometimes people's opinions were a bit more moderate. Two women delegates from a small cement factory (140 workers, 90 per cent women) told me: "I don't know this new Prime Minister. So I can't judge him. But I hope that Gierek is right when he says that he's a capable man, and that he understands our problems. I hope he treats us properly." And what was their main demand? "The free union, of course!"

So, convinced of a coming victory, people awaited the return of the government commission. Every now and then messages of solidarity were read out. Delegations brought more money for the Inter-Enterprise Strike Committee, for the monument to the victims of 1970. People were losing count of the numbers of factories which were coming out on strike one after the other. On Saturday 23 August the Inter-Enterprise Strike Committee covered 388 factories; one week later, there were more than 600. "Soon there won't be enough space to fit them all in this hall," somebody said. People also had high hopes of support from other parts of Poland, in particular Silesia. On Saturday two workers from Tarnowe Gory, representing committees from a dozen big factories in the region, explained: "We have sent a personal letter to Gierek. If the government plays for time with this seaboard strike, if it does not grant your demands, then on 1 September we too will strike, in solidarity." Another delegation, from Swidnik, read an identical motion. "I hope that all the Polish miners will say the same, as well," commented my interpreter, a delegate from an electrical construction firm. But he quickly added: "We're not looking for a general strike. That would cost Poland too dearly. By refusing to listen to us the government is squandering millions of dollars a day. But if we have to, then the whole country will come out on strike." So, there was no doubt that this organisational strength was extending, and also that it did not believe a word that the government was saying. People had come a long way from the illusions of 1956, or even 1971. Now their defiance was total.

Within the Party — at first in the striking regions, and then throughout the country — the workers' movement aroused a growing sense of unease. To start with, there were numerous Party members among the strikers and among the Inter-Enterprise Strike Committee delegates. One Party official in Gdansk told me that between 30 per cent and 40 per cent of the delegates were card-carrying Party members. This statistic could not be proved, but at least it reveals how a local official, himself a supporter of the strikers, saw the situation. At any rate, it is undeniable that the apparatus lost any influence over the membership. For example, it proved incapable of organising even the smallest of mass demonstrations to support its policies. This malaise was described by a member of the provincial committee's secretariat in Gdansk in a confidential letter sent to the 24 August plenary session of the Party's Central Committee. He noted the popular mobilisation around the strikers, and the ineffectiveness of the Party's propaganda. "People are convinced that the talk of 'losses' due to the strike is an argument that carries little weight. Yesterday and today holy masses were celebrated in the principal workplaces of Gdansk and Gdynia. Similarly, workers have been continuing to hand in their old union cards in section W1, W2, W4 and W5 of the *North* shipyard. Inter-Enterprise Strike Committee leaflets are still being distributed throughout the province. The sectoral industry-based discussions undertaken by the government commission have not resulted in any return to work. New enterprises have been submitting motions and proposals. (...) Yesterday discussions took place with a section of the strikers from the *North* shipyard, with the repair yard at Gdansk, and Unimor. (...) The public relations campaign embarked on by Party militants and the administration becomes more and more difficult to carry out. (...) Support is growing. (...) In general the Party membership feels that we must call an end to this dangerous and complicated political situation as quickly as possible." This letter was published in *Solidarnosc* No. 4, where it 'showed the powerlessness and the disarray of all the Party's organisations' and encouraged the strikers that they were on the right lines. Furthermore, at the Central Committee plenary session, the speeches by the Party members from the Gdansk and Szczecin shipyards were also indicative of the malaise. Three of them are worth quoting.

Jan Labecki,[21] First Secretary of the Polish United Workers Party for the *Lenin* shipyard section, began by describing the atmosphere of this strike which was "supported and aggravated by illegal publishing activity and by elements of discontent in Poland". The strike was due to the "conviction on the part of workers that the decisions of the VII and VIII Party Congresses have not been implemented in any real manner. I can say this because of my daily work among both Party members and non-Party members. Independently of any agreement which may be reached on this seaboard strike, we must undertake a deep analysis and draw the necessary conclusions." He then put forward a number of immediate reforms that were very close to the spirit of the Inter-Enterprise Strike Committee demands. "I have seen these people, I have lived through this drama with them. There is no doubt — the majority of workers, including Party members, never imagined that the strike would spread to such an extent. We must have the courage to say what a number of comrade members have been saying for a long time: the Party must make an effort to shake off a lot of the dirty laundry that it carries on its back. This is a matter for all Party members, whatever the post that they occupy. What counts is work, and not fine words.'' Then, after a plea for reforms and the granting of the strikers' demands, he concluded: ''I have to say that I have spoken with Party members in the street, in the works — I go there every day. I don't know how, or why, but nobody has mistreated me, either physically or verbally. Perhaps this is because, in my work, I have always tried to match my words with deeds. For that reason I have no enemies. It's for that reason that during these seaboard events nobody has had a bad word for me. (...) Of course, the workers do object to some people — but these are mainly the careerist militants, the arse-lickers who use their Party membership to get to the top.''

Stanislaw Miskiewicz, Party First Secretary at the Warski shipyard in Szczecin, asked himself whether the strike could have been avoided: ''The militants and the workers think that it could have been. The events of 1976 had pulled the alarm cord. We hadn't stopped to think. We had to draw suitable conclusions and then apply them. People's opinions were unanimous: nothing was done. On the contrary, the mistakes made were aggravated still further, and everything began to take a turn for the worse — a turn quite opposite to that which was being proclaimed officially. To confirm what I am saying, I would turn to the demands drawn up by the workers. In the realm of economics, they want to see improvements on two fronts: 1. A continuous supply of raw materials, so that the organisation of work can be improved and continuous production ensured. In addition, an increase in production for the home market and for export; and increased wages. 2. The improvement of supplies to the market, not only as regards food products.

''Unfortunately, the general movement of criticism which accompanied the preparations for the Party's VIII Congress, and the conclusions that were drawn, have not had any effect in the sense of a programme of measures which should have immediately been submitted to the nation. Instead of improving, the workers' standard of living is getting worse. (...) To this must be added the never-ending queues, arising from the lack of supplies, queues which are tiring and difficult for people to put up with. We have to say that the majority of workers' demands are of an economic nature. The shipyard strike committee has declared several times that it draws the line at any activity touching on questions of socialist politics or Poland's constitutional entity. In the Inter-Enterprise Strike Committee conference hall there is a banner on which you can read: 'Progressive socialism, yes! Deformed socialism, no!' We stand for order in our country, in order to develop the responsibility of those in government. The rank and file, the workers, are complaining about the absence of a long-term programme capable of winning society to its side. They are demanding meaningful action, so that words are followed by deeds. (...) The general conclusion that one can draw from this situation is that there is a total lack of confidence in the regime. (...) Comrades, I would like you to know that neither Party militants nor the shipyard management have been badly treated by the strike committees. We enjoy freedom of action. But the bitterness and the mental state of the workers after this conflict will have a tremendous influence on our future work. Brutal confrontations in our country have been becoming more and more frequent: 1956, 1970, 1980. None of these was provoked by the rank and file of the Party!''

Finally, Edward Pustelnik, a locksmith at the Szczecin repair yard, confided his doubts to the assembly: ''I have spent six days and nights with the strikers of the 'GRYF' shipyard. Thanks to the intervention of comrade Brych, the strikers allowed me to leave the yard. They suspected that I was coming to today's meeting. In these six days, I have taken part, I have heard hundreds of workers speak, both Party members and non-Party members. All of them, with bitterness and feeling, have spoken of their conditions of work, of their deteriorating standard of living, of the lack of any determination at governmental level to draw up a programme of improvements. (...) As a worker, and as a member of the Party, I have to say that there are certain things which I do not understand. Because, when all is said and done, the majority of the problems at present being raised by the strikers have already been raised several times within Party meetings, in particular in the meetings preparatory to the VIII Congress of the Polish United

Workers Party. The non-Party members knew this, and they supported us; furthermore, they believed that our voices would finally be listened to. Unfortunately this proved not to be the case. This is what I cannot understand: why is it that the demands that were put forward at that time were not treated with the seriousness that they deserved? It's only now that they're being looked at, now that we're forced to do it. This, surely, is what is happening. But to carry on like this gives the lie to what we have been saying and repeating in public, viz., that the Party listens to the opinions of its members, as well as to those of non-Party members, and that it draws from these opinions the necessary conclusions.''

These speeches were in no sense exceptional. They revealed, at the highest level, the mood of very many Party members. They also showed the vulnerability of an institution which oppresses the working class while pretending to govern in its name. They foreshadowed the crises to come.

In the same way, the turning point of 22 and 23 August, arising from the balance of forces, was inevitably to lead Jagielski, after a week of negotiations, to capitulate on a number of basic points. However, the Minister still had a few cards up his sleeve.

His first had no direct means of effect on the workers' militancy. It came from outside the Party — in the form of support from the Catholic Church. The statements from the episcopate, while they were discreet, are worth noting here, because later on some people tended to discount them. On 27 August the PAP press agency issued a communique from the General Council of the Polish episcopacy. This communique was in line with the earlier statements of Cardinal Wyszinski and the Bishop of Gdansk. Obviously it raised the question of the democratic rights sought by the workers (without however uttering the phrase 'free union'!). But at the same time it advised moderation on both sides, and mutual understanding. It hoped for a rapid end to the strikes. Using deliberately vague formulas, it stressed the necessity of national unity: ''The people of Poland need a real moral and social renaissance, in order to regain confidence in themselves, in their future, and in their own strength, as well as to awaken the moral energy and the spirit of sacrifice which will be necessary to accomplish the tremendous effort which awaits us all. We must, without delay, re-establish mutual confidence between society and the regime, in order to construct, by joint effort, a better future for the country, and in order to guarantee the interests of both nation and State." Given the context, everybody saw this communique as an attempt to moderate the strikers' positions. Its influence was minimal, but it revealed the basic policies of the Catholic hierarchy. At that moment it provided only feeble assistance to a beleaguered Jagielski.

In fact, the only argument of any weight which Gierek and his government had was the permanent threat of a Soviet military intervention. This was summoned up on every possible occasion in official statements. Inevitably this argument influenced a section of the non-striking population, in particular in Warsaw. In more general terms, it established certain limits, a barrier which could not be crossed in the course of the negotiations. The Inter-Enterprise Strike Committee experts tended to set rather too much store by this threat, and as a result, occasionally advised the negotiators to err on the side of moderation. The threat of a 'fraternal aid' from the Soviet Union, was in the final event, Jagielski's only card.

However, the shipyard workers were quite unconcerned. Endlessly harassed on this point by journalists, they tended to give irritated answers. When I raised the point with a delegate from the *Paris Commune* shipyard in Gdynia, he immediately said:

"That is impossible. Impossible."

"But why?"

"This is something very difficult to explain," he answered, smiling. "I am quite sure of what I'm saying, though. What I'm saying is based on a very powerful impression, backed by the history of our country. The risk is of the order of between one per cent and three per cent... We know that the present historic moment is good for us... very good. I can't explain... I can see that you're still worried..."

"Not really. But everybody's talking about it in Warsaw..."

"It is impossible that a government as corrupt as this one would invite the Russians in."

"And if they came of their own accord?"

"Oh no! They couldn't"

"But these strikes are having a certain effect in the USSR,

aren't they?''

"That's their problem, not ours.''

It was pointless to go on arguing the point. On another occasion I broached the subject with a group of workers relaxing on the grass. They did not like my question.

"We don't like that sort of question here,'' one old man said.

A younger worker cut in: "Czechoslovakia will not happen again.''

"We keep a clear separation between politics and our strike,'' the first worker continued. "And anyway, when you look at the international situation, it's not really such a clever solution, to bring tanks in here.''

Encouraged by his comment, I tried another line of argument.

"Do you believe that the Russians would put up for long with the existence of a free and uncontrollable trade union?''

"I had the impression that they've been doing precisely that since the start of this strike! Even if it's not particularly convenient for them.''

Obviously...

I ventured further: "In Czechoslovakia they didn't intervene straight away.''

"No, no, it's not a problem...''

"We don't really want to talk about this. At the moment we are fighting for our own problems; we've got enough on our plate.''

"But to set up a free trade union is to bring about a political change,'' I insisted.

"Yes... but... no!''

"Our union will not be political,'' the older man said. "We don't want to have anything to do with politics.''

"Anyway, people are frightened: there's nothing like the word 'politics' to frighten people,'' a third man added. "We live in the socialist camp, we want to stay within it, and we want to have the workers' rights that we are fighting for.''

The whole group nodded in agreement. They all brought up various arguments, and finally they told me what they really thought.

"For us Poles, the important thing is that nobody should meddle in our affairs. We've got our clever people, and we've got our Pope. We don't need the advice of Big Brother. These Russians don't frighten us."

"No," another worker corrected. "Some people are frightened."

"You're introducing politics now," someone else interjected. This started an argument.

"But we need to know whether we are free to negotiate or not."

"If you're frightened of talking, then..."

Then the old man stepped in, in a low voice: "We're not getting involved in politics. We are just simply telling you what we think, honestly. As you know, with their Afghanistan, they've got problems too. And coming here would cause too many repercussions..."

"But Poland is just a small country," someone objected.

"We are in the right," replied the old man. "We want nothing more than what was signed by our representatives in Helsinki. And the Russians signed there too."

That day they convinced me of one thing: not to ask that question any more.

8. A Difficult Agreement

They were expected at any moment. A guard of honour had been waiting there in the late summer sunshine. Their yellow helmets traced a pathway through the parked, silent crowd. In the background stood Gate 2, with its flags and flowers. It was 11.00 am on Tuesday 26 August: the strikers had prepared a first-class welcome for the government commission. But the welcome was turned down. We heard that the commission had entered discreetly via Gate 1, packed into their minibus. With the vice Prime Minister at their head, they crossed the shipyard. But they were nonetheless recognised by the workers, who watched them pass.

This second meeting was only made possible by laborious negotiations during the evening and the whole night of the preceding day. At 7.30 pm the government had contacted the Inter-Enterprise Strike Committee with a view to an immediate meeting. The strikers had refused, because telephone communications had still not been reconnected with the rest of the country. After several hours the regime gave way. Thus negotiations could begin that Tuesday morning, in the small hall of the Inter-Enterprise Strike Committee building. Newspaper photographers took photos from every single angle through a large plate glass window, while the delegates followed the discussions as they were re-broadcast into the other hall, and throughout the shipyard. Public negotiations like this are a historical rarity, but here they had become almost an everyday matter. Secret negotiations would have been impossible. At one moment technical problems cut off the relays to the outside world, and within the yard and its confines, people got very angry and were just about ready to break down gates. They thought the government had banned the use of the loudspeakers. The vice Prime Minister himself asked for the breakdown to be repaired. He interrupted his speech to this end, and did not start again until the broadcast — that is to say, workers' democracy — had been re-established. Everyone could see that the regime was on the defensive, stuttering, getting tangled up in technical details. People's faces were alight with joy, with pleasure even. They listened patiently to the minister. They applauded warmly the proposals made by members of the praesidium, who had no desire to repeat Saturday's experience. They came straight to the point: "We will have to discuss everything," Walesa explained, "but let us start with the first demand — the free trade union." Jagielski hesitated, but then he outlined the resolution of the Party's Central Committee. He stated: "In a few days new elections will be taking place in all enterprises in the region. If they show that the Inter-Enterprise Strike Committee is in a majority, then it will be up to you to take charge and change the unions." This was his reply, although, as he explained, here he was only expressing his own personal opinion. In short, nothing really new. Then, after a number of Inter-Enterprise Strike Committee speakers had spoken, the minister asked for a ten-minute break. This was to last for an hour and a half. In the end they agreed on the setting-up of an ongoing commission, bringing together experts from both sides. "As you wish," Walesa agreed, "but this commission will have no power. It will not commit anybody."

The main thing that this second round of negotiations revealed was the determination and radicalisation of the strikers. This development was quite obvious from the speeches being made by members of the praesidium. The demand for the free trade unions was now taking on an increasingly political meaning. It became a shorthand for people's hopes, for change that was progressive, self-aware and democratically controlled. Bogdan Lis was very clear on this: "We are seeking all the rights we demanded, at every level. (*Applause*) (...) We want a guarantee of freedom of action." Andrzej Gwiazda took the point up at length: "The population here, and the workers, have reached an age of maturity. Their calm behaviour at the time of the Pope's visit last year was the first demonstration of this... I think that Poles have had enough of listening to speeches about mistakes and errors-which-one-could-not-avoid. (*Applause*) ...To such an extent that it is now virtually necessary to bring about a sort of revolution in this country. I believe that if society's voice is heard, if it is no longer thwarted, then these mistakes will no longer be repeated. For this to happen, society needs its own set of organisations. The workers must have the freedom to express themselves, whether they are right or wrong. A debate can only take place when all voices are able to make themselves heard. (*Applause*) The question is: who is to decide? Up until now only the authorities had the right of decision. That is why we, the seaboard workers, want to set up new trade unions which are free and independent. (*Applause*) Certainly, the economic situation is very complicated. It will have to be approached at a number of levels. But who else, other than those who work, are able to say where truth lies, or who is right? A new trade union will avoid a lot of mistakes. The government must not let their reply drag on forever."

In the opinion of Florian Wisniewski, an electrician, if the workers had a guarantee of control over the situation, they would be prepared to accept certain sacrifices. "Many of our investments are unproductive; we're spending our money badly. Polish workers, everyone, must be able to choose what is and what is not necessary. Some reforms will probably be difficult, but a free union under democratic control will be the only guarantee that we can get out of the situation. We want all economic decisions to be taken in the light of calm and rational understanding."

Finally, and this was the opinion of the majority of delegates with whom I talked later, the new union was to have all the prerogatives of a real working-class power. Lech Walesa took an example to explain this. He quoted the case of a factory producing prefabs, which was producing at only 50 per cent of capacity. "The government decided to build another one, right next door. This is pointless. It's ridiculous. Maybe the Central Committee doesn't realise this, but we workers see this happening everyday. The free trade union means the exercise of control over economic choices at all levels: local, regional and national. A new plan is required, and this is the way that it is to be drawn up." This, then, was the substance of the first demand: the idea that, throughout the country, people could take matters into their own hands, that the working class, with its self-awareness, could guarantee this process. This was what the vice Prime Minister heard on that Tuesday morning. It was the one burning hope of the whole of working-class Poland. Lech Sobieszek, a praesidium member, made the

152

point clearly, to the accompaniment of thunderous applause. "The problem which we are discussing here concerns the whole of Poland. Obviously, we want a free trade union for the whole of the country." The Minister: "This is your point of view, not mine. Here we are discussing Pomerania." Lech Sobieszek: "Don't try to divide us from the rest of the country. If you do, you will have a general strike on your hands."[22]

This understanding was confirmed throughout the course of the struggle. In the space of a fortnight the strikers had changed. Now they were aware of their own strength, they were sure of themselves, and they all knew that what was at stake in the movement went beyond simply the making of demands and agreements. While, on the one hand, they still avoided talking 'politics' with journalists, on the other, their proposals tended towards drawing the lessons of the past 35 years, tended to a future, tended to a new situation that would be changed by the strike. In fact, every question they broached was a political question.

I observed this at my ease during the hours of waiting for the government delegation, and in particular during the final days, when it became clear that victory was at hand. But the happiness on people's faces was tinged with a caution. An old delegate from the *North* yard told me not to get too carried away: "It's too early to really start rejoicing. There will have to be many more struggles. This is just a good beginning. We will have to keep our finger on the pulse, so as to take matters further." This sense of realism left all questions open. How will the new union function? How will it be set up? A delegate from the *Paris Commune* yard outlined a number of possibilities. "It's too early to discuss details. It will take three, four, maybe five months for us to clarify our ideas and discuss it in our newspapers. Then there will probably be elections in all the factories, and a big meeting of delegates who will elect a leadership, officials, and one person for the whole country, our leader." Why a leader? He didn't know... "I'll have to think about that". The second possibility would be immediate elections, followed by a national Congress. But he preferred the former. "I think that first we will have to consolidate our influence, discuss with the workers, keep them informed, negotiate with the government, and then, in those conditions, the elections will go off well. Because, you know, undesirable characters could quite easily get in if we are not careful. We have to protect what we have won, and the best protection is preparation.''

Another day, in the canteen, I was eating a plate of sausage and beans at the same table as a group of young delegates from Gdansk-Pruszcz. We passed the time of day, and my interpreter was telling typically Polish jokes. And then we came on to the subject of the government.

"From the start the strike committee has been clear on this. We are not interested in who's who in the government.''

"We are here to make sure they keep in line,'' explained a young woman. "The important thing is not personalities. We're not interested in personalities. The important thing is their relations with the unions.''

"Yes, but what exactly do you mean by good relations between the government and the free trade unions?''

"Very simple. We will elect a leadership of determined people, people who will not give way, hard-liners, intelligent people.''

The speaker was a teenager, proudly sporting his 'strikers' beard', who had no intention of letting himself be talked round. His eyes shone, and his workmates eagerly supported him. Then they started on the Polish jokes again.

In all these discussions I found the same kind of mood: a determination not to be manipulated a third time; a sharp awareness of their collective strength, of their solidarity; a hatred for corruption, for shoddy work and for waste. On the faces of these men and women there was a kind of smile, which some might say was simple-minded, but which is the smile produced by revolutions in progress. The devastating smile of great moments of working-class history.

On 28 August *Solidarnosc* published a long document which summed up the strikers' intentions. In the first place, they reminded their readers, there was no question of challenging the system's basic principles. Almost half the document was devoted to this theme, which was in no sense a 'tactical concession' to the regime. "The Polish worker of 1980 is a conscious, reasoning member of our society, who needs neither the big stick nor the placebo, because he is not afraid, and he is not out to cause trouble. The best proof of this has been the calm, the restraint and the discipline shown by the seaboard popula-

154

tion during recent years. Furthermore, the support for our positions, despite the inconveniences that people have had to put up with, is the proof that our positions are correct, as are the forms in which we have chosen to express them. The aim of our demands is not to question either the foundations of the socialist regime in Poland or Poland's position within international relations. We would not support anybody who tried to exploit the present situation to that end. On the contrary, we would oppose them." What was being contested was 'bad management policy', bad planning and bad management of the economy. As workers they were demanding the right to participate in decision-making. "It is for these reasons that our basic demand relates to the creation of free trade unions, because this is our only chance of avoiding major blunders in the future." This would mean that 'social injustices' would be abolished, and 'waste will be eliminated'. "We believe that a rationalisation of our economy will prove capable of satisfying our demands and also recovering the losses arising from the work stoppages — which were necessary for us to make our voices heard. (...) Above all, we have to create the conditions which will guarantee that these losses will not be repeated." Thus, the basic hopes of socialism were reconfirmed: "Nobody denies that the aim of socialism is the transformation of social relations. But the results that have been achieved thus far have been considerably lessened by the emergence of unfairly privileged groupings, by the imbalance between rights and obligations, by the gap which exists between the extent of power and the sanctions which would limit its utilisation. Anyway, we can no longer accept the present state of human relations in Poland, and the way in which our superiors treat their subordinates." In fact, "we want the regime to listen to the authentic voice of the working class, and not merely to the echo of its own words". This statement effectively summed up the principles of a true socialism.

On the same day, 28 August, the 'ideology and pedagogy section of the Central Committee of the Polish United Workers Party', published the Party's reply to the workers' first demand. Its line of argument revealed a characteristic bureaucratic narrow-mindedness. Its first postulate was as follows: 'Socialism, by eliminating class antagonisms, at the same time eliminates the socio-economic base for an opposition.' Second postulate: However, differing interests of different groupings (regional, professional) continue to exist, and the 'leading role of the Party constitutes a mechanism which guarantees the possibility of bridging these differences of interest at the level of the interests of the working class as a whole, and at the level of society's interests in general'. Conclusion: Setting up trade unions independent of the Party 'would give rise to a situation of dual power. Their activities would be contrary to our most urgent present needs, and would also tend to affect Poland's constitutional unity, our alliances, and consequently the balance of power in Europe and the world at large'. This line of reasoning had the merit of formulating two of Stalinism's principal dogmas, and of clearly defining the target: namely the monopoly of power held by the Party's apparatus. This principle is exactly the opposite of the principles of socialist democracy.

In fact, to imagine that socialism had 'eliminated class antagonism' was particularly absurd in Poland, which, in the course of 35 years, has known four big working-class uprisings. On the contrary, true socialism should guarantee to the working class *all* the necessary means for it to express itself in its *diversity*. In other words, the creation of parties, of unions, a diversity of associations, etc. To claim, as the Polish United Workers Party text does, that only the Party can handle these oppositions and differences is blithely to confuse political democracy with police repression. All the more so since this Party tolerated no opposition in its ranks. In conditions such as these, who other than self-proclaimed leaders could best appreciate the true interests of the working class?

The strikers had a very simple answer for this dogmatic-Stalinist gobbledygook: only the working class can decide what are the 'interests of the working class as a whole'. This split was not particularly an ideological argument; it merely concentrated two antagonistic points of view. Thus, the outcome of the negotiations between the government commission and the Inter-Enterprise Strike Committee would depend on the balance of power. Jagielski retreated when forced to recognise the extent of the working-class mobilisation, but he sought, and sometimes obtained, verbal concessions from the Inter-Enterprise Strike Committee, in the hopes that later, once this mobilisation had diminished, he would be able to dredge these words up in order to recover, by other means, the ground he had lost. For their part the strikers saw the existence of a free trade union and a working-class self-organised within it as the only solid guarantee of any final agreement. They had no confidence in fine words. And they also understood (by looking at the international context) the limits of their strength: they knew that they would have to seek a compromise. In conditions such as these, any final agreement would be the outcome of a subtle interplay in which words did not have the same meaning for the two protagonists, and where the only thing that counted was each party's assessment of its own strength. It took a week to get this agreement. A difficult week in which the pre-negotiations within the commission of experts did not always correspond to the needs of the thousands of workers gathered at the *Lenin* shipyard.

On Saturday 30 August the minister finally gave his agreement in principle to the first two demands. But this was by no means plain-sailing. Andrzej Gwiazda opened the session by reading the text which had been agreed by the commission of experts, on the first demand:

"1. The activities of the trade unions in people's Poland have not matched the hopes and aspirations of the workers. We think that it would be useful to create new, autonomous trade unions which would provide an authentic representation of the labouring class. We do not question the right of workers to continue to be members of the old union, and, for the future, the possibility of cooperation between the two unions will be studied.

"2. In creating new, independent and autonomous unions, the Inter-Enterprise Strike Committee undertakes that these will respect the principles outlined in the Constitution of People's Poland. The new unions will defend the workers' social and material interests, and have no intention of acting as a political party. They will be based on the principle of the social ownership of the means of production, the basis of the existing socialist system in Poland. They recognise that the Polish United Workers Party plays a leading role within the State, and they are not opposed to the existing system of international alliances. They wish to achieve for the workers suitable means of determination, of expression, and of defence of their interests. The government commission undertakes that the government will guarantee and assure that the independence and self management of the new trade unions will be respected, both as regards their organisational structures, and as regards their operations at all levels. The government will guarantee the new trade unions the fullest possibility of carrying out their basic functions in the defence of the interests of workers, with a view to satisfying the material, social and cultural needs of the workers. At the same time, it guarantees that the new unions will not be subjected to discrimination.

"3. The creation and function of the independent self-managed trade unions are in line with convention No. 87 of the ILO regarding trade union freedoms, and convention No. 97, concerning the right of association and collective negotiation; — these two conventions having been ratified by Poland. The proposed plurality of trade union representation will require changes of a legislative nature, in particular involving the laws of trade unions, workers' councils and the Labour Code.

"4. Strike committees at the level of individual enterprises will be enabled to transform themselves into institutions representing the workers, either as workers' councils, or workers' committees, or founding committees of the new self-managed unions. The Inter-Enterprise Strike Committee, as a founding committee of these unions, is at liberty to choose a suitable form of a trade union or an association covering the Gdansk seaboard. The founding committees will operate up until the statutory elections for the new union authorities. The government commits itself to create conditions which will permit the registration of the new trade unions outside the central Trade Union Council.

"5. The new trade unions must have a real possibility of intervening in the key decisions that affect the living conditions of workers, as regards the principles of allocation of national revenue between consumption and accumulation; the allocation of social consumption funds between varying objectives (health, education, culture); the basic principles for forms of remuneration and the orientation of incomes policy, particularly regarding the principle of automatic indexation of wages to inflation; the long-term economic plan, the orientation of investment policy, and changes in prices. The government undertakes to provide the necessary conditions for these functions to be carried out.

"6. The Inter-Enterprise Committee will create a centre of socio-professional research, whose aim will be an objective analysis of the workers' situation, of workers' living conditions, and of the means whereby their interests can be correctly represented. This centre will also produce expert research on the question of indexation of wages and prices, and will propose forms of compensation. The centre will also publish the results of its research findings. In addition, the new trade unions will have their own publications.

"7. The government will guarantee the respect of Article No. 1, paragraph 1, of the law on trade unions, dated 1949, which guaranteed to all workers the right to associate freely in trade unions. The new trade union being created will not be a member of the central Trade Union Council (CRZZ). We undertake that the new law on trade unions will respect these principles. At the same time, we will guarantee the participation of Inter-Enterprise Strike Committee representatives, or of representatives from the founding committees of the self-managed union and other workers' representatives in the drawing up of this law."

Then the Deputy Prime Minister made the following contribution:

"Ladies and gentlemen, I think we should call it a day for today. The negotiations have been long and difficult, with real differences being expressed. Let's start with the fundamental questions (...). In particular I refer to point No. 1 on the list of demands. As you have said yourself, Mr Chairman (*speaking to Walesa*), this point is the keystone of our agreement, and it is also the most difficult to put into practice. That is why we have had to discuss it in such minute detail. (*Wondering aloud*) I don't know what others will have to say on this subject...

"I would also stress that the other questions raised by you — and I think you will not disagree — are all equally important. They relate to wage demands, social demands, and the way of life of the working class and other social groups.

"Maybe some of you are not yet exhausted by these lengthy negotiations. The representative who welcomed us today told me: 'You don't come here often enough, Mr Minister'. Well, I don't think it's quantity that counts, but rather the fact of sorting out concrete questions. And I shall certainly be coming back more often... But we must be clear that the position which we take up today will be essential and fundamental in character. The content of the resolutions adopted will have a crucial effect on the degree of activity of the working class and other social strata in both the long and short term. (...)

"Gentlemen, I would like to mention two principal groups of problems. The first relates to the... how can I put it... political and ideological orientation of the new union... of the autonomous unions and other forms of worker-representation. I note with satisfaction that the Inter-Enterprise Strike Committee has taken a clear position on this. It stresses that these unions will be founded on the principle of social ownership, which is the base of the existing socialist system in Poland. They will also recognise the leading role of the Party within the State, and the continuation of the present system of international alliances. This means that they do respect and will continue to respect the constitution of the People's Republic of Poland. (*Applause*) The second group of problems concerns... how shall I say... the fullest, most democratic forms of representation of the workers; corresponding to the best possible defence and protection of the interests of the workers. This will be the role of the independent trade unions, and we will have to create the suitable conditions for them... as has already been said. Obviously we realise that before they can be registered, one will have to settle the details of their statutes, as well as setting up a founding committee for the new union. On the other hand, the strike committee already in existence could transform themselves into an ongoing form of working-class representation, which could be called.. one could give them various names: workers' committees, work committees, or maybe commissions. (...) I would just like to add one thing. On the basis of the political platform adopted here, the plenary of the Party's Central Committee wishes to clarify its position on the questions that involve us here. And I think I can say — I have come from Warsaw — that such a clarification will give a guarantee at the highest level that our agreement will be carried out. I heard one of you say: 'Today it's Jagielski who chairs the government commission, but in two or three weeks it could be somebody else.' Alright — so it should not be Jagielski, but the Party meeting in plenary session, who takes up a principled position on this business. Mr Chairman, I suggest that we initial the first point. And also the second point.''

Gwiazda: "I suggest that we read it out loud first, so that everyone is clear."

Jagielski: "Certainly, go ahead."

Gwiazda: "This is the agreed formulation on point No. 2.: 'The right to strike will be guaranteed in the new trade union law which is being drawn up. The law will define the conditions within which strikes can be called and organised, the methods by which one will resolve conflicts, and penalties in the event of violation of the law...' (*Noise in the hall*) Excuse me — we don't have a proper copy, I'll have to read from where it's been written in the margin. 'Articles 52, 64 and 65 of the Labour Code will not be used against the strikers. Until the new law is passed, the government guarantees to the strikers and to the people helping them individual security and the continuation of their conditions of employment.' "

Walesa; "As you have said, we can now take these two points as agreed. We can now sign."

Jagielski: "Yes... in short, Mr Chairman, I can accept them, but may I suggest... do we really need to write 'to the people helping them'? (*Uproar: shouting from the delegates' hall*) Think about it, gentlemen. I'm not expecting an immediate answer today... I'm asking you to reflect on this question carefully."

Walesa: "But we want this to be guaranteed by law. We will have to..."

Jagielski: "Alright, I accept! So as not to waste time."

Walesa: "Mr Deputy Prime Minister, there are people of goodwill who have assisted us; they have helped us..."

Jagielski: "I don't deny that. I have even thanked them myself..." (*Laughter, applause*)

Walesa: "Alright. Shall we sign?"

Jagielski: "I have no objection, none whatsoever."

Walesa: "Let's sign these two points, then."

Jagielski: (*Slowly, weighing every word*): "I simply wish to give you a guarantee, a guarantee from the highest level."

Walesa: "For my part, it is difficult to formulate things in that manner. I would say that... In short, at this moment it is not the highest level... (*Silence, followed by prolonged applause*).

Jagielski: "Right, shall we sign?"

It was seven minutes past eleven, on Saturday 30 August. They handed across their respective copies. Jagielski leaned over to write his initials. Their conversation then became muffled and inaudible to the delegates in the other hall. There appeared to be shouting, with the voices of Jagielski and Walesa coming over the top. Quite simply, the minister had removed from his text the word 'independent', in relation to the unions. Walesa pressed the point, repeating several times: 'independent, self-managed unions', and then he added: "this is the same formula which they signed in Szczecin". The conference hall applauded Walesa's every word. Jagielski gave way.

Jagielski: "Right, shall we sign?"

Walesa: "Let's sign!"

But the minister had not finished with his last-minute manoeuvres. For example, he suggested that the other demands should be handed over to a commission, on the basis of an agreement in principle, which he would very willingly give. There was no question of this. His suggestion was met with uproar in the hall. He did not press the point. Then he made another proposal.

Jagielski: "Let us adopt the following principle: I am now going to Warsaw, to the plenary session of the Central Committee. I shall report back on the first point, as we have initialled it — the essential point. Now, wouldn't it be better... here I am asking for an initiative from you... wouldn't it be better if we had... I hear that this is what they did at Szczecin; wouldn't it be better if we were to put out a communique on the basic points that we have considered. We could then end the strike and go home. I have an outline here; we could leave it to our experts, as last time. They could discuss them, couldn't they. As for myself, I shall come back this evening — now I might be late, but I shall try to be here by seven o'clock, even though it's not easy, as you know. It's Saturday, and... as they say, on Saturday you have to take pot-luck. (*Applause*) So, gentlemen. Either we commit ourselves to discussing every demand point by point, spending several hours on each one, or we accept what I have just said and we begin to implement it..."

Walesa: "Mr Deputy Prime Minster, there really is not much more work. We have made a lot of progress on the essential questions. Today it's Saturday, tomorrow it's Sunday...

Well, let's all do what we have to do. You will come back tomorrow, you will explain to us how things stand there, and we'll arrive at some sort of an agreement. Why run the risk of misunderstandings? (*Applause*) On Monday, we might be back at work, but first we want everything in black and white."

Jagielski: "It will be in black and white."

Walesa: "Let's not jump to conclusions. We will wait and see! (*Applause*) We're 90 per cent in agreement, but there are still a lot of things left hanging..."

Jagielski: "If we were to put something on paper..."

Walesa: "Mr Deputy Prime Minister, since we have almost reached agreement, since we are reaching an understanding, I would ask for the arrests in Warsaw to stop (*Applause*), so that they don't spoil what we have achieved. We're keeping in touch with Warsaw. If those arrested have done nothing wrong, I would ask that they be released..."

Jagielski: "But as soon as I heard of problems in Wroclaw, I sorted the business out. As regards Katowice, it's been settled. So..."

Walesa: "We've got a list here, for Warsaw — many arrests."

Jagielski: "Really?... But look, I was suggesting a final communique. The commission could be working on it till I get back."

Walesa: "Yes, of course..."

The minister read out his communique, but did not get much of a hearing. He was pressing for a return to work, as if not grasping the meaning of the mass of workers who had mobilised in the shipyard.

Walesa: "Mr Minister, I would suggest that we stop there. I'm sure that you still have a lot to do. The commissions will stay here and I hope that they will work as fast as possible. You say you will be returning, and I am sure that you will... While you are there, you should raise the problem of the people who have been arrested, so that this doesn't start again. We've almost reached an agreement, and those arrests really are pointless. In my opinion we could possibly end the strike even before Monday."

Jagielski: "Mr Chairman, it's my opinion that we really ought to settle matters today..."

Walesa: "If the experts manage to finish their work in

time. I can't really say... I don't know all the problems they're having to deal with."

Jagielski: "Let's all make a resolution. As president of the government commission, I commit all the members of that commission, and our experts, to do everything that is possible to settle this business, and to sign. There you are."

Walesa: "Mr Deputy Prime Minister, tomorrow is Sunday. I see no reason to hurry at this point. Let's do our best to make sure that both parties are satisfied... without hurrying too much."

Jagielski had to leave. It was 11.25. He drove off. Around the building where the strike committee was in session, the crowd was dense. They literally lifted Walesa off his feet and carried him towards Gate No. 1. They made the 'V for victory' sign, and chanted "Leszek! Leszek! May he live for a hundred years! A hundred years!"

The Inter-Enterprise Strike Committee chairman climbed up into a mechanical excavator and addressed the enormous crowd packed on both sides of the flower-decked gates. "We are continuing the strike today. The important thing is that this business is settled in a manner that we all decide together! (*Long applause*) The strike has produced results. Finally, alongside the so-called 'unions', we now have independent and self-managed unions. (*Ovation*) As regards the other points, we will be deciding on them soon. (*Ovation*) We have every right to be happy, because we have achieved a tremendous task — something that we still haven't got the measure of. But don't let anybody think that the rest will come as easily as this. Given all the problems, I didn't agree that we should try and settle all this in five minutes flat. (*Ovation*) We have held out for so long... and we will hold out for another day or two more, but calmly, slowly, discussing among ourselves, democratically (*Ovation*), as and when we need. Now, as you have seen, Mr Deputy Prime Minister has left for Warsaw... to do battle. (*Laughter*) All things considered, what he has done, he has done well... Also, we told him: 'If you don't come back, our next demand will be: We want the Prime Minister!' (*Ovation*) Right... I will have to excuse myself. Believe me, we've really got a lot of work. Now we have to start fighting for the other points. Points number three and four, on censorship and the Church, two very important points for us. (*Applause*) As regards censorship, we almost have an agreement. We will have our independent newspaper! (*Applause*) Once we've settled these four points, we will immediately have to decide on the rest, decide our sticking points, and where we can afford to be more flexible. But the essential point, which will enable us to make sure that the other points are put into effect, is the fact of what we have already got in black and white: the independent, self-managed trade unions! (*Ovation*) This is what we're going to have to knuckle down to now — we already have an outline of a statute for the union — the sort of statute that *we* want. But it was drawn up a bit too hastily, and we are probably going to have to modify it.

"One more thing. I'm sorry if this sounds a bit authoritarian, but we don't want to see any more bloodshed like in 1970. I would like to make a permanent rendezvous with you. Every 16 December we are going to gather again, here... yes, under the monument. (*Applause*) That date is set and fixed for ever, and the gathering will take place at some time between half past two and four o'clock in the afternoon. If I'm not there, well come and find me! (*Ovation*) OK. I must go now. I have to go and work. As soon as there is something to report, I shall come and tell you, because I am at your service. You can call me your servant!" (*Ovation, long applause*)

The crowd sang the Polish national anthem, and an ancient hymn. Their joy matched the magnitude of their victory. Tens of thousands of men and women, the whole population of the town, stayed there, as if surprised by a result which all had taken for a certainty. They talked in small groups; they hugged each other; they sang; they wept. Within the shipyard the praesidium members could hardly move for being harassed by strikers, and they patiently answered their questions. Everywhere they moved they were surrounded by groups of strikers. They signed people's copies of strike posters, as souvenirs. It was memento time. Throughout the yard people were taking leaflets, posters, notices, even religious pictures, to be signed by Walesa and the other members of the praesidium, and even by foreign journalists and by their workmates. After several attempts I finally managed to put a few questions to Anna Walentynowicz. What did she think of the agreement? "We are very happy, very happy. We have won a lot. In essence, all our demands are going to be met." Gathered around us, a group of about thirty strikers were listening. It began to rain. Somebody brought out an umbrella to shelter us. "On Monday," explained Anna, "we are going to found the new union. We will hang a huge banner over our temporary headquarters: 'Free and Self-Managed Trade Union'. We will even have a telephone. The only thing which is not very clear is how we will arrange a printing press for our newspaper." The newspaper will be an essential part of the new union. "Our work depends on it. It will inform, it will open its pages to discussion, it will allow us to argue a case. Up till now, we have only had *Robotnik Wybrzeza*, which has been semi-clandestine, often seized by the police, and put together with makeshift means." The paper would probably continue, but the trade union newspaper was a far more ambitious project: "We want to produce a daily, which will be on sale at newspaper kiosks. It will keep the title of the *Solidarnosc* strike bulletin. It will have to be printed officially, and we will pay for it from the new union's subscriptions. And if they refuse us access to the printing presses, we shall buy our own printing machines."

Her face looked tired after eighteen days of little sleep, but it still bore all the happiness of this strike. "All our prayers have basically been answered. The rest will come with the union. It is already operational. We believe that our victory will be total, and supported by everyone. My first stop when I get out of here will be to go to church, to thank God, who has helped us to bring all this about. You know, none of this was organised or planned. Everything happened spontaneously. It's been amazing. People understood immediately what had to be done. That was the miracle of our seaboard strike. It will bring about a great change for our people. And in the most difficult periods, I have to say, we were protected by the Czestochowa Madonna. We will have to pay homage to her too." But at the same time her optimism could not conceal a certain worry. This worry began to nag all the more insistently when the government commission still had not returned by late afternoon.

At four o'clock a group of actors from the Gdansk Wybrzeze Theatre put on a show in the Inter-Enterprise Strike Committee hall. People were in a happy, festive mood. Backed by the enthusiasm of the thousand or so people jammed into the small hall, they read pieces by Milosz, Mickiewicz and Norwid, as well as anonymous poems written by the strikers. The show was interrupted at about 5.00 pm so as to allow those who wanted to attend the short daily religious service in front of Gate 2. The hall emptied, the windows were opened to let some air in. Only a few groups of delegates stayed behind to discuss, in a shaft of sunshine that filled the hall, while in the corner others were preparing sandwiches. People were coming and going. Some of them proudly wore the new T-shirts, printed with the *Solidarnosc* logo. One French journalist was bartering with a pretty young woman delegate, to swop her T-shirt — and he succeeded. In the hall UPI's special correspondent dozed in a chair, unshaven, with his white check suit crumpled. A peaceful scene. Journalists, delegates and members of the praesidium alike were savouring this moment of relaxation.

Suddenly voices were raised. The evening's peace was broken by a man shouting angrily. First it was two people, having an argument. Then more joined in. "I tell you, it's contained in the text!" one speaker shouted, only to be drowned out by another: "No... the text says nothing precise on this." The argument spread to others, running through the hall like wildfire. As delegates returned peacefully from their prayers, they got caught up in it. One man got up: "We will have to go and find Leszek!" People packed into the hall.

Before long all the delegates, and all the journalists had arrived. The praesidium members also arrived. Discussion began immediately, without formalities. Outside, people were trying to hear, but there was a fault in the sound system. The atmosphere began to get tense. People were saying that the agreement was bad, that it recognised a leading role of the Party, that they had no guarantees on the political prisoners, and that the free union would be limited only to the seaboard. People were worried. Doubts had begun to affect the delegates. Walesa took the microphone and once again explained what the agreements meant. He analysed every detail, pointing out where compromises had been effected, and stressing the importance of the free trade union. He concluded: "It is not a total victory. Everything will depend on us." He was applauded at length, but a sizeable majority still protested. The delegates were tense and excited. The chairman of the strike committee, speaking closely into the yellow ball of the microphone, tried again to answer the speakers in the body of the hall.

"The other union? It will continue to exist... if it still has any members! No, you will not be paying for it. There will be two unions within each enterprise, that is all! The release of political prisoners? I have an assurance from the vice Prime Minister. That's enough for me.''

"We want it in writing,'' someone shouted. Others applauded.

The hall: "In writing! In writing!''

Walesa: "Let's vote on it.''

Everyone's hands shot up: the minister would have to commit himself in writing. The hall was momentarily pacified. The platform took advantage of this to read out messages of solidarity. Representatives of seven enterprises had just arrived from Krosno Odrzanskie. They explained that down there they had organised a warning strike, with the threat that if the seaboard workers' demands were not met, they would go on strike again. People applauded. The delegation from the University of Gdansk explained how their official trade unions had been transformed into a strike committee. They also called for autonomy for the University. Again, people applauded.

Then the debate restarted. Andrzej Gwiazda, as usual, spoke in a calm voice. The delegates listened attentively.

"I agree, and I understand your reservations. I was in the negotiating commission. It was very difficult. We had to fight over every sentence. It was impossible to extract more. In my opinion, despite a number of omissions, the text is not bad. They wanted a union which was only regional, but we refused to accept this. However, as a result, we had to accept a certain vagueness in the text. But nobody will be able to prevent us from collaborating with others. We know that other firms want to contact us; we have already received many letters, many telephone calls. Many small workplaces are saying that they want to take up our 21 points. This is excellent. Nothing can stop our agreement being picked up by others. As regards censorship, we have achieved important, concrete results. Unfortunately, censorship will not be totally abolished...! But it will be public, and controlled by a law. People will be able to make an appeal to tribunals, and the censors will be forced to justify themselves.''

Somebody interrupted him. He listened, and answered.

"Yes, I know. We are still far from an abolition of censorship, and it's not much, compared with what we wanted. But

168

it's a lot when you compare it with the present situation. (*Applause*) This is how it has been during the negotiations: you don't get everything that you want. Believe me, these negotiations have been really difficult... Will the new union be totally free and independent? The only guarantee is us ourselves... Even if there is not enough down in writing. In 1956 we achieved some good things, but in the end, everything disappeared. Believe me, this time it won't happen like that again. But if you now leave the Inter-Enterprise Strike Committee on its own, here, if you go home and go to sleep, then there will be a repeat of 1956. The workers' councils gave tremendous reason for hope, but in the end they were made ineffective. (*Applause*) We know that hundreds of thousands, millions of people think the same as us. And there too we have a guarantee. If we have accepted compromises, we knew that this was not the end of the story. It will continue. We know that the word 'solidarity' will stay; we will continue to defend our rights. Thank you." (*Applause*)

Henryka Krzywonos: "At the beginning, we had an agreement among ourselves: all for one, and one for all... (*Applause*) I am here to represent the UPK (*urban transportation*). They told us that they would grant all our demands. We refused, because we knew that we were too weak. We knew that we had to carry on. Now it's the same: if we all go home, we will lose everything!"

A voice from the floor: "That's right!" (*Applause*)

Gwiazda: "We have just sent the provincial government our list of people who have been unfairly persecuted. He will give the list to the Party plenary. It would be scandalous if we were to desert these people. While the whole of Poland remained silent, they were the only ones there to defend the workers. And they have been charged. We hope that they have already been released!" (*Applause*)

Florian Wisniewski: "The text of the agreement says that the Inter-Enterprise Strike Committee will not dissolve itself, and that it will be up to the Inter-Enterprise Strike Committee to create these new unions... But we should not be too smug. We cannot afford to sit back in our work until the unions see the light of day. There's no danger of getting isolated — everybody supports us. At the start, when we elected our delegates, we used to say: 'The right people in the right place'.

The same thing should apply in the unions. We will have to elect people we can depend on, people who, in difficult situations, will prove capable of making decisions in line with the interests of those who have elected them. Everybody knows that written declarations are no guarantee. The only really solid guarantee consists of all those who we have been able to rely on, all those who have their place here.''

Henryka Krzywonos: "One thing is clear: until we are certain that all those imprisoned have been released, until we are sure that the demands of every firm have been satisfied, I say: not a single bus will leave our depot!'' (*Ovation*)

Zdzislaw Koblynski: "Huta Warszawa has just telephoned. Their delegation is arriving. They are ready for strike action. The same goes for Nowa Huta, and the Jastrzebia mines. (*Applause*) It would be really crazy if those who have been helping us didn't get the same as us. It's impossible to imagine that we should have the right to form strong unions on the seaboard, and that they should not! (*Ovation*) We cannot agree to any document that says that the free unions will be limited to the coastline. I suggest that this phrase should be crossed out of the agreement. I'm not asking for a general strike, because that would cost Poland too dearly. But what we have won must be applicable to the whole country!'' (*Ovation*)

Gruszewski: "Listen. Today has been long and difficult. I have talked with a lot of people, and I understand that some people here want everything, straight away... so that they can go home happy in the knowledge that they have done a good job. But this is not possible. Our activities are only just beginning. We will have to take action again, because we can't hope to get everything straight away. For this, I think that our solidarity and our sense of responsibility, the things that have brought us all together here, are our principal strengths. Let's not start setting up factions now, committees of dissidents etc. Let's not start showing mistrust. I appeal to all of you. Now, as never before, we need solidarity...! Otherwise, we run the risk of never achieving our objective.'' (*Applause*)

There followed two hours of confused and passionate debate, in which arguments intermingled with solidarity messages, news announcements, rumours and sometimes demagogy. The delegates too were very tired. Behind all these words lay a lot of worry and uncertainty ("Were we right to call a halt there?'' one delegate asked me), a bit of discontent, and maybe also a feeling that it was still going to take a long time to really change things. It was nine o'clock in the evening; the hall began to empty. Outside night had already invaded the shipyard. There was a chill in the air. Everyone felt like getting some fresh air.

"People are uneasy, very uneasy," one woman delegate told me. "They're telephoning all the time; no one knows if they're going to come tomorrow... Also, there are people here who have not joined the strike, but who have got in here anyway. Nobody knows who they are."

Another woman told me: "We've already won a lot. But some people want to risk everything by insisting on getting every last point."

The atmosphere was not improved by rumours about what was happening at the Party's plenary in Warsaw. Jagielski had not arrived as he had promised. Had he gone back on his morning commitment? A Dutch communist journalist just returned from Warsaw seemed fairly well informed. He told me that at two o'clock that afternoon it seemed certain that Gierek was going to be replaced by Olszowski. What was being prepared? A showdown with the strikers? Who would come tomorrow morning: Jagielski, to sign an agreement, or the army to evacuate the shipyard? A lot of people would sleep uneasy in their beds that night.

Walesa went to reassure the enormous crowd which was waiting in front of the gates. His voice echoed comfortingly in the night: "(...) If, as some people are saying, the Party is hoping to impose its views on the union, and to run it, they are mistaken. The agreement is clear. The free unions will be those that we elect democratically, those that we decide. Each of us will have the union that we ourselves create. To be sure, there will be problems in small enterprises, because they will need at least one hundred workers before they can register. But they will have to cooperate with each other. We suggest that small enterprises combine among themselves, so as to build up enough strength in order to be recognised. We already have two outlines for a statute for the union, but these are only outlines as yet. It's possible that they may be wholly revised; they will certainly be improved. When people say: 'Improve them', then we will improve them. It's true that not everything is perfect. But believe me, we'll get there... We can already see the light at the end of the tunnel... We will get there. I hope that there's going to be no trouble, no outrages. We know that there are provocateurs in our midst; there are people who don't like what is happening. But they will not be given the chance. We must prevent them from acting. We might still lose. We must not let slip our chance of winning, because it is just possible..." The crowd listened to him, silently at first, and then warming to his speech. Their chants and their hymns warmed the heart.

The next day, Sunday 31 August, after a mass attended by many thousands of people, Deputy Prime Minister Jagielski reappeared. He too was very tired. He confirmed his undertaking of the preceding day; he promised that the political prisoners would be released; and within an hour, he had signed the agreement drawn up by the commission of experts on all the other points. By four o'clock in the afternoon it was certain that all the people detained would be released within 24 hours. The Deputy Prime Minister and the Inter-Enterprise Strike Committee praesidium proceeded to the delegate hall for the signing ceremony. It would be broadcast that same evening on national television.

In their closing speeches Walesa and Jagielski congratulated each other on the way the negotiations had gone — 'as between Poles'. But while the minister was stressing the necessity of a return to work in order to make up for lost time, the chairman of the strike committee was pointing out the importance and also the limitations of the agreement. "We have achieved everything that it was possible to achieve in the present situation. We will also go on to achieve what we still have not achieved, because to that end we now have one most important thing: our independent, self-managed trade union! This is our guarantee for the future. We have not only fought for ourselves, for our own interests. We were fighting for the country as a whole. You all know the tremendous solidarity we have received from the working people. The whole country has been with us. In the name of those working class forces who went on strike, I would address myself to all those who have supported us: we have fought together, and we have also fought for you. We have won the right to strike, we have received guarantees of certain civil liberties, and, most importantly, we have won the right to an independent trade union. All working people are now able, *voluntarily*, to form their own unions. They have the right to create an independent and self-managed union!''

Thus the final agreement was a compromise, but a compromise which was favourable to the workers. In order to appreciate its value, one would have to examine the balance of forces in Poland on that day of August 31. The determination and the level of organisation of the workers in Gdansk, Gdynia and Sopot had reached their highest point. From all over Poland messages of support were arriving, together with ultimatums to the government. Already some of the main enterprises in Silesia, Warsaw, Lublin and Wroclaw had struck for several hours, some of them for the whole day, and were ready for a general strike on 1 September. In fact in Silesia, this general strike went into effect for the first four days of September. Without the Gdansk agreement, it would also have been inevitable, even if this was not what the workers particularly wanted. It would have cost Poland very dearly. In addition, at Szczecin and Elblag the first signs of weakness had appeared; the strikers had signed separate agreements, so reducing the strength of the movement. While there was postal contact between the Inter-Enterprise Strike Committee and the principal strike centres, there was, however, no national representation of the movement. Gdansk effectively acted as the mouthpiece, the spearhead of the movement, but there was no organisational cooperation between the various strike leaderships. So, they couldn't coordinate a general strike. In addition, it was bound to lead to a showdown with the regime, in a context where the only way that the State apparatus could save itself would be via 'fraternal aid'. While the working class had a number of good tactical positions, it was still too weak to engage in such a confrontation with any hope of victory.

For the regime, the situation was even worse. It appears that the plenary session of the Party's Central Committee that weekend had been taken up with bitter factional infighting. For the first time in a long time the meeting was held totally in closed session. Contrary to normal custom, for example, the shorthand writers who usually took down the proceedings were not allowed into the hall. None of Gierek's speech was published officially. People were expecting his resignation, which had already been reported unofficially. The only thing to come out of this silence were the names of the speakers: the two Deputy Prime Ministers who had negotiated at Gdansk and Szczecin, and Stanislav Kania, secretary of the Central Committee, member of the politburo and responsible for the police. We will probably never know the details of that meeting. However, it is public knowledge that one group was very strongly in favour of a confrontation. According to a number of 'rumours' circulating later in Warsaw, this group (which apparently included Gierek) had won a majority, against a minority which had comprised, in addition to Barcikowski and Jagielski (the negotiators), the functionaries responsible for police (ie Kania) and army, who were not too sure of their troops. This was the reason why they eventually carried the day. According to other reports, on 31 August the State of Emergency was already at an advanced stage of preparation, and some people were predicting that the port of Gdansk would be blockaded and the *Lenin* shipyard evacuated by force. In the streets of Gdansk itself, the police presence was not particularly evident, but a number of university cities already housed numerous reinforcements of special militia groups from the Golendzinow school, which trains anti-riot units. It was even claimed that they were preparing to use paralysing gases in order to wipe out any resistance. But these official plans foundered somewhat on the rocks of a more complex reality. Within the army, there were signs indicating a degree of sympathy for the strikers' actions. A number of units had received the Inter-Enterprise Strike Committee bulletin, and on the Sunday a group of soldiers came to the *Lenin* shipyard to inform the workers that a number of their comrades were starting a hunger strike in support of them. In front of the shipyard it was not unusual to see sailors standing and watching the course of events. In other towns manifestations of discontent were also reported among the militia. At Lublin, for example, certain militiamen refused to go to Gdansk as reinforcements. Finally, within the Party itself, as we have seen, the repercussions of the strike were enormous. Many meetings in workplaces limited themselves to gathering people's opinions. Sometimes even cell meetings, or secretariat meetings, were not held, often 'for fear of not being able to answer people's questions'.

Thus, neither of the two parties in the situation had, at

that moment, sufficient means to defeat the other. But each held a number of trumps which would force the other to compromise. The strength of the strikers lay in their unity, and the support which their struggle had aroused within the country as a whole; the strength of the government was reduced, basically, to the support it could expect from abroad.

The future will show who holds the best hand.

9. Solidarity in the Countryside

André had spent most of the month of August near Saint-Lô, in Britanny. He was a technician, currently unemployed, and earned his living by doing research for the agricultural census bureau. He was also a trade unionist, a member of the CFDT. It had been a miserable summer, with nothing much to look forward to — not even a steady job for September. Like thousands of many young agricultural workers in the region, he faced an uncertain future. But a ray of sunshine had shone through the rainy summer — the fact of the strikes in Poland. The newspapers were full of them. André read them all, and told himself that it would be a good idea to go to Poland, to see things at first-hand. Anyway, he needed a holiday, and he still had some savings left...[23]

Warsaw, early October: André climbed to the second floor of No. 5 Szpitalna Street. A bustling crowd packed into the three rooms of an old apartment which served as the new union's local headquarters: there were notice boards covered with leaflets, messages, and addresses which people were copying down. Behind the tables two young people patiently answered questions, and handed out information to people who had come to register their unions. Did they have the right to demand a notice board in their factories? How do you organise a meeting? Is it true what the plant director has been saying, that if you join Solidarity you lose your social benefits? A mass of problems, to which a young Ursus worker — presumably an old hand in the free unions — was paying careful attention. In Mazowsze (the Warsaw region), the building of the new independent organisation was a slow process. There were a large number of small enterprises, and their managements were behaving arrogantly. Obviously, in big factories like FSO, Ursus or Huta Warszawa the union was organised very quickly. There was already a tradition, and strike committees for the general strike had already been set up at the end of August. But elsewhere there was a lot of fear to be overcome.

André looked for someone who would be able to help him. Marta, who spoke French, pointed out Wieslaw Kecik to him. Kecik was a KOR member responsible for the agriculture sector. This was the reason that had brought André to Poland — to find out about the situation in the countryside, so that he could report back to the peasants in his own region, perhaps to organise some kind of support action. Wieslaw welcomed him warmly. With a mixture of French and English they managed to make themselves understood.

The following day André and Wieslaw took the road to Torun, travelling by bus, by train, and by hitchhiking. It was a fine day, and they had time to spare. Wieslaw was looking to set up a network of contacts in order to establish the new peasant union. At the end of the afternoon they arrived at the house of a young farming couple, Michal and Anna, who farmed 5 hectares of land in Dobrzejewice commune. They had two children. As Wieslaw had explained to him during their journey, "In Poland the majority of agriculture is private, but the farms are small." This farm was medium-sized. They had a milk-cow and a horse; they raised 24 pigs per year, as well as harvesting corn, potatoes and beet.

The house itself looked fairly dismal. You reached it by an earth track which obviously would not carry any kind of large load. A number of cows were dozing in the middle of a field. In an unfenced orchard there were apple trees and five or six plum trees. It was a low-roofed house, and the out-buildings were too small to shelter machinery during the winter. They were mainly used for storing fodder and the animals.

Inside were a television, a radio and a fridge, but no running water. A nearby well provided water for the house and the animals.

They had a drink, and Michal immediately went off around the village on foot to gather some of the peasants. Out of the fifty or so families living in the village, Michal and Anna were among the youngest.

"There are only two young couples in this village," Anna explained. "It's not easy to get started. In some ways we were lucky. Michal first worked for 20 years in factories: six years at Gdansk shipyard, and then fourteen years in a factory in Torun.

He used to live here, and helped my father in the fields. Anyway, he didn't really have any choice. It was impossible to find lodgings in town. When my father died, he wanted to take over the farm. But it was impossible to find long-term credits. We had to take out two successive loans of six months apiece, at an interest rate of 1 per cent per month. Luckily we were able to find an interest-free private loan, in the end. Otherwise it would have been impossible to survive on the farm.''

André was amazed: "Not very encouraging..."

"For children, for example, the situation is incredible! We've only got one primary school for all 34 villages in this commune.''

Wieslaw was worried about the effects of the rainy summer. The rain had been almost continuous, and the harvests must have been very bad.

Anna exclaimed: "It's shameful! We have slaved away all summer, in dreadful conditions, and do you know what they have offered us as compensation for the bad weather? A starvation-level subsidy! And even that only applies for 'improved' land. As if we could afford to improve the output of our land, with the money that they give us...''

She explained to André:

"We have to fight for everything we need — chemical fertilisers, fodder, feed for our pigs. You can't even get coal. Imagine it, in Poland, one of the biggest coal producers in the world! The other day Michal sold a pig. This gave him the right to a voucher to buy 350 kilos of coal. Well, we couldn't find a single gramme of coal. There's none left! And on TV they say the production has been *up* this year.''

In Warsaw, Wieslaw had heard that the peasants of this village had protested against the government's selective subsidy policy.

"That's right," Anna replied. "We got together to demand that everybody should receive the same amount. This farm will eventually receive an indemnity of 40,000 zloty.''

A small victory then, even though, every year, they have to find 4,000 zloty just to insure themselves against fire, accident and bad weather. Since 1972 this insurance had also covered sickness.

"The truth is that it's very hard to live here," Anna confessed.

André inquired: "Do you ever think of moving into town?"

"From a strictly economic point of view perhaps that would be better. But at least in the country you know who you're working for. You're independent, you run your own business, despite harassment from the administration. So we stay here. And just so as to make ends meet, Michal has to work several days a month for a neighbouring peasant. He's helping him to build greenhouses."

"And if the situation continues to get worse?"

"Well, we will be forced to move into town," she answered sadly.

André was familiar with this preference for independent work, where you can measure precisely the results of your own efforts. It's the same feeling that motivates many young farmers in France — sometimes André himself.

It was eight o'clock. Michal returned and took his guest to the house of a neighbour, where a dozen or so farmers from the village were waiting. Some men, and two women, almost all over the age of 50. They met in the kitchen, where all the chairs had been brought down from various parts of the house. The decor was sober: a sink, some furniture dating from the 1950s, and a big stove which heated the whole house. They were served tea — no alcohol. The farmer's son acted as secretary, and took notes. André sat at one end of the table. The meeting began immediately. Everybody put their point of view. The women were very forceful. Wieslaw was a bit worried at the low attendance, but they explained: "Everybody here will join the union, but this evening we didn't have time to notify everyone." Those who were free had come spontaneously, with no hesitation. The others, they assured him, were in agreement. Then they gave reports on their individual situations, and talked about demands.

"I've got seven hectares," said one woman. "I sell a hundred pigs per year. I have no cows. Now, everyday, I have to queue from five in the morning so as to get five kilos of food for the animals. When I get there, there are already thirty people waiting."

Somebody else, with only five hectares, explained: "Our farms are small. I'm the only one working on my land. My son works in the factory, and I'm not sure that he will take over the farm when I retire. Should I leave it to the State?''

"Me, I'll never retire," interrupted a sixty-year old farmer. I'll always live better by working, even if I have to leave part of my land uncultivated."

And so it went on, for more than an hour. This was the second meeting of this kind in the village. At the first there had been about fifty participants. But it was difficult to notify everyone. To set up the union, Wieslaw still had to depend on the network of addresses which had been drawn up by KOR. Wieslaw had thought of making the union platform known via the offices of the Church, but would that really have been sufficient?

André asked whether the Gdansk strike had had a big effect.

"It changed everything," they all replied at once. "Previously we could only think about things, and talk among ourselves. It was difficult to say publicly what we wanted, because of the way the administration and the police used to react. Now, though, it's like a breath of fresh air."

"What's more, the administration has become a lot more careful, a lot more polite in its dealings," an old woman added. "You no longer see the militia out in the streets."

"It's a new era, we feel more free," a young man confirmed.

"But are all the peasants going to follow you?" André asked.

"The state of agriculture in Poland is tragic, catastrophic. Economic life is at a standstill. There are no more goods, no more fertilisers, no more fodder for livestock. We have no coal, no sugar, no coffee, no bread... We're very worried about the winter."

"All the peasants are in agreement with us. The situation is the same everywhere."

"We don't believe in the administration's methods. There is only one solution to get us out of this: to rely on the new social situation developing, and on the peasants' union which is being set up."

André wanted to know the demands of the peasant union, so that he could report back to his friends in Normandy. He wrote in his notebook. They gathered round him, all speaking at the same time. Wieslaw only just managed to keep up with his translation.

"Individual farmers must be guaranteed the ownership of their land."

"Higher prices."

"We need coal, fodder for our livestock, fertilisers and electricity."

André continued writing.

"We need credits without excessive interest rates..."

"And longer term," added someone else.

"Agriculture is going to have to be mechanised, but not too much," a third added, cautiously.

"So you want to change everything?" André asked.

"And how!" replied a woman who was somewhat younger than the others. "When you see the way they treat us when we're sick! No medicine, no doctors..."

"We are demanding true equality with the rest of the population," said Michal. "Too often people accuse the farmers of not working, of only thinking of themselves, of being responsible for the present level of poverty..."

"And what do you think of Kania?"

"Kania? He will do the same as the others — he will let us down. No confidence!"

The atmosphere was becoming heated, and the presence of a French trade unionist encouraged people to speak. "That's it, that's what we ought to be saying". André could see that these men and women were worn out, and that they lived no better than their counterparts in the most remote corners of the French countryside. But one demand had amazed him: this attachment to individual property. The next day he talked about it with Wieslaw, on the road.

"The land is their tool. But the government has a right to take over any piece of land that falls vacant, or is put up for sale. There is a permanent threat of 'collectivisation'. Also, when a peasant 'farms his land badly', they can take it away from him. If you add to that the amount of wastage on the State farms, you will begin to understand. To demand a guarantee of individual ownership is, in a sense, to demand a guarantee of employment and of control over your work."

After a few more visits André was also to realise that if the small peasantry were opposed to cooperatives, this was mainly because of State favouritism. They were not opposed to cooperation as such, to the sharing of machinery, etc, but they wanted to manage things themselves. This feeling was also stimulated by the mobilisation under way in Poland. Nonetheless, behind this demand he sensed a trace of conservatism, an attachment to this 'privilege' of not selling yourself as a worker would sell himself to management. This sentiment was particularly common among the older peasants, who made up the majority.

In fact, Poland, together with Yugoslavia, is one of the few 'socialist' countries where the majority of agricultural production derives from family farms. In 1978 the socialised sector provided 20.9 per cent of agricultural production, 17.5 per cent from State farms (PGR) and 3.4 per cent from the cooperatives. The rest, that is to say almost 80 per cent, was produced by more than 3 million individual farms, with a size ranging from 0.5 to 10 hectares or more. However, as in all the 'people's democracies', the regime had at first attempted a general collectivisation. After having distributed the lands belonging to the large landowners to the small peasantry in the post-War period, it began in 1950 a campaign of restructuration. The 1950-55 Six Year Plan embarked on an intensive programme of industrialisation, matched by punitive measures against the 'remnants of the capitalist class'. It forced farmers to deliver part of their potato, corn and meat production to the State, which bought them at low prices. In this way it hoped to provide itself with a source of accumulation to assist its industrialisation effort, which was centred on heavy industry. At the same time, it launched a drive for the collectivisation of land, encouraging by every means the formation of cooperatives. The results were disastrous. This policy represented neither a voluntary choice of the peasantry nor an appreciable improvement of the situation. On the contrary, the priority given to heavy industry resulted in lower and lower prices for agricultural products, and did not favour the production of chemical fertilisers or machinery. The peasantry began to withdraw into themselves, and produced only for their own consumption. Only six per cent of small farmers joined cooperatives, despite the official pressure to do so; the others tended to farm only for their own needs, and overall agricultural production levels sank dangerously low. In 1956 Gomulka tried to reverse the situation. A short while later, the III Congress of the Polish United Workers Party denounced the mistaken policies, which had been characterised 'by excessive charges; by an unsatisfactory supply of means of production to peasant farms; by an assault on the principle of freedom of association, at the time of the creation of production cooperatives; by the bureaucratisation of the management system; and by the underestimation of the self-managed socio-economic activity of the peasantry.' By then the cooperatives were increasingly being deserted.

Gomulka's new agricultural policy envisaged a gradual and flexible socialisation, in line with principles which, in broad outline, were also common to earlier governments in Poland.[24] This entailed, on the one hand, progressively reducing charges that weighed on the individual farmer (credits, taxes, compulsory tithes), and investing more in machinery and fertilisers, and, on the other hand, encouraging mutual cooperation among the peasantry by means of 'agricultural clubs'. These clubs, which were inherited from the peasants' traditional cooperative organisations, were, from 1956 onwards, to become a social, political and economic lever for the government. Thus, for example, the difference between the market price of agricultural products, and the lower price at which the State bought within the framework of compulsory tithes, was reversed by means of a development fund linked to these clubs. Seventy five per cent of this money was required to be used for purchasing machinery which would be made available to everybody by the inter-village clubs.

However, this new orientation, despite some improvements in incomes, mechanisation, fertiliser supplies and availability of funds, was to founder because of the power politics and machination of an all-powerful bureaucratic apparatus. The head of the commune and the local Party secretary reigned as autocrats, deciding on every issue. The various agricultural reforms made no provision whatsoever for farmers to be democratically involved in decision-making. In addition, choices made in the industrial field were not always designed to match decisions relating to the countryside. Thus, on a number of occasions, agriculture was to run into serious difficulties.

First, in the mid-1960s, despite a considerable amount of investment, supplies of building materials were never sufficient, and this put a brake on modernisation of livestock buildings. Furthermore, there was a permanent shortage of fodder and the socialised sector had first claim on agricultural machinery — which was produced in small quantities and which was often unsuited to the structure of Polish agriculture. Finally, the food industry remained notoriously backward, at a time when, with the growing urbanisation of the population, it should have been playing a decisive role in feeding the cities. Gomulka succeeded in aggravating the crisis further still in 1956, by deciding to reduce imports of cereals and increasing their price to farmers by 20 per cent. The prices of animal products, on the other hand, hardly changed at all. The consequences of this move for pig production were catastrophic, and the government had no other choice than to raise the consumer price of meat suddenly in 1970. We know what that led to.

Gierek attempted to correct the situation by completely abolishing a new investment programme, and by embarking on an enormous programme aimed at the 'improvement of supplies to, and the development of, agriculture' (adopted by the Sejm in November 1974). However, yet again, after a slight improvement, the overall results were to be disastrous. Gierek was effectively trying to kill two birds at once: on the one hand he was trying to bring agricultural production back to a level where it could adequately supply the country's needs; on the other hand he was trying, despite all the disappointments of the past, to accelerate the socialisation of the countryside. His experts were working on a forecast for 1990 of an agricultural sector comprising 50 per cent socialised farms, and 50 per cent family farms of 20 hectares apiece, all profitable and adequately mechanised. This second objective, which corresponded most closely to the interest of local bureaucrats and the large peasantry, was to take the upper hand. At first, the abolition of compulsory tithes encouraged the small peasantry to expand their output. They could now get a better price for their animals. But the State still remained the principal customer for most of their production. And the State itself fixed prices. In addition, selling to State bodies was an indispensable precondition for obtaining the tokens necessary to acquire fodder or coal. The free markets bore witness to the poverty afflicting these small farmers. André saw it for himself in Lipno. Two old peasants were laying out on the pavement the scanty produce of their farm: a crate of pock-marked apples (which would have been unsaleable in France), a few pears, potatoes, flowers... They had arrived, as they did every week, in their horse-drawn cart, as sad as their surroundings.

The political choices made by the regime in no way helped matters. The systematic priority given to State farms and cooperatives in the allocation of fertilisers, fodder and equipment, only increased the difficulties of small farmers. Suspicious, and lacking in the necessary means, the small peasantry began to reduce their production of animals, and turned to mixed farming (particularly of vegetables). At the same time production in the socialised sector did not show a corresponding growth. As a result meat production stagnated. Whereas, in 1970-74, Poland's cattle population had risen from 10,843 thousand head to 13,023, in the years that followed it no longer progressed.[25] Even worse, in 1976 and 1977, because of a lack of fodder and of energy, there was a massive slaughtering of pigs, which was hard to make up for in the years to come. And those were years during which the population's food requirements continued to increase. Finally, 'in order to maintain consumption levels, in 1977 the government was obliged to reduce traditional exports of meat and meat products, and in 1977 and 1978 even resorted to massive imports of meat. The balance of trade for agricultural and food products, traditionally in the black, went into deficit in 1978.' The deficit was accounted for largely by purchases of cereals and fodder. All this introduced a new factor of instability, inasmuch as agricultural prices were spiralling upwards on the world market, as a result of the crisis which was raging in the capitalist world. But in addition to these miscalculations, the lack of progress in the food industry (despite large-scale investments) and the energy industry were to act as a continuing brake on the growth of agricultural production, including that of the large farms.

André, whose trip had now taken him to the north-west of the country, visited a farm of some 18 hectares near Lipno. The owner, a 50-year old man, spoke French. He worked alone, while his wife was a judge in the town. The house was large and comfortable: television, central heating, a fridge... Cultivated people, with a well-stocked bookcase.

He had 15 head of cattle, of which seven were milk cows.

They each produced, on average, 4,500 litres of milk per year. A good output, thought André, compared with the Calvados, where the average is 3,500-4,000 litres per year. On the other hand, production from the land was not so successful. The farmer grew corn, potatoes and sugar beet, over an area of 12 hectares. He produced only 35-40 quintals of corn per hectare (compared with 56 that year, in Calvados).

This farm was a model for those 50 per cent large family farms that Gierek's experts dreamed of. It enjoyed a number of advantages, including good equipment. "Here we have everything we need," the farmer explained to André, "a harvester, a haymaker, a trailer, an elevator, etc. But it has cost us a lot!" He had been the first person in his commune to possess a tractor. He had to pay 200,000 zloty for it (cultivation of one hectare would bring him an average of 15,000 zloty per year), and getting it involved long hours of bureaucratic procedures. "If you want to get stuff, the only way to get it is to grease the palm of some official. You won't get anything for less than a 1,000 zloty backhander." And that was not all. The man led André to the end of a barn and showed him a brand new milking machine, lying there. "We can't use it, because there are too many electrical blackouts..." Also a lot of farms still did not have 30-amp power supplies. This, then, was the situation in the best farm out of this commune which comprised five villages, and where, on average, each farmer farmed between 10 and 12 hectares.

The fact is that Gierek's policy — continuing that of Gomulka — had more than just a passing influence on people's consumption patterns in Poland. Its effect was a profound remodelling of the Polish countryside. A number of its 'innovations' were now a brake on any short-term improvement.

While successive governments were working towards a development of the socialised sector, and of the large modern farms, at the same time one was seeing an increasing subdivision of the land. Between 1950 and 1978 the proportion of small farms of between 0.5 and 2 hectares increased by ten per cent (from 20.9 per cent to 30.5 per cent, while the proportion of large farms of ten hectares and more only grew by one per cent (12.8 per cent to 13.7 per cent). At the same time, medium-sized farms diminished in number by 11 per cent (66.3 per cent to 55.9 per cent). In addition, in 1978 most available cultivated land belonged to farmers aged 55 or over. The only farms managed by young people were those of between 15 and 20 hectares.

The small farms gave rise to the phenomenon of the 'peasant-worker', that is to say a section of people who split their time between the factory and the fields. The existence of these people inevitably influenced both the nature of agricultural production (vegetables rather than livestock) and its productivity.[26]

Finally, it is estimated that today between 900,000 and 1,000,000 hectares of cultivatable land are lying fallow, inasmuch as a Party directive has forbidden them to be sold to the peasants after the death of an owner with no heir. It would be impossible for all this land to be taken over by the cooperatives or the State farms. In general it consists of small, dispersed strips of land. In recent years that Party directive has been relaxed somewhat, but its application depends on the local administrators, who are often shortsighted in their attitudes.

As their train wound its way across the plains of Poland, Wieslaw pointed out some new houses to André. "The old peasants," he said, "are frightened that the State is going to take their land. So they spend all their savings. These houses have every comfort: central heating, running water and toilets. They will be used for their children, who have difficulty finding accommodation in town." These buildings were by no means splendid. They were just boxes, scattered here and there on land that had been left fallow.

Rather than an accumulation of capital, one was seeing a decapitalisation of private agriculture. In France, for example, a peasant would invest his first savings in order to buy a milking machine or a shed for his cows. Some of them even have hot water in their milking hall before they have it in their own apartments.

Profiteers doubtless exist within Polish agriculture, but they are only rarely to be found among the small farmers. For this, one would have to look among large landowners, like the market gardener whom André and Wieslaw went to visit near Gdansk. The man was about 40 years old. His wife did not work, and he employed a worker. His house was large and new, built in the style of a French doctor's house. The rooms were decorated to excess, and in bad taste. Here was a nouveau riche, showing off his money. He showed them into the living room: wall-to-wall carpeting and a well-stocked drink cupboard — champagne, liqueurs, aperitifs... Outside, the lawn was impeccable. The garage was equally well-stocked, with a small lorry and a smart Mercedes. He took his guests to visit the greenhouses. They were well-maintained: according to the season, they housed flowers or vegetables.

The market-gardener was in favour of the peasants' union, and in fact had already joined it. André inquired of the vice-president of the union, who had come along with them:

"Don't these kinds of members pose problems for you?"

"All peasants have the right to join the union."

However, he had to admit that this one was a bit of a special case.

André found it hard to forget the poverty which he had repeatedly encountered as he crossed the plains of Poland, past lakes and enormous forests. He was haunted by the enormous number of small plots of land which surrounded the few large State farms. On the road he still came across people travelling on foot, on bicycles or in horse-drawn carts — being overtaken by the occasional bus, by cars and lorries. He had a general impression of a poverty which was not improved by those rainy autumn days.

He wasn't particularly enthusiastic about the 'socialist' sector either. He did not in fact visit those 8,000 hectare State farms of which the regime was so proud. But people showed him the grey apartment blocks, on the edges of villages, where the agricultural workers lived. Not particularly cheerful.

The fact is that for years that sector had made little progress. In 1978, as we have seen, it provided only 20.9 per cent of overall agricultural production (compared with 18 per cent in 1970). But the important thing was that it was constantly in deficit, and was a source of enormous waste. There was no overall study which would allow one to assess the extent of this waste, but some examples published in the press were indicative in themselves. On the basis of official inquiries undertaken in the south-east of the country, the weekly *Kultura* quoted a number of cases. For example, at the Smerek cooperative the cost of producing one kilo of meat was 175 zloty, instead of the 28 zloty planned for. A litre of milk on a State farm in

Lutowiska cost 35 zloty to produce (and would be worth 4 zloty on the market!). These were particularly bad examples, uncovered by State inspectors, but they were not exceptional. On the contrary, on State farms and cooperatives it was customary to plan your losses. And as usual, loss forecasts were always exceeded. At Gruszowice a State farm had forecast a 15,800,000 zloty loss for 1979; in fact, despite millions of zloty injected in loans and subsidies, it turned in a loss of more than 58,000,000. At Lubaczow another PGR (State farm) which had planned for 41,900,000 zloty losses, had losses of nearer 115,000,000. In cases like these grant aid from the State served to make up for money wasted. At Medyka, one of the best PGRs in the region, which had forecast a 35,000,000 zloty loss, received 38,900,000 subsidies in order to cover its losses (in fact it was only to lose 21,600,000 zloty). The *Kultura* article quoted other examples of this kind, in which losses exceeded grant aid: at Lubaczow, Rzeszow and Stubno. The author then demonstrated how the farms that were least wasteful were those which took the lowest subsidies. This led to absurdities like the following, observed at Lubaczow: a kilo of meat cost 2,250 zloty to produce on a State farm, and 28 zloty on a private farm. In effect, the price of fodder for a kilo of meat on the hoof differed according to whether the fodder was produced in a PGR, or by an individual farmer. In the former case, a ton of hay cost around 5,000 zloty, and in the latter 2,200. This fact led to a ridiculous situation. The cooperatives preferred to leave their land fallow and buy their fodder from the small peasants, because it was less expensive. This was the case, for example, at the Chorkowka and Korcyn cooperatives. Each of them bought in their fodder from outside, at an overall cost of more than 4,000,000 zloty. Another cooperative, at Krzywcze, left 16 hectares of land lying fallow. The output of that cooperative was a lot less than the next-door farm which belonged to an individual peasant. The cooperative produced 7.5 quintals of barley per hectare, compared with 22 quintals produced by its neighbour. The same difference applied to rye: 12.1 quintals per hectare, compared with 20 quintals next door. Moral: the cooperative used to buy its barley and rye from its delighted neighbour. At Rozwienica the inspectors discovered a similar situation. At Zagorze the cooperative's harvest achieved something like half the output produced by individual farmers, even though it received the best grains, mineral fertilisers, machinery etc. As regards livestock, the picture was no better. The article's author concluded: "We must say loud and clear that farms like this should not be allowed to exist. We cannot accept having to pay for excesses like these. We are short of meat, milk, and bread — and with waste on this massive scale, it is hardly surprising."

This picture of the socialised sector is certainly exaggerated — even though nobody could give you a precise assessment of the situation in the country as a whole — but at least it shows one thing: the priority given to the socialised sector is a priority for corruption and waste. It has put excessive strain on agricultural production as a whole, and discourages individual small peasants from combining together in cooperatives. They see absurdities like these every day with their own eyes.

Finally, the productivity of Polish agriculture was the lowest out of all the socialist countries, with the exception of the USSR. The daily *Zycie Warszawy* published in September 1980 a comparative table of the average harvest in 1977-78. In Poland the average output was 28.9 quintals per hectare for barley (USSR, 17.1; Czechoslovakia 38.6); 30.7 quintals per hectare for corn (USSR, 17; Czechoslovakia 42.3); 297 quintals per hectare for sugar beet (USSR, 248.5; Czechoslovakia 353); and finally 182 quintals per hectare for potatoes (USSR, 120; Czechoslovakia 170).[27] Polish figures were among the worst in Europe, even though Poland has one of the best soils for growing potatoes, for rye and for sugar beet. Probably the corn producer is the only one who could argue poor natural growing conditions. But even then, the country's two main granaries — the regions of Poznan and Bydgoszcz — have very favourable conditions. Not surprisingly those two regions contained two thirds of all the agricultural cooperatives in Poland.

It is hard to be surprised at the shortage of foodstuffs in Poland. It is the inevitable consequence of the waste, malfunction, power politics and corruption which have for years governed the regime's agricultural policy. This was the situation denounced by the Committees for Peasant Self-Defence, formed in the past two years, in their message to the striking workers at Gdansk: "If they continue to destroy our agriculture, there will be no meat and no food on Polish dinner tables."

This declaration also called for unity between workers and peasants. "Disagreeable though it may be, there is one thing that we must discuss. For 35 years the government and the Party have been encouraging people to hate the peasants. They choose not to value our work, and our role as providers of food. People see us as 'boors', 'louts' and 'tramps'. We are treated with contempt in offices; we are hated when we go and queue in shops in town, even though where we live there is only bread, sugar, salt and groats. People in the towns take it out on us whenever we buy anything at all. Stories about our supposed income and wealth are allowed to fester, but all you have to do is to go to any village, any house, to see these are only myths. The regime tries to divide us and provoke quarrels between us. So we are going to have to do everything we can to unite." The peasants, like the working class, were subject to the whims of bureaucratic power politics, and they demanded a radical reform. "After the stabilisation of the national economy, we will have to embark on an agrarian reform. We are not asking for a new division of land, but for new legislation, new autonomous institutions and real cooperativism. Peasants are going to have to be free to decide what to do with their land, except as regards questions of national defence. Otherwise we will always be threatened with a return of famine. If changes are not made in line with what we suggest, there will be fewer and fewer young people in agriculture, and therefore less and less production. Very soon the State and the Party will have achieved their strategic aim — they will have destroyed family farming in Poland.

"The worries of family farmers should be the worries of the whole nation. You who live in the towns, who work in the factories, you do not yet have a real union; your rights are not respected. But we in the countryside, we are treated as slaves. The head of the commune and the commune's Polish United Workers Party secretary exercise unlimited power over us. At any moment they can take away our land, expropriate us, transfer our children to schools far away, refuse us permission to complete the construction of a house, call up our boys into the army to send them off to work in a State agricultural farm. The head of the commune decides on our behalf what we are supposed to grow and when we are supposed to harvest it, without a thought for our profits. Often they send us State machinery without our prior agreement, in order to reap our harvests before they are even ripe. In certain regions they give us new land and take away our old land. So, we are dependent on the whims of the commune head, even over simple matters like buying a sack of cement, a plank of wood, or other materials. In order to get any of these things we have to write out a request, take it to the commune head, and buy tax stamps. We waste a third of our production time in carrying out formalities, waiting endlessly in corridors. In practical terms there is no way of exercising control over the commune head, and no appeal from his decision. He is capable of ruining a commune very quickly, and we have no means of recourse.'' Three peasant self-defence committees signed this statement, which on 20 August was sent to the Inter-Enterprise Strike Committee in Gdansk. These were the committees of Lublin, Grojec and Rzeszow, communes situated in the south-east of the country.

In this region, ever since the Sejm had voted a new law on disablement insurance for farmers in October 1977, protests had been under way. This law was aimed at speeding up the socialisation of land belonging to older peasants. It gave the State priority of acquisition. More than 250 farmers spontaneously refused to pay, and when, in July 1978, the tax collector came to visit villages around Lublin, he was driven out. A committee was organised, which held meetings of several hundred people. The clergy, which had often led struggles for the right to build churches in the countryside, supplied logistical and moral support. Sunday sermons were transformed into indictments of the new law. Some of the organisers of this movement were detained by the militia, but the peasants responded by stopping deliveries of milk, and within 24 hours they had won their release. The same scenario occurred in September 1978 in Grojec district, where the delegates from 18 villages had formed a self-defence committee arising out of a meeting of several hundred people. At Lowisko, in the district of Rzeszow, in the month of November, a third committee was founded to resist seizures of land by the State. For a year and a half, the farmers kept watch over one particular piece of land. When the administration's tractors arrived to work the land, the guards blew a trumpet and the whole village rushed to the scene. The official reason for this land seizure was that it was unprofitable under private management. The State had wanted to build a specialised farm there.[28]

However, even though these movements expressed a discontent which was general in Poland as a whole, they were still scattered and limited to certain regions. A number of attempts were made to centralise them. In September 1978 KOR members set up a national committee for the foundation of a Farmers' Union, along the lines of the committees that had been created within the working class. But this was to remain principally a centre for discussion. It circulated its ideas via a periodical, *The Independent Farmer*, which was published in 2,000 copies and ran to 25 editions. Another similar magazine, *Placowka*, was produced in Warsaw (2,000 copies, 20 issues). And finally, each local committee published its own bulletin in two or three thousand copies.

Thus this movement was characterised from the start by organisational difficulties and the individualism of the peasantry. However, the August strikes were to give it a considerable boost. The farmers were to give massive support to the strikers, leaving their harvests to go and take food to the gates of the occupied factories. At the end of the month of October the first peasant assemblies were held, with a view to forming what was later to become Rural Solidarity. However, the disintegration of previous mobilisations, and the absence of a recognised trade union leadership (as represented by the Gdansk team in the case of the workers' movement) were to result in a long and laboured birth.[29]

10. A Wind of Hope

On 1 September, as a strike was coming to an end, a crisis was beginning. The Gdansk and Szczecin agreements, followed by those of Jastrszebia in Silesia, set their seal on a given balance of power, and introduced a fundamental source of instability into the Polish political system. They recognised the principle of the independence of the working class in relation to the regime, a regime whose only source of life, legitimacy and power was supposed to derive from that entrusted to it by the working class.

If the Polish United Workers Party had hoped to confine the crisis to the seaboard region, it soon had to come to terms with the reality of the situation. Within just a few weeks the majority of workers, particularly those in industry, left the old trade unions linked to the Party, and joined what was soon to be called Solidarity. The movement, albeit uneven at first, was rapid, massive and unanimous. Long queues formed up at Solidarity's temporary headquarters. People were bringing in membership applications by the packet. The numbers were hard to assess: five million, then seven, then eight, finally levelling out at around ten million members. One of the most powerful independent trade unions in the world had been created in one fell swoop. Every enterprise and every trade, from metallurgists to priests' housekeepers, set up trade union commissions.

The atmosphere of the seaboard region during the month of August was to spread to the whole of the country. Those two weeks of strike action were not only the starting point, but also the laboratory of a revolution, a powerful process of development. All the confusions, all the contradictions which were to blossom in the following months were already present at Gdansk. Stripped bare by this remarkable working-class mobilisation, these conflicts were to become interwoven in the fabric of society in such a way as to lead inexorably towards more conflict and fresh confrontations.

We have seen how the working class moved from the cautious establishment of workers' commissions, and from the economic demands of 1 July, to an exceptional level of self-organisation, and to demands that were both radical and *political*, such as the free union, the right to strike, and the release of political prisoners. This process was to widen and spread. The first phase saw its consolidation in each region; then, in mid-September, the new union set up national structures. On 17 September, 500 representatives of the founding committees met in Gdansk, and on 22 September they agreed a founding statute. Seventeen regional federations were in operation, coordinated by a national commission based in Gdansk. Later on the plan was for this commission to have half its members elected by a congress which was to be held every two years. But for the moment its membership was made up of volunteers and delegates from the first founding committees. Solidarity officials felt that it was necessary to wait a number of weeks before proceeding to elections within the union.

The expectations of the *Lenin* shipyard strikers were confirmed. They would have to fight, and fight hard, to ensure that the summer agreements were fully applied. The Party, which now had a new Secretary General, wanted to limit their impact. But, as usual, it succeeded in bringing about the opposite result to that intended. Kania and his officials certainly defended their privileges and their monopoly of power, but through this battle the working class was to develop its political awareness.

The workers had to fight on several fronts. At the local level the bureaucracy set up a series of pitfalls. Managers of enterprises, Party secretaries and the officials of the old trade unions put up resistance. They banned meetings, and despite the national statements issued by the Polish United Workers Party, often refused to allow 'their' workers to organise. They threatened to withdraw the advantages of social benefits which were traditionally managed by the union. They also continued to receive union subs by virtue of deduction at source from workers' wages. The putting up of posters and access to the local media were banned, and so forth. The workers responded with strikes; they forced recognition; they drove out certain directors, and occupied union offices. In the end negotiations were opened. It was agreed (at first in Gdansk on 25 September, then in the whole country) that the two unions would co-manage social benefit funds. Directors retreated, one after another, abandoned by the central administration, and by the government, which, in the end, dissolved the CRZZ (the old Trade Union Council).

At the national level the first big trials of strength were to come over the question of the legal recognition of Solidarity, the application of wage agreements, and payment for the days lost by strike action. Here too the regime balked. Its pretext was the absence of any explicit reference to the leading role of the Party in the union's statute, in order to reject its legal registration. On 3 October Solidarity got angry, and organised a one-hour 'warning' general strike over four demands: their agreements to be accepted; access to the media to be granted; wage levels to be raised; the unions to have freedom to organise. On 29 September the union's national committee had stated their objective quite clearly: "Let us not forget: a 'warning strike' is only a manifestation of our strength, of our sense of responsibility and our discipline. We must show that during this strike we will be capable of maintaining calm, order, the protection of public property, as well as effecting a return to normal working at one o'clock. We must be ready to foil any attempt at provocation, calmly and firmly. If the warning strike fails to produce the desired results by 20 October, the national liaison commission will examine the question of a full general strike." And the demonstration was only too clear.

On 24 October the Warsaw tribunal finally went into session. The union won its right to registration, but the judges introduced a number of amendments to the union's statute, without the agreement of the union. There was outrage. The mobilisation built up again: Solidarity sent the Prime Minister an ultimatum on 27 October; Walesa met with Kania; a new meeting of the tribunal was scheduled for 10 November. Solidarity went into detailed preparations for a general strike. The national commission fixed 12 November as the first day of a rotating national strike. Two regions (Gdansk and Warsaw to start with) would stop work, on a rota basis, every two days. At the end of a week of warning, if the regime still refused to give in, there would be a national general strike.

On 10 November the High Court saw reason. It revoked the

Warsaw tribunal's decision. Solidarity was to be registered without any modification of its statute. The court pronounced itself satisfied with three documents, in particular the first articles of the Gdansk agreement, which recognised the leading role of the Party and Poland's international alliances. The matter was settled but on this point only.

The obduracy of the regime and its administrators was to lead to new conflicts. They defended their privileges tooth and nail. Points of dispute began to pile up. Point No. 16 of the Gdansk agreements provided for an increase in the public health budget and improvement of health amenities. However, the delegates in the health sector were forced to occupy the provincial government building in Gdansk on 8 November in order to gain a hearing. The medical students were all ready to declare a general strike in sympathy. This had already begun, in fact, in Gdansk. The situation was similar in the education sector, and on the question of the work-free Saturdays which were supposed to come into effect on 1 January 1981. On this point a compromise was finally reached, granting three out of the four Saturdays originally promised, but once again even this compromise was only won under the threat of a general strike. As the strength of the working class continued to grow, their demands began to become broader. People were beginning to question everything. A huge groundswell was shaking Poland's bureaucratic system. Aims and objectives began to become political. At Czestochowa in the month of November, then at Bielsko Biala and Jelenia Gora in January/February 1981, the local administration became the target of protests. Workers demanded the dismissal of the Party's local officers and secretaries. They called a 'state of preparation for strike action', followed by a strike. At Bielsko Biala it was to last for ten·days.

On 20 November the militia arrived to search Solidarity's headquarters in Warsaw, and arrested two trade unionists, J. Narodniak and M. Spolena. They were accused of having stolen and distributed a confidential circular from the Ministry of the Interior. What a circular! It explained in detail how to organise provocations in order to arrest 'anti-socialist elements' — that is to say, KOR militants. However this confrontation turned out badly for the regime. The Warsaw workers mobilised and threatened strike action. Ursus stopped

on 24 November, and on 25 November the other three largest
enterprises in the town also went on strike. Negotiations began,
Jagielski spent another two sleepless nights, and at dawn on 27
November the two trade unionists were released. Solidarity
also demanded that negotiations be opened on ways of controlling the State's repressive apparatus. These negotiations
were postponed indefinitely, but this general strike, which had
been both political and aimed directly at the regime, had a lot
of support. After the event a poll among 1,000 delegates from
the Warsaw region found that 95 per cent of them would have
gone on strike without hesitation.

The economic crisis, the wastage, and the food shortage
encouraged the development of a movement of workers' control over distribution, which was to prove effective during the
Christmas holidays. At the workers' request, the government
distributed meat rationing tickets. However, Solidarity had no
confidence in the government's organisation, and spontaneously, as from 18 December, its local organisations took charge of
the distribution of ration books. In Warsaw they realised that
the inhabitants of neighbouring towns were to fare less well
that those in the capital: Warsaw residents were to receive 800
grammes, and those in neighbouring towns 500, or even 300.
Also, the shops supplying the Radom militia were receiving ten
times the amount of meat that was destined to ordinary shops.
The union reacted promptly, and forced a fairer distribution of
foodstuffs. In a number of towns it proved necessary to occupy
the government buildings: at Piotrkow Tribunalki, and Chelm,
for example. In the latter instance, despite the fact that an agreement had been reached, the workers still went ahead with a one
hour warning strike on 23 December, in order to teach the
authorities good manners. On the first day of the occupation
the authorities had sent militiamen armed with sub machine
guns to intimidate the trade union's militants.

This workers' control movement also took institutional
form. At Ursus, when the management refused a wage rise,
Solidarity decided to publicise the extent of management incompetence. They set up a committee to carry out a census of
useless stocks and machinery. They suggested that these should
be sold to other enterprises. After the results of the inquiry in
the factory had been published, the union won its case. There
was another form of control too — control of production. Once

again, at Ursus, the workers had been discussing with members of Rural Solidarity the planned schedules of tractor production. After a number of inquiries they came to the conclusion that overall tractor production should be reduced by ten per cent, and that the manufacture of spare parts should be increased, given the fact that they were in extremely short supply. Thousands of broken-down tractors were rotting on farms, because of shortages of such parts. A similar movement developed in the steel industry. At that time the government was proposing to freeze a large planned investment. The workers sought to contest the point. At the Huta Katowice steelworks Solidarity set up a number of commissions. These worked on the planned investments, and examined the workers' working conditions. As the union president wrote in the factory bulletin: "In future there will be no central planning that does not include us."

At a more general level, the new union set up national and regional commissions in order to control prices and wages. They were to oversee the application of the 'threshold system', which had theoretically been won in August, and they were to alert the workers in the event of abuses. By the same token Solidarity demanded that a commission should be set up, answerable to the Sejm, on workers' working conditions. It also negotiated with the authorities the drawing up of a plan for the rational distribution of electricity with a view to ending the wastage arising from frequent blackouts which were playing havoc with production.

Workers were also throwing out incompetent directors. This was a 'speciality' of Henryka Krzywonos, who by this time was a member of Solidarity's regional commission. She told me good-humouredly how she set about it. This was in mid-November: she had already organised the resignation of six post office directors in Konin region, and at that moment was working on a seventh, in Poznan. Obviously she did not consult the government. "I say to them: 'You cannot stay here. The enterprise cannot work with you around. You are incompetent.' And he goes. Then the workers elect a new director. This movement is only just beginning. The provinces are afraid. We should spread this method of workers' control. And anyway, why shouldn't directors work as workers for a month or two every now and then? Then at least they would under-

stand our conditions better.''

"And do all these expulsions take place with no problems?''

"Oh, you know, in general by the time I arrive the director has already left. I usually warn them in advance by telephone.''

The working-class movement was expanding its means, and was developing its strength and its unity. It was spreading in a remarkable manner, in conflict with an administration that was becoming increasingly demoralised. The movement was becoming radicalised.

The Party, for its part, was evolving in an opposite direction. The internal differences noted at the time of the August strike became more acute. On 6 September the factional struggles which had taken up whole days and nights of plenary sessions during the summer were resolved on the Central Committee by the nomination of Stanislaw Kania as Secretary General. Kania was known for his role in having organised the police, and was not a particularly striking personality. Gierek, suffering from heart troubles, gave up the leadership. In fact a persistent rumour in Warsaw claims that it took the use of force by two security employees in order to get him out of the hall. That evening he had not wanted to go.

Kania aimed to act on three fronts: first of all, to recognise the Gdansk agreements, and to promise that they would be put into effect (while at the same time attempting to limit their impact); then, to renew the attacks against the 'anti-socialist elements', who were supposed to be leading the union astray (this meant making KOR and its leader, Jacek Kuron, his principal targets); and finally to take the Party in hand again, closing its ranks by purging one or two corrupt elements who could be made scapegoats. His aim: to re-establish the authority of the Polish United Workers Party and little by little to win back the ground that had been lost in August. He gave assurances to Poland's 'fraternal' countries, who, as he never tired of telling, were eager to avoid 'the worst'.

In practice these policies were to appear as an absence of policy, a ship lost in a storm, a string of half-measures. Kania defended his prerogatives in a state of retreat; he maintained with difficulty an unstable situation which was threatened on the one hand by the mass movements and on the other hand by the apparatus, which was becoming prey to rebellions and was

beginning to fall apart. In addition, at the Party's rank and file level, Solidarity's arguments were increasingly finding an echo among dissatisfied militants who were beginning to speak in the tones of 1956, and were demanding the calling of a democratic Congress.

We have already highlighted the Kania leadership's attitude towards Solidarity. We should also note that it was not until 15 December that the Gdansk agreements were officially applicable to the rest of the country, and 21 December before Mass was broadcast on television. But in February 1981 the new Union still did not have its legal national newspaper; its access to television was still limited; and a number of other points of the agreements had still not been put into effect. Kania himself, on the occasion of the Central Committee plenary, proposed a wholesale renegotiation of the agreements.

At each step of the worsening crisis, the attacks on the democratic opposition movement intensified. Despite the fact that ROBCIO had disbanded, seven former members were arrested in mid-November and charged. The principal KOR leadership, Jacek Kuron, Adam Michnik and Antoni Macierewicz were libelled and slandered by name in the Press and in official speeches. They were threatened with imprisonment several times, but their close links with the Solidarity leadership would have made this a difficult operation. Jacek Kuron, for example, had become one of the most popular people in Poland: when he spoke it was often to crowds of many thousands of people. The union's national commission warned, on 24 September, that any reprisals against Kuron would be seen as a provocation against the union as a whole. At the economic level the government was scarcely more effective. The Prime Minister presided over a commission which was supposed to formulate reforms and draw up urgent measures. Their first decisions were to bring a confrontation not only with the workers, but also with resistance from the apparatus and from an obdurate administration. Thus, the October Party plenary promised reforms in agriculture, with a better distribution of economic aid between State farms and the private sector. In fact, at a local level the commune head and the Party secretary would contine to behave like corrupt potentates, following their own preferences and those of their clients.

The new Secretary General's difficulties would have been

less acute if his Party had been winning back a measure of confidence among the people. But the crisis in society at large was only aggravating the tension. Superficial improvements were not going to be enough. The resignation of Gierek and his team was followed by a number of spectacular measures. These began with the arrest of the ex-director of Polish radio and television for misappropriation of funds. Mid-September saw a reshuffle of regional secretaries. Some were changed, and others, as at Poznan and Katowice, were dismissed. On 26 September around 100 judicial inquiries were begun against senior officials accused of corruption. However, the effect was not all that might be desired. On the one hand this use of scapegoats created no illusions, because people knew that a lot of similarly corrupt officials were still in their posts! On the other hand, which was worse for the regime, the purges began to be taken seriously. Workers began to make their own contribution, demanded more purges, and (as in Silesia at the end of September) went so far as to organise strikes and people's tribunals. Within the apparatus all this created fear, and an aggressiveness against the working class. These resulted in factional infighting at the top of the apparatus. Without going into detail one could outline three broad reactions which Kania was attempting to reconcile.

The first was the reaction of General Moczar. He had been off the political scene since 1970, but on 3 November he made his return. He was re-elected president of the organisation of ex-soldiers, the ZBoWID, in which he had worked during the 1960s. He made a long speech which was broadcast on television and published on the front page of *Trybuna Ludu*. He addressed himself to the nation, and appealed for order and a return to normal: "The political atmosphere in Poland is returning to normal, but too slowly. There is a lot of ferment still, and a lot of enterprises have still not returned to normal working." His policy aimed to combine firmness with diplomacy: he stressed the positive role of Solidarity, while at the same time advising a purge of anti-socialist elements. He also attempted to alter his image, which had been heavily stamped by the chauvinist and anti-semitic campaign he had led in 1967-68. As ex-Minister of the Interior he also had a reputation for having repressed students and workers. So he went out of his way to offer hypocritical homage to the Jews 'who have participated in the creation of our history', to salute the Soviet Union whose friendship was 'inestimable', and to preach moderation. Thus he took a 'firm line', but without descending to provocation. He continued to improve his position: on 1 September he entered the Politburo, and then, at the start of 1981, he was elected president of the National Unity Front, which linked the Polish United Workers Party with its satellites. Above all he could count on a faithful team of allies in the Party apparatus and the police. Some of these even occupied key positions. The new director of national television, for example, Kazimier Kakol, had distinguished himself in 1968 by his anti-semitic and anti-intellectual diatribes. The same was true of the men responsible for propaganda and for cadre training, Klasa and Rokoszewski. Not to mention Namiotkiewicz in the Central Committee's ideology section, and Wojtczak at the Ministry of Culture. In short, a number of individuals on whom Moczar could rely. Furthermore, as president of the Polish United Workers Party, he had accumulated a number of dossiers, and had more than one State official in his pocket. Finally, he had a lieutenant in a man who was younger than himself, but equally ambitious, and with a less blemished past. This was Stefan Olszowski, who had managed to portray himself as one of Gierek's victims for having spoken out too publicly about the state of the economy. He too was in favour of a firm line, but at the same time he attempted to keep his reputation as a new man and as a reformer. Whatever the tactical nuances and the temporary concessions practised by Kania, it was clear that Moczar and Olszowski, presumably each for their own reasons, were polarising the aspirations of a hard-line fraction within the apparatus. Also, despite their nationalist past, it appeared that they enjoyed a certain confidence in Moscow.

At the opposite extreme stood a more moderate fraction, around the Gdansk Party secretary Tadeusz Fiszbach. His openings towards Solidarity, his speeches and his participation, together with Jagielski, in the shipyard negotiations, had earned him this reputation. On 10 November he made a programmatic speech to the provincial party committee's plenary session. He took exactly the opposite view to that of General Moczar: "Change must come fast, and all those who have dealt in corruption must leave the Party." He protested against those who sought to identify the new union with 'anti-socialist elements'.

He said that the Party should recognise Solidarity and should undertake democratic reforms. He called for an early Congress, to be arranged according to new and more democratic rules. Finally, he described the kinds of economic reforms that the country needed, which should be adopted by the communists as fast as possible. In short, he was developing ideas that were very close to those of Dubcek and Sik at the time of the 'Prague Spring' twelve years earlier. However, his audience within the apparatus appears to have been more limited than that of General Moczar. His appointment to the Politburo (as substitute) on 1 December was intended to provide a counterbalance rather than to represent an influential faction.

In the event the rank and file militants who might have been open to such a line of argument were rather more attracted by the activities of Solidarity. A number of them (approximately 1.5 million) had joined the union, and saw themselves more as Solidarity militants within the Party, rather than the other way round. When they began to organise within the Polish United Workers Party in the lead up to the extraordinary IX Congress, they set up a coordination which was 'horizontal', and based on a politics far more radical than that of Fiszbach. At Poznan, Lodz, Torun, Warsaw etc, Party cell secretaries were beginning to meet outside the usual hierarchical structures, and were producing and circulating documents. Some of these even appeared in the local press. At Poznan, for example, the weekly *Kujawy* reprinted in its 5 December issue an interesting article entitled: 'How to win at Congress'. The article appealed to militants to take a stand in favour of 'authentic change'. In Warsaw the 'political work centre' of the Sigma club (part of the University's youth organisation) collected a number of similar texts and circulated them within the Party. At Torun the regional apparatus reacted by expelling one of the officials responsible for these horizontal coordinations. His factory cell refused to ratify this decision, and informed the administration that comrade Iwanov had just been elected Party first secretary for the factory. The Torun coordination brought together militants from eleven of the most important enterprises in the region (metal-working, chemicals, textiles), together with school-teachers and railway workers. It elected an ad hoc praesidium. It published a regular journal. In the November issue, there was an interesting article

204

entitled 'A Last Chance for the Polish United Workers Party'. Its two authors, Roman Backer and Andrzej Zybertowicz, welcomed the 'real socialism' which was being lived in Poland at that time, in which the struggle of the strikers and the work of the unions were a real 'school of politics'. "Marxists must put forward a programme for reconstructing from bottom upwards a true workers' party which will get society out of its present situation without committing the same mistakes as the Polish United Workers Party." They went on to say: "The time has not yet come to tear up our Party cards. Perhaps it will, after the IX Congress, if this does not take a decisive step towards change, if it is not won by the working class." After a critique of the apparatus's various excesses, the authors proposed that sincere militants should set up a coordination. The final paragraph took the bull by the horns: "The changes in the Party's structure and methods which we propose might lead to fractional struggle. This is quite likely to happen, at least in part. Is this in conflict with the Party rule which bans fractions? We do not think so, because this rule is a matter of limiting their importance. In the context of the Party's normal functioning, such fractional struggles are harmful. But in periods of crisis, when the Party requires a change of face, then the political struggle inevitably creates fractional struggles." Such documents were not exceptional. Dozens of them were circulating. In Lodz, for example, B. Rogowski's document, prepared for the Polish United Workers Party executive committee in the Fonica radio factory on 14 November, became a reference point for numbers of militants. Its title was Leninist in inspiration, and provocative: *'What is to be Done?'* The article contained the following description of the events under way: they 'are revolutionary in character. Workers in heavy industry are their principal initiators and their main driving force. They have been joined by wider and wider circles of society at large. This movement tends towards a definitive rejection of the present system whereby power is exercised, and of current methods for the construction of socialism. What is at stake is the fact that the dictatorship of the proletariat should not be a dictatorship *over* the proletariat; that the right of self-expression of the broad masses must be guaranteed both by the law and in practice'. The author suggested 'electing a new, properly competent leadership. All its members will have to be known to the nation as honest and proper people. The Polish United Workers Party is compromised to such an extent that unless it is radically changed from top to bottom, it will never regain the confidence of the masses. We are proposing to transform the Polish United Workers Party into a new party: the Polish Socialist Workers Party'.

So the Kania leadership had a difficult job on its hands. Its internal policies could not count either on the docility of the workers' movement or on the unity of the Party. The slightest re-emergence of social crisis constantly endangered the stability that had been achieved with such difficulty in August. The Secretary General's task appeared impossible, inasmuch as he controlled none of the basic factors of the situation. Furthermore, from outside Poland, he was constantly under the eagle eye of 'big brother' Russia, who had no intention of allowing the situation to get too far out of hand. Moscow was calling for a rapid return to normality, and threatened military intervention. The leaders of neighbouring countries, in particular G. Husak in Czechoslovakia and E. Honecker in East Germany, repeatedly issued warnings and alarmist statements.

On 19 September Deputy Prime Minister Jagielski went to meet Leonid Brezhnev in Moscow, and, on 30 October, S. Kania and his Prime Minister J. Pinkowski made the same trip. The joint communique issued at the end of the second meeting expressed the USSR's confidence in the fact that Polish communists and workers would be able to resolve their problems on their own. In fact, according to generally reliable East European sources, Brezhnev had used the occasion to give precise instructions to the Polish leadership. He is supposed to have explained that for the Soviet Union the crucial point was the maintenance of the socialist regime and of the leading role of the Polish United Workers Party, in addition to the safety of its military lines of defence and its communications with East Germany. Within that context, Brezhnev is supposed to have promised that the Poles would be given a free hand to sort out their problems as they thought fit, and to undertake the economic and social reforms that they felt were necessary. If they wished, they could draw on the Hungarian experience, or even the Yugoslavian model. However, all this required the situation to be taken in hand.

This, however, did not happen. Even worse for the regime,

as we have seen, the movement was beginning to become more radical and the contradictions more acute. With every intensification of conflict, the mass media in the USSR and the people's democracies became more agitated. At the start of December, after the political strikes in Czestochowa and Warsaw, the Polish authorities added their own voice to these regular threats. On 3 and 4 December the PAP agency published a number of alarmist communiques, including an appeal from the Central Committee to the people of Poland: "The fate of our people and our country is at stake." Klasa, Moczar's friend and the man responsible for propaganda, stated that in the event that socialism in Poland found itself under threat (and there were "reasons to believe it"), Polish communists would possibly "ask our closest friends and neighbours for assistance". On 5 December a summit meeting was held in Moscow, bringing together the leaders of the seven member countries of the Warsaw Pact. Their final communique was perfectly clear: "Poland has been, and will remain, socialist, and a solid link in the socialist family (...). The workers' Party and the people of Poland can count on the fraternal aid and solidarity of all countries in the socialist community." A similar level of international tension was created in mid-February 1981, after the confrontations in Bielsko Biala and Jelenia Gora. Kania changed his Prime Minister, bringing in a military man, General Jaruszelski, who asked that strike action be suspended for three months. Once again the source of this threat was the fact that the workers were challenging the *political* power of the Party.

These factors had existed at Gdansk during the summer: a radicalisation of the working class, divisions within the Party, and Moscow's impatience. But the forces in play now encompassed the whole of Poland. The Solidarity leadership and the various opposition tendencies now had to face up to considerable responsibilities. Their tactics had to become more acute. They had to elaborate new aims and objectives, as well as taking the movement towards victory, rather than coming up against a brick wall. Poland's way of life had changed in the past 35 years, and millions of workers were now finding it intolerable. Real change was needed. Three broad areas were central: the organisation of the union, the restoration of the economy, and relations with the central authorities and their allies. Any resolution of the crisis opened by the Gdansk strike would depend on these being solved.

To organise the union meant to ensure that the democratic tendencies initiated in Gdansk were continued; it was to guarantee the independence, the sense of responsibility and the strength of the working class. When, within the space of a few months, ten million people join an organisation, and when, at the same time, these men and women had virtually no experience of democracy, then the job is not so simple. The new trade union leadership was to understand this very fast, as it came up against a thousand problems. It was no longer a matter, as in August, of finding a set of rules for the effective conduct of a working-class mobilisation on immediate objectives. On the contrary, it was a matter of finding ways of working that would be valid in the long term, in order to avoid the bureaucratic deformities whose consequences one knows only too well. For this the imagination of a few individuals would not suffice. The Solidarity leadership had embarked on a democratic process of recreating trade union democracy. The months to follow showed how difficult it was to achieve this objective, and how much patience was required. At first they decided on a national trade union structure, based on regional groupings, and not on branches of industry. This system, they thought, would have the advantage of avoiding corporatist reactions and the leap-frogging of demands. Control would be more collective. It would be exercised in the overall interests of the working class in all its diversity. Each region would enjoy a large measure of autonomy. In addition, trade union sections would make their contribution to all decisions. A union officer from one factory in Warsaw explained how this would happen. In the local *Niezaleznosc* ('Independence') bulletin, published by Solidarity, he answered a number of questions.

Question: (...) Would you say that struggle is contradictory with having democratic rules?
"Full democracy is, for the moment, a question for the future. The union is organising itself, and unfortunately certain decisions are going to have to be taken from the top."

Which decisions?
"In particular technical decisions affecting how the union

is organised, the process of the union's advance. This could be, for example, the adoption of an electoral system, of means of conducting elections. But any such decision would be based on the union's statutes, which have been discussed and adopted democratically. At the same time each enterprise is free to modify its electoral system to fit with its own needs.''

Another question, perhaps more important: Which decisions can only be taken by the workers themselves?

"All decisions on strikes, and on blackings. Each enterprise has the right to make its proposals to the regional section of the union, which in turn will communicate them to the national commission. By the same token, the regional commissions and the national commission will be able to make their own proposals, and enterprises accept them. But nobody is obliged to. A given enterprise may adopt another form of action. For example, it may decide, instead of a blacking, to draw up a petition and send it to the authorities. Thus democracy will work on a two-way system: from the national commission to the regions and from these to the workers; and also back again by the same route.''

And how long is this going to take?

"This depends on the capabilities of the given enterprise, on their level of organisation. If it is a mess, it may be that the workers will not know whether they or not they are supposed to take strike action. Information will not get through. On the other hand, in enterprises where the trade union structure is well organised, information will get through very quickly, and decisions will be taken fast.''

Which decisions have been taken in this way in your place of work? And how many of these have been in response to proposals from the national commission?

"First of all we ratified the union's statutes. Then there was the warning strike of 3 October 1980. Since then there have been no further proposals. The national commission is not yet very well organised, and it is not easy for it to arrive at decisions. But let's get back to the question of the warning strike. As Solidarity representative at ZM-Nowotko I accepted this proposal, and expressed my personal agreement with it. But in order for it to become effective it had to be put forward at our section meeting, which, in turn, via representatives from the various sectors of the enterprise, then sought agreement from all the workers who were members of the union. Agreement was unanimous, and the strike was supported not only by the sectors which had been selected, but by the enterprise as a whole. However, a strike in the whole of the factory would have had serious economic consequences. This was not what we wanted, and so we picked on sections which, in that period, were not working to full capacity. This, for example, was the case in engine-assembly. They had a shortage of parts, and so were not able to work. In this way the one-hour strike did not cause losses."

One more question: the question of democratic practice. On the one hand lies ideal democracy, and on the other lies practice and concrete activity. How to organise a meeting, how to organise elections, how to conduct a debate successfully etc. Can you say something on this. How has this been resolved in your factory?

"Yes. For each meeting of our union section we get together to sort out an agenda in advance, picking out the most important points to be discussed. The leadership in our union section is simply those people who are better informed than others about what is happening. In the agenda we also leave space for proposals from sector representatives. Then we try to follow this agenda strictly. If somebody gets up to raise a point which is not on the agenda, they are automatically asked to sit down. This means that we don't stray from the subjects on the agenda, or from subjects raised by sector representatives at the start of the meeting. We don't want our meeting to go on for ever."

The elections within the union also raised new problems. The national commission circulated a document at the start of December in which it summarised the electoral rules which had been adopted, on the understanding that each enterprise could tailor them to fit local conditions. The election was to be organised by the union's founding committee, which, depending on the size of the enterprise, would decide whether one single section would suffice for the whole factory, or whether several should be set up. At this stage delegates were to be elected ('trustworthy people') in a proportion of roughly one for every

fifty workers. They were to be chosen on the basis of a programme, on the basis of what they were proposing to do. These
delegates would then go to make up the works commission.
From among their number they would then elect the members
of a departmental commission (one delegate for every five
members), which would then elect its representatives to the
national commission.

The electoral process began at the end of November, and
by the end of February had only reached departmental level. It
was carried out with minute care, and aroused many points of
debate, as Solidarity's bulletins bear witness. These discussions
revealed how difficult practical democracy can be. It demands
enormous effort. All Solidarity's circulars and explanatory
articles explained in detail: how to assess a candidate; how to
proceed to a vote; what is an abstention; what is a simple
majority; what are absolute and relative majorities. They
pointed out the many pitfalls. Via practical experience the
trade union leaders were setting in motion a long process of
education. They sought to thwart bureaucratic manoeuvres, as
well as the 'false friends' who were infiltrating the union in
order to take control of it and integrate it within the State
apparatus.

This struggle demanded patience, time and perseverance.
But it was a necessary precondition for guaranteeing that the
victories of Gdansk would be maintained and developed. This
was not a foregone conclusion, particularly because the very
dynamic of events was incessantly raising the stakes.

The second problem which the union leadership had to
face was the economic crisis. The Party's passivity and
negligence, as well as sabotage by the apparatus during those
months, and the permanent state of mobilisation of the working class, meant that winter 1980-81 was one of the hardest yet
seen by the Polish economy. The overall volume of production
dropped, and queues lengthened outside the shops. Food shortages developed, of a kind not seen since the Second World
War. And, as people queued, one thing was becoming clearer
and clearer in their minds. The government promised
measures, but nothing ever happened.

Within the union there were a number of points of view,
but the discussion remained very confused. Conferences were
organised in Gdansk and Lodz. Economists, sociologists and
jurists painted a catastrophic picture of the overall situation.

The questions raised dealt firstly with the economic system and the structural reforms required. Nobody was suggesting that large-scale means of production should be returned to private ownership. On the other hand, State planning was roundly criticised. All the arguments of the 1950s and 1960s, about the relationship between the plan and the market, came to the surface. The Hungarian and Yugoslav experiences were both invoked. The discussion was complicated by the fact that for five or six years the Polish economy had no longer really been planned. The objectives fixed by the planning bodies were never respected — in fact they were frequently undermined by decisions made by the government. But at the same time the central administration continued to make all decisions. For all their attention to detail, the net result tended to be economic anarchy. Therefore workers tended to identify planning with excessive centralisation by the authorities.

The majority of Solidarity's economists were in agreement that, while structural reforms were absolutely indispensable, in the short term they would be impossible to achieve. First, order would have to be re-established, temporary reforms would have to be enacted, and limited objectives fixed.

As regards the tasks of the unions within this situation, two tendencies developed. The first, which was to dominate the union bulletins published in the autumn, saw Solidarity as limiting itself to traditional trade union activities and defending the interests of workers without worrying about overall reforms. This reaction can be explained in part by the absence of reliable information on the management of the economy, and therefore as a desire not to take responsibility as long as the country's resources remained an unknown quantity. A second viewpoint, on the other hand, proposed that Solidarity should take part in the debate on reforms, and should formulate its own positions. This was not to be equated with co-management, of which people were very suspicious. At first this was a minority position, but it gained ground as the movement began to radicalise itself. Before the August strikes Jacek Kuron had written: "In our opinion, our most urgent task today is the examination of economic reforms."

It then remained to decide the content of these reforms, and the priorities which they should encompass. This brought up many varying proposals, and, without going into detail, one can say that there were certain basic lines of argument: first, that the government, in accord with the 31 August agreement, should undertake a census on the state of the country's resources, equipment, and its most urgent needs. Then choices were to be made. For example: to increase investment in agriculture in order to do away with the food shortages; to speed up housing construction; to increase public spending on schools, creches and hospitals.

At a certain point, the debate on the economy merged with the debate on democracy: who was to decide? By whom and how was the plan to be drawn up? In the opinion of many people broad economic choices should henceforth be taken from *below*, and no longer from the top of the Party. This was the implication of the extension of workers' control that had developed during the struggle. The 'self-managed' structures which would enable such a collective drawing-up of a proper economic plan were not yet clearly defined. They would have to be distinct from the union. Kuron, for example, envisaged 'assemblies of workers organised by the unions, or, more precisely, motivated by them. In these assemblies the workers will have to discuss a broad range of problems, inasmuch as they will be co-managers of the enterprise, or even of the whole sector. (There is presently a plan for mass assemblies of construction workers). Responsibility for the decisions of these assemblies will lie with the participants themselves, and with the authorities with whom they are negotiating, and not with the unions'. However, he was rather vague on the nature of the relationship between the self-managed institutions and the State apparatus. And this brings us to the final but fundamental question posed by the Polish crisis: the question of power.

The political strategies drawn up in the mid-1970s effectively now had to face a new situation. It was no longer a matter of fighting to win the major democratic freedoms (right of self-expression, right to organise etc), but of maintaining what had been won, extending it, and ensuring the realisation of the tremendous aspirations which at that moment were the driving force behind a mobilisation of millions of workers. Above all, Gdansk was not to be betrayed.

Despite the growing polarisation in society, would it be possible to maintain the compromise that had been achieved in August? The forces in play were formidable. On the one hand, the organised working class was drawing into its wake all those sectors of society who had been victims of bureaucratic power, in particular the peasantry. On the other hand stood a State apparatus and a Party which were sick, and which were watched over by the ever-threatening power of the USSR and its allies. In a situation like this the results of any major confrontation would be dire. This meant that each party was attempting to moderate the other, in the hopes of avoiding a confrontation. But was this really a possibility?

This was the line taken by the Church, by intellectuals from the Catholic Intellectual Clubs within Solidarity. It preached moderation and repeatedly appealed for calm. The Pope himself took advantage of his Xmas message in order to call for fair cooperation 'as between Poles'. The episcopate was thus pursuing the same policy that it had always pursued in times of major crisis in Poland. It preached good behaviour.

Good behaviour was well and good. But the Church as an institution had no intention of disturbing the existing world order, and was particularly concerned to maintain its religious influence. As it had already shown in the past, it could accommodate itself very easily to a state of co-existence with bureaucratic power.

Could the same be said of the working class? The experience of the past 35 years, as well as the recent developments, tend to prove otherwise. In 1956 and in February 1971 the workers put their trust in compromise. It set to work — as we have described — and took literally the statements by the various new Secretary Generals. On each occasion the experience proved negative. Workers lost their already poor possibilities for self-expression and organisation; their working and living conditions worsened; and inequalities increased. In short, fresh revolts were needed in order for the class to make itself heard. On 31 August the strikers signed a compromise at Gdansk. They were right. Given the power balance at that time they could not do otherwise. Jagielski promised to put the agreement into effect. Six months later, what did the government do? It had manoeuvred ceaselessly in order to erode the concessions that had been made at Gdansk. The situation revealed one of the basic factors of this crisis: that the two opposing forces were inextricably linked. When one retreated, the other advanced, and vice versa.

Any demobilisation within the working class, the smallest sign
of weakness, and the regime would advance anew. It nibbled
away, little by little winning back what it could, when it could.

But might the working class not yet get a grip on this see-
saw situation, this progress from truce to conflict, and from
conflict to fresh truces? Might it not do this, not by giving back
what had been won, but by avoiding the worst, and by stabilising what had been achieved? And to this end, might they not
seek to consolidate the movement, with all its internal democracy, its independence and its unity? This was the basis of
KOR's strategy. Jacek Kuron defended it in the course of
numerous speeches following the August events. He began
from a obvious fact: within its dynamic the movement carried
the seeds of the disintegration of the ruling political system.
"In order to avoid this disintegration the apparatus has two
choices: either to put down the self-managed social movements
by depriving them of any real content, or by democratising the
system, and this to be done as quickly as possible. The first
solution appears unlikely." So, indeed, did the second. "The
regime is paralysed in the face of a society so well organised. It
has no social base, and it has no social groups on which it can
call. All it can do is make use of the army, and in this situation
that would have to be a foreign army. (...) Such a course of action would very soon lead to a Soviet intervention. The regime
is inclined to exaggerate this threat. But obviously one cannot
say that the threat is not real. However, should we hold the
movement back in order to stave off the threat of an intervention? In order to answer this question we have to remember
that the social movement has its own dynamic, and that it cannot simply be directed at will, whether from within (on the in-
struction or advice of leaders), or, even more so, from outside
(by the warnings of 'advisors') (...). If the movement for the
democratisation of our society does not bear this fact in mind
in its programme, (i.e. the disintegration of the system), it
could suffer a defeat with incalculable consequences. To the
extent that the regime is weak, and (which amounts almost to
the same thing) to the extent that it is not capable of adapting
its policies to the situation, to that extent the democratisation
movement will become more radical. And radical in this case
means clashing directly with the regime and with its political
structures. Every step forward, despite the various threats,

lessens one's sense of the danger. (...) Is it possible today to set limits on the dynamic of this movement? Yes. And it is also necessary. But the only way of doing this would be with a programme which would allow the movement to develop while at the same time being aware of its own limitations. (...) We have embarked on a voyage of no return. I think that today the USSR will accept a democratisation of Poland, arising from the base, so as not to be forced into a military intervention. Tomorrow it may even accept that this democratisation is taken a stage further, as long as, in exchange, it has certain guarantees regarding its military interests. But the day after tomorrow... one would rather not think about it. It is important that Polish society is ready to exploit every present opportunity, and self-organisation within independent and self-managed movements is precisely one of those opportunities.'' Today it is up to the worker-members of Solidarity to seize this opportunity. Many divergent points of view are being debated and tested within experience and democratic discussion. Working-class Poland will henceforth have to choose the best path to guarantee a successful future.

References

1. See C. Milosz, *The Captive Mind*, (Penguin 1980). The author provides portraits of a number of intellectuals of this period, including J. Andrzewski, today a member of KOR.

2. Some accounts claim that he was victimised after the June 1976 strikes, but in fact he no longer worked in the yard at that time.

3. I have reconstructed this course of events by using information that I gathered on the spot, together with information published in *Robotnik Wybrzeza* and material gathered in November 1980 by T. Dussart, journalist working for *Le Point*, whose assistance I acknowledge. On the subject of E. Myszk, K. Wyszkowski wrote in *Robotnik Wybrzeza* No. 4 (September 1979) as follows: "In my opinion, E. Myszk is a sick man. It has been his complexes and his mythomania that have made him an easy prey for the secret police. This is no joke. I was his tutor. In the opposition movement I met him every day, and even though at our first encounter thought him unstable, I still saw him as a friend. To the last I was protesting his honesty to the world. I did not even end our collaboration when he stole some of our funds, or when I uncovered a number of his amazing lies. Why? Because we needed him. I didn't want to believe that he was financed by the secret police. I always had faith in his abilities and his intelligence, hoping that it could be put to good use in our opposition movement."

4. Petr Uhl, Vaclav Havel and their friends, organisers of the Defence Committee for People Unjustly Persecuted (VONS), who were given heavy sentences in 1980.

5. This is not entirely certain: some organisers, such as Anna Walentynowicz, insist that the movement was wholly spontaneous. However, on the basis of statements I have gathered, I would say that this was unlikely.

6. List of party members to whom preference is given when certain key posts become vacant.

7. See 'The National Question and Autonomy' in *Selected Writings* by R. Luxemburg, edited by H.B. Davies (New York and London, Monthly Review Press 1976). While Luxemburg's position on the national question is debatable to say the least (see her polemic with Lenin), she remains one of the most interesting sources on the development of capitalism in Poland.

8. See I. Deutscher, *Trotsky, The Prophet Armed*, (Oxford University Press 1954). Trotsky's opposition to the war was not merely formal. He was strongly against the positions taken by Lenin and Tuchachevski. He considered that the advance on Warsaw would "destroy the Russian revolution's goodwill with the Polish people, and will play into Pilsudksi's hands". (See Deutscher, *op. cit.*, page 464). In this he was supported by a number of Polish communists (themselves divided), including Radek, Marchlewski, and, contrary to general opinion, Dzerjinski.

9. On 11 November 1918 Pilsudski came to power, and Poland regained her independence after two centuries of partition.

10. See the writings of M.T. Staszewski and CISR Strasbourg, quoted by A. Swiecicki in 'La Religiosité Polonaise entre L'Est et L'Ouest', in *Nous Chrètiens de Pologne*, p. 48. In Yugoslavia, where the post-war relationship between town and country, and the standards of education, were comparable with Poland, there were, in 1977, 50 per cent believers in the countryside, and 29 per cent in the towns.

11. In May 1978 Moczulski and Czuma split up. The former set up (in September 1979) the Confederation of Independent Poland (KPN), while the latter built up a ROBCIO around the non-official review *Opinia*. Arrested in September and November 1980, along with 5 other militants who had come out of the ROBCIO, they were still in prison as of February 1981.

12. 'Young Poland' edits *Bratniak* ('Brother'). It originally comprised school students from Gdansk. It followed Dmowski without (they claim) taking up his anti-semitic and hitlerite activities.

13. *Aneks*, a quarterly review published by the Uppsala-London Polish Scientific Club, was founded in 1973 by young Polish intellectuals exiled after 1968. Its director was A. Smolar.

14. The Trotskyist Left Opposition led by Stefan Lamed and Isaac Deutscher formed a pre-war Bolshevik-Leninist Group in Poland. Its members were for the most part exterminated by the Nazis and the Stalinists. One of them, Ludwik Haas, after 17 years spent in a Soviet gulag, had an important influence on Kuron and Modzelewski. He too was sentenced to a number of years' imprisonment in 1966.

15. His theoretical break with Marxism dates from the end of the 1960s. It is expounded by L. Kolakowski in his three-volume work *Main Currents of Marxism*, Oxford, 1978.

16. At the time of his trial in 1968, he had stated: "I do not agree with my friends Kuron and Modzelewski on one fundamental question, namely their mode of envisaging the working class in relation with other social strata. This means that I cannot envisage their book as my own political programme. However, this does not mean that I do not have a high estimation of their *Manifesto*... This is the first Polish essay to be published on the problems preoccupying people who are attempting to build socialism (...)"

17. In 1956, together with other PAX 'fringe elements' T. Mazowiecki had publicly attacked the organisation's pro-Stalinist orientation, and had declared his support for democratic currents within the Party.

18. *Main Currents of Marxism, op. cit.*, Oxford, 1978.

19. KOR officially dissolved itself at the first congress of Solidarity in September 1981. Announcing the dissolution at the congress, Professor Lipinski said that he believed that the tasks undertaken by KOR would be carried out by the independent and self-managed union.

20. The so-called 'liberal' faction of the Party which brought Gomulka to power comprised, in addition to this generation of worker-militants, old-time Communists of the resistance movements who did not have Moscow's support, and who had grouped around Gomulka during the War; it also included those who had served in the International Brigades — and were still alive. See the comments by G. Mink in *Le XXe Congrès, mythes et realité de L'Est en 1956*, Institute for Slavic Studies, Paris 1977.

21. Elected onto the central committee in February 1980, Labecki was promoted onto the political bureau of the party at the special Congress in July 1981.

22. These speeches and the speeches that follow are transcribed from tape recordings made at the time.

23. Many thanks to André Gasson for having told me the tale of his travels, and for having made available to me his notes and interviews.

24. At the start, Gomulka's agricultural policy was very empirical, and its principle of 'gradual socialisation' was only systematised by Polish economists at the beginning of the 1970s.

25. The figures for livestock are as follows: 1975, 13,254 head; 1976, 12,879; 1977, 13,019; 1978, 13,115; 1979, 13,000.

26. Estimates for the number of worker-peasants vary, according to definitions used, between 500,000 and 3,000,000.

27. These figures need to be taken with care since the agrarian structures of the countries are very different.

28. Documents relating to these struggles have been published by *Labour Focus on Eastern Europe*, Vol. II No. 5, and Vol. III, Nos. 1 and 4, London.

29. Rural Solidarity was officially founded on 14 December 1980. It does not include the workers of State farms. The Rzeszow Agreement of February 1981 will satisfy a number of the peasants' demands. See issue No. 1 of the Rural Solidarity bulletin in *L'Alternative* No. 9, March-April 1981.

The Twenty-One Demands

of the striking workforces represented on the Inter-Factory
Strike Committee of Gdansk Shipyard

The following are the Committee Demands:

1. Acceptance of free trade unions independent of the Communist
Party and of enterprises, in accordance with convention No. 87 of
the International Labour Organisation concerning the right to form
free trade unions, which was ratified by the Communist Government of Poland.

2. A guarantee of the right to strike and of the security of strikers
and those aiding them.

3. Compliance with the constitutional guarantee of freedom of
speech, the press and publication, including freedom for independent publishers, and the availability of the mass media to representatives of all faiths.

4. (a) A return of former rights to:
— People dismissed from work after the 1970 and 1976
strikes.
— Students expelled from school because of their views.
(b) The release of all political prisoners, among them Edmund
Zadrozynski, Jan Kozlowski and Marek Kozlowski.
(c) A halt in repression of the individual because of personal
conviction.

5. Availability to the mass media of information about the formation of the Interfactory Strike Committee and publication of its
demands.

6. The undertaking of actions aimed at bringing the country out of
its crisis situation by the following means:
(a) Making public complete information about the social-economic
situation.
(b) Enabling all sectors and social classes to take part in discussion
of the reform programme.

7. Compensation of all workers taking part in the strike for the
period of the strike, with vacation pay from the Central Council of
Trade Unions.

8. An increase in the base pay of each worker by 2,000 zlotys (?£30)
a month as compensation for the recent rise in prices.

9. Guaranteed automatic increases in pay on the basis of increases in prices and the decline in real income.

10. A full supply of food products for the domestic market, with exports limited to surpluses.

11. The abolition of 'commercial' prices and of other sales for hard currency in special shops.

12. The selection of management personnel on the basis of qualifications, not party membership. Privileges of the secret police, regular police and party apparatus are to be eliminated by equalizing family subsidies, abolishing special stores, etc.

13. The introduction of food coupons for meat and meat products (during the period in which control of the market situation is regained).

14. Reduction in the age for retirement for women to 50 and for men to 55, or after 30 years' employment in Poland for women and 35 years for men, regardless of age.

15. Conformity of old-age pensions and annuities with what has actually been paid in.

16. Improvements in the working conditions of the health service to insure full medical care for workers.

17. Assurances of a reasonable number of places in day-care centres and kindergartens for the children of working mothers.

18. Paid maternity leave for three years.

19. A decrease in the waiting period for apartments.

20. An increase in the commuter's allowance to 100 zlotys from 40, with a supplemental benefit on separation.

21. A day of rest on Saturday. Workers in the brigade system or round-the-clock jobs are to be compensated for the loss of free Saturdays with increased leave or other paid time off.

Notes on People and Organisations

In December 1981, all the leading members of Solidarity and the opposition movements were interned under martial law. Censorship in Poland has made it impossible to give more information.

AK — Armia Krajowa (*National Army*) Military resistance organisation under the leadership of the Polish government in exile in London (from 1939 to 1942 known under the title ZWZ, Armed Struggle Association). In 1944 AK units undertook the liberation of (pre-war) Eastern Poland. On 1 August 1944 it launched the Warsaw Uprising. The National Army was dissolved on the orders of its commandant on 19 January 1945. Many members of the AK were imprisoned by the Stalinist regime after the war.

Babiuch, Edward Born in 1927, he joined the Polish Communist Party in 1948. His career developed first in Katowice, then in Warsaw. Member of the Politburo after the working-class riots in 1970. Appointed Prime Minister in February 1980, he replaced M. Jaruszewicz, following the VIII Congress of the PUWP. Removed from his post by the plenary meeting of the Central Committee on 24 August.

Bahro, Rudolf East German dissident, philosopher and author of a marxist critique of actually existing socialism (see *The Alternative in Eastern Europe*, NLB-Verso 1980). After his imprisonment he was deported, and currently lives in West Germany.

Bierut, Boleslaw (1892-1956) An old-time Communist militant of the Stalinist school. General Secretary of the Communist Party (1948); President of the Republic (1947-52); Prime Minister (1952-54). Died in Moscow shortly after the XX Congress of the Communist Party of the Soviet Union.

Borusewicz, Bogdan Born in 1949; history graduate from the Catholic University of Lublin; student movement leader in 1968 (imprisoned for two years), and a member of KOR and of the editorial committee of *Robotnik Wybrzeza*. Member of the Solidarity leadership in Gdansk until August 1981.

Bratkowski, Stefan Communist journalist; editor of the weekly supplement of *Zycie Warszawy*. Sacked for his anti-establishment views. An initiator of DiP, and President of the Union of Journalists since October 1980. Expelled from the PUWP in October 1981.

Catholic Intellectual Clubs (KIK) Discussion and education clubs, linked to the Catholic parliamentary group created after 1956. Split in 1976. One component of the intellectual opposition movement.
DiP, *Doswiadczenie i Przyszlosc (Experience and Future)* A study group set up in November 1976, comprising people of very different professions and political views (principally Communists and Catholics). Their first two reports are published as *Poland: Report on The State of the Republic* (Pluto Press 1981).
Duda-Gwiazda, Joanna Technical engineer at the Ceto shipbuilding enterprise in Gdansk. Joined PUWP in 1962, left in 1968 because of its repression of students. In 1971, returned her membership card of the metalworkers' union. First contacts with KOR in 1976. Founder member of the KWZZ (Constituent Committee of Free Trade Unions of the Baltic) and of the editorial committee of *Robotnik Wybrzeza*. Member of the MKS praesidium, and later of the Solidarity leadership in Gdansk with responsibility for the newspaper.
Gierek, Edward Secretary General of the PUWP from December 1970 to September 1980. Born in 1911; worked as a miner; emigrated with his family in 1923. Returned to Poland in 1948, to pursue a brilliant career. Secretary of Katowice voivodie in 1951; moved on to the Politburo, July-November 1956; Secretary to the Central Committee, 1957-64; member of the Politburo since 1959. Taken off the Central Committee in January 1981. Interned under martial law in December 1981.
GLOS Bulletin of the democratic opposition movement. Edited by Antoni Macierewicz.
Gomulka, Wladyslaw Born into a working-class family in 1905; joined the Communist Party in 1926; leader of the trade union Left, particularly around Lodz; spent time in Moscow, 1934-35. Returned to Silesia and elected to the Central Committee at the end of 1935. Arrested in March 1936, he spent several years in prison. Escaped in 1939 and took refuge in Lwow, then under Soviet Army occupation. Took part in the reconstruction of the Party; member of its Politburo until September 1948. Victim of the 1949 purges. Sentenced to life imprisonment. Triumphant return in October 1956. Ruled Poland for fourteen years. Removed from his post following the seaboard strikes in 1970.
Gruszewski, Wojciech Chemical engineer; Inter-Enterprise Strike Committee (MKS) delegate representing the Gdansk Engineering School; member of the MKS praesidium; Solidarity leader in Gdansk.
Gwiazda, Andrzej Born in 1935; electrical engineer in the laboratories of the Elmor factory in Gdansk. Founder member of KWZZ (Constituent Committee of Free Trade Unions of the Baltic); member of the editorial committee of *Robotnik Wybrzeza*; member

of the MKS praesidium. Vice-president of Solidarity's national commission.

Jagielski, Miroslaw Former Deputy Prime Minister; minister responsible for the government commission which negotiated with the
MKS. Born into a peasant family; member of the government since
1970; member of the Central Committee since 1959; substitute
member of the Politburo from 1964-71; became a full member in
1971.

Jaruzelski, Wojciech First Secretary of the PUWP since October
1981. Born into an intellectual family, he enlisted in the Polish army
in 1943. Assistant Minister of Defence in 1962, he became a
member of the Central Committee of the PUWP in 1964 and of its
political bureau in 1971 — part of Gierek's team. Appointed Prime
Minister in February 1981, he combines the premiership with com-
mand of the defence ministry. In December 1981, Jaruzelski
declared martial law.

Kania, Stanislaw First Secretary of the Central Committee of the
Polish United Workers Party (PUWP) since September 1980. Born
into a peasant family in 1927. A worker, he joined the PUWP in
April 1945. He began his career in charge of rural youth in the
Rzeszow region, then, from 1958, in Warsaw. Joined the Central
Committee of the PUWP at the time of the V Congress, and joined
the secretariat of the Central Committee since the VII Congress in
1975. Close to Gierek, he was known for his talents in organising
both the Party and the police. First Secretary of the PUWP from
September 1980 to October 1981.

Kecik, Wieslaw Agronomist; member of KOR; spokesperson of the
Founding Committee of Agricultural Trade Unions set up in 1978;
one of Rural Solidarity's experts, and editor of its newspaper.

Kobylinski, Zdzislaw Warehouse worker in the PKS factory in
Gdansk; member of the MKS praesidium.

Kolodziej, Andrzej Born in 1960; welder; sacked from the *Lenin*
shipyard at the start of 1980; member of the Constituent Committee
of Free Trade Unions of the Baltic; President of Strike Committee
of the *Paris Commune* shipyard in Gdynia; Vice-President of MKS;
member of the Solidarity leadership.

Krzywonos, Henryka Tram conductor; WPK (urban transport)
delegate on the MKS; member of the MKS praesidium.

**KSS-KOR (Committee for Social Self-Defence-Committee for
Defence of the Workers)** The main organisation of the Democratic
Opposition movement, set up in September 1976 on the initiative of
thirty-one intellectuals. KOR published various independent
bulletins, including *Biuletyn informacyjny* and *Robotnik*, a number
of journals, and also established a publishing house, Nowa. Its
militants were frequently arrested, and played a decisive role in the

strikes and in the building of Solidarity. KOR announced its
dissolution in September 1981.

Kuron, Jacek Founding member of KOR; principal target for the
regime. Born in 1934; expelled from the Communist Party in 1953;
rejoined for a brief period in 1955; organiser of the 'Red Scouts' in
1956, and of the short-lived Union of Socialist Youth. Together
with K. Modzelewski, author of the Open Letter of 1964, *A Revolutionary Socialist Manifesto* (Pluto Press 1972). For this he was
sentenced to three years in prison. Released at the end of 1967, he
joined the student movement in 1971. A founder of KOR in
September 1976, as well as author of a number of articles. He was
arrested several times and spent the whole of the end of the month
of August 1980 in prison. Released, thanks to the Gdansk
agreements, and became one of Solidarity's experts.

KWZZ (Constituent Committee of Free Trade Unions of the Baltic)
Founded in 1978 in Gdansk by A. Gwiazda, J. Duda-Gwiazda and
B. Borusewicz. Published seven issues of *Robotnik Wybrzeza*, each
in 2,000 copies. Brought together the future organisers of the
August 1980 strikes. Similar committees existed in the same period
at Katowice and Szczecin.

Lis, Bogdan Born in 1952; labourer at the Elmor factory in Gdansk;
joined the PUWP at the time of his military service in 1975; Vice-
President of the Union of Socialist Youth in his firm. Elected Vice-
President of the Trade Union Council in March 1980; KWZZ sym-
pathiser; Vice-President of the MKS and national leader of Solidarity.
Expelled from PUWP in October 1981.

Mazowiecki, Tadeusz Journalist and Catholic militant; born in
1927. Split with the PAX group in 1956. Editor of the monthly
review *Wiez* from its beginning in 1958. Several times elected deputy
in the *Znak* group. President of MKS's commission of experts;
editor of Solidarity's national weekly.

Michnik, Adam Historian; born in 1946; organiser of KOR and its
Flying University. Member of the 'Red Scouts' in 1956; arrested for
the first time in 1965 for having set up the 'Club for the Seekers
after Contradictions'; expelled from University in 1968, he spent
two years in prison. Worked in a factory in Warsaw; then became
secretary to the writer Slominski. Imprisoned several times as one of
KOR's organisers. Author of various articles, and of the book *The
Church and the Left* (published in French by Seuil, 1979); editor of
the independent review *Krytika*, and one of Solidarity's experts.

Moczar, Mieczyslaw Army general, born in 1913. Joined the Communist Party in 1937. Arrested in 1938, and released in September
1939. Commander of the Communist Resistance Groups 1942-45.
After the war he took on important functions within the security
organisations. Deputy Minister, later to become Minister of the

Interior 1956-58. Member of the Central Committee, later of the
Politburo; he led the big anti-semitic, anti-intellectual campaign
which led up to the repression of the student movement in March
1968 and to the purges which followed. He left the Politburo after
the workers' revolt of December 1970. President of the Supreme
Control Chamber (NIK). Returned to the Politburo on 1 December
1980; President of the National Unity Front, and of the Organisation of Ex-Soldiers (WBOWID).
Modzelewski, Karol Born in 1937. Historian specialising in the Middle
Ages. Organiser of the student movement in Warsaw in October
1956. Together with J. Kuron, author of the Open Letter in 1964,
(*A Revolutionary Socialist Manifesto* Pluto Press 1972) which got
him three-and-a-half years' imprisonment. Sentenced again after the
student movement of 1968. Author of a well known book about
mediaeval Poland. Wrote an open letter to Gierek in September
1976. Worked in the Nowa publishing house; member of the MKS
praesidium in Wroclaw and of the national commission of Solidarity.
Olszowski, Stefan Member of the Politburo of the PUWP since
September 1980. Born in 1931, he was elected to the Central Committee in 1964, where he was in charge of the press up until 1968. In
this role he played an important part in the anti-semitic campaign
orchestrated by the 'partisans' of General Moczar. Entered the
Politburo in 1971; removed by Gierek at the VIII Party Congress in
February 1980.
Pienkowska, Alina Nurse at the Elmor factory; born in 1954.
KWZZ militant and member of the editorial committee of *Robotnik
Wybrzeza*. Member of the MKS praesidium.
Pinkowski, Josef Prime Minister from August 1980 to February
1981. Born in 1929; officer in the Polish Army; joined the Central
Committee in 1971; substitute member of the Politburo in February
1980; became full-time member in August 1980.
Robotnik Workers' bulletin published by KSS-KOR. Set up in 1978;
published 20,000 copies. Its main editors were: B. Borusewicz
(Gdansk); L. Gierek (Radom), F. Grabszyk (Nova-Huta), J. Litynski and H. Wujec (Warsaw), E. Zadrozynski (Grudziadz).
Walentynowicz, Anna Born in 1929. Welder, later crane driver at
the Gdansk shipyard. Leader of the strike movement of 1970-71;
militant in KWZZ, and one of the editors of *Robotnik Wybrzeza*.
Sacked a few months before retirement; reinstated following the
strike by the shipyard workers. Member of the MKS praesidium.
Walesa, Lech Electrician; born to a peasant family in 1944; began
working at the *Lenin* shipyard in 1967; led the 1970-71 strikes; sacked
in April 1976; member of the KWZZ and of the editorial board of
Robotnik Wybrzeza; sacked several times, and arrested; President
of the MKS and of Solidarity's national commission.

Wielowieyski, Andrzej Born in 1927. A Catholic militant, secretary of the Warsaw Catholic Intellectuals Club; MKS expert, then one of Solidarity's experts.

Wisniewski, Florian Electrician at the Elektromontaz factory in Gdansk. Member of the MKS praesidium.

Chronology of Events

1980
Stages in the recognition of Solidarity
31 August : The Gdansk agreements are signed. *6 September* : S. Kania replaces E. Gierek as First Secretary of the Polish United Workers Party (PUWP). *15 September* : The basics of the Gdansk agreements are extended to the whole country. *22 September* : The independent trade unions set up a coordination in Gdansk, under the name of 'Solidarity', and with Lech Walesa as President. *28 September* : Organising committees of peasants submit a constitution for an independent union. *3 October* : One-hour national strike to enforce implementation of the agreements. *24 October* : Solidarity's constitution is registered, but with unacceptable alterations. Threats of strike action for 12 November. *10 November* : Solidarity is legally registered.

22 November : A Solidarity militant is arrested in Warsaw; spontaneous strikes, and threats of a general strike. *27 November* : The militant is freed. *5 December* : An important delegation from the PUWP attends the Warsaw Pact summit in Warsaw. *8 December* : Meeting of the joint State-Church Commission. *16 December* : Tenth anniversary of the 1970 Gdansk killings. Unveiling of the monument which the strikers had demanded in August 1980.

1981
The question of work-free Saturdays
5 January : Meetings between L. Walesa and M. Jagielski, on the problem of work-free Saturdays. The government attempts to backtrack on the August agreement which granted four free Saturdays. *10 January* : Mass support for Solidarity's line of not reporting for work on this 'work-free' Saturday. *22-28 January* : Strike action throughout the country; threats of a general strike. *31 January* : After 14 hours of negotiation Solidarity and the government reach a compromise: three free Saturdays out of every four. *12 December* : Under martial law, the six-day week is re-introduced.

Rural Solidarity and the Bydgoszcz affair
12 February : General Jaruzelski nominated as Prime Minister. *16 February* : Negotiations begin at Rzeszow, between the govern-

228

ment and representatives of Rural Solidarity, which has still not been recognised. Lech Walesa is present. *17 February* : In Warsaw the NZS, the independent student union, is officially registered. *19 February* : The Rzeszow agreements are signed, granting the basic elements of the peasants' demands. *4 March* : Kania meets Brezhnev in Moscow. *10 March* : The first Congress of Rural Solidarity ends in Poznan. *19 March* : Incidents in Bydgoszcz. During negotiations, police harass Solidarity militants. The union's national commission calls for preparations for a general strike. This is the most serious crisis since August 1980. *20-31 March* : The whole country mobilises for a general strike. *27 March* : A four-hour warning strike receives massive support. *29 March* : Plenary session of the Central Committee of the PUWP; confrontation between progressives and conservatives. *30 March* : The Warsaw agreement is signed, and Lech Walesa withdraws the call for a general strike. *31 March - 1 April* : Stormy meeting of Solidarity's national commission. Karol Modzelewski, spokesperson for the union, resigns. *2 April* : Publication of the union's national weekly newspaper. *17 April* : The government signs an agreement recognising Rural Solidarity. *11 May* : Legal recognition of Rural Solidarity by the Warsaw Tribunal.

The Ninth Extraordinary Congress of the Polish United Workers Party (PUWP)
15 April : In Torun, twenty or so 'horizontal structures' meet. These represent a rank-and-file reforming tendency within the Party, deriving from autumn 1980. *26 May* : Formation of the 'Katowice forum' representing conservative positions within the Party. *28 May* : Death of Cardinal Wyszynski, later to be replaced by Mgr Glemb as the head of the Polish Catholic Church. *9-10 June* : Eleventh plenary session of the Central Committee of the PUWP, which rejects a letter from the Communist Party of the Soviet Union supporting the positions of the conservatives. *14-20 July* : Ninth Extraordinary Congress of the PUWP, in an atmosphere of change. S. Kania is re-elected as First Secretary, albeit with some difficulty. The Party's leading personnel are radically changed (new Central Committee), although the basic balance of forces remains the same.

Solidarity's First National Congress
25 July : The deepening of the economic crisis results in the first hunger march in Kutno. *30 July* : Thirty thousand women and children embark on a hunger march in Lodz. *3 August* : The centre of Warsaw is occupied, to protest against the reduction of meat rations. Negotiations are opened. *10-11 August* : Plenary session of the PUWP Central Committee, condemning the street demonstrations

and threatening a "bloody confrontation". The union's national commission meets and calls for a programme of self-management. *15 August* : Kania, Jaruzelski and Brezhnev meet in Crimea. *16 August* : The march on Warsaw in support of political prisoners is called off. *19-20 August* : Strike in newspaper printing and distribution houses. *3 September* : The Central Committee proposes a restrictive law on self-management. *5 September* : The first session of the Solidarity Congress opens in Gdansk. The constitution is adopted, along with an "appeal to workers in the Eastern bloc countries". The union demands that Parliament organise a referendum on self-management. *10 September* : The first session of the Congress ends with a declaration demanding the organisation of free elections. *24-25 September* : A parliamentary battle over the question of self-management. Parliament adopts a text which is closer to the union's position than to the Party. *26 September-7 October* : Second session of Solidarity's National Congress. Walesa is elected President, with a 55 per cent vote. From now on a National Commission will represent the union's delegates. The Congress adopts a programme for the establishment of a "self-managed republic" and a "new social contract".

16-18 October : A plenary session of the Central Commission names General Jaruzelski as Party head, to replace S. Kania. *12-14 December* : Jaruzelski declares martial law that, he says, will be temporary. He claims that this is needed, given that the country is "on the edge of the abyss".